Auctions: Theory and Practice

CW00550941

with

your help and advice on this

Paul Klemperer

Auctions: Theory and Practice
IS A PART OF THE SERIES
TOULOUSE LECTURES IN ECONOMICS

Jacques Crémer, Series Editor

The series *Toulouse Lectures in Economics* is an annual joint project of Princeton University Press and the Institut d'Économie Industrielle of the University of Toulouse. The volumes are based on lectures presented over a week at the University of Toulouse by leading international researchers.

We invite scholars we admire and whom we want to hear discuss in depth their current research both during the lectures and through the week they will spend with us enjoying the Toulouse hospitality. Reflecting the broad range of interests of the Institute the lectures will call on microeconomists, macroeconomists, and econometricians both theoretical and applied. Behind this diversity the reader will find a constant intellectual rigor and attention to the real world consequences of economic theories.

The IDEI is very grateful to the City of Toulouse and National Economic Research Associates, who kindly cover some of the local expenses incurred in the organization of the lectures for this series; neither of these institutions has any role in the selection of authors or themes for the series.

Paul Klemperer, *Auctions: Theory and Practice* is the first volume of this series

Auctions: Theory and Practice

Paul Klemperer

PRINCETON UNIVERSITY PRESS

PRINCETON AND OXFORD

Library of Congress Cataloging-in-Publication Data
Klemperer, Paul
   Auctions: theory and practice / Paul Klemperer
      p. cm. — (The Toulouse lectures in economics)
   "Inaugural (2003) Toulouse lectures"—Table of contents.
   Includes bibliographical references and index.
ISBN 0-691-11426-9 (alk. paper) — ISBN 0-691-11925-2 (pbk.: alk paper)
      1. Auctions. 2. Auctions—European Union countries—Case studies. I.
   Economic theory of auctions. II. Title. III. Series

HF5476.K54 2003   2003061019
381$'$.17—dc22

British Library Cataloging-in-Publication Data is available

This book has been composed in Times

Printed on acid-free paper ∞

www.pup.princeton.edu

Printed in the United States of America

10 9 8 7 6 5 4 3 2 1

To Meg, David, Katherine, and William

Contents

Preface

February 2000 was a stressful month for me: the UK 3G auction was about to begin. For over two years I had been working with the UK government to design the world's first auction of spectrum for "third generation" (3G) mobile-phone services. A lot was at stake. If our auction worked well, it would allocate the spectrum efficiently and raise a lot of money, but many previous auctions had been embarrassing flops that had failed to generate the sums expected. This time the politicians were hoping for billions of dollars.

We had written numerous papers, developed theories, and tested prototype auction designs in experiments. But would it all work on the day? What might go wrong? The bidders all had armies of consultants and lawyers. What loopholes in the rules might they find to exploit? Could they find a devious way to coordinate their bidding and so avoid competing against each other? Or might our rules actually have discouraged some potential bidders from entering the auction at all—so destroying competition for a different reason?

The 1990s had been littered with examples of auctions—especially of new products or services—that had gone disastrously wrong. Several US auctions had fallen down because bidders signaled to each other by including lot identification numbers and even phone numbers as the final digits of their bids. The winner of a New Zealand auction had bid $7 million, but the rules required it to pay only $5,000. Only three bidders had turned up for a German auction of three blocks of spectrum, which therefore sold only at the tiny reserve price. Closer to home, an auction of UK television broadcasting rights sold licenses for some regions of the country at prices less than one ten-thousandth of others. UK electricity auctions were widely criticized for yielding collusive prices. So would our new auction end up as just another humiliating giveaway?

The tension only mounted over the seven weeks the auction ran. The auction started well. Day after day the prices climbed, but we continued to worry about what we might have missed, and what could still go wrong. As the prices kept rising through 150 rounds of bidding, and records started falling, nerves gave way to astonishment. Still, it was an enormous relief when the gavel finally came down on five bids totaling over 34 billion dollars—our auction had raised more money than any previous auction in history. It was even more of a relief when the bidders all paid at the appointed time, and the sale process was finally over, without a hitch.

In the following months, other countries held 3G auctions. The results were very different. Whereas our auction raised almost 600 dollars per head of population, most countries earned far less revenue, and the Swiss made only 20 dollars per head. The key reason was, quite simply, how the auctions were designed: good auction design matters enormously.

This book is in large part a story of the thinking behind the United Kingdom's auction. I survey the basic theory of how auctions work; emphasize the practical lessons that can make the difference between successful auctions and catastrophic ones; and discuss the 100 billion dollar 3G mobile-phone auctions as a case study.

I also explore the connections with other areas of economics that originally drew me into studying auctions. The increasing use of auction theory to develop insights into *other* parts of economics has been one of the most exciting parts of my professional life. So I look in detail at the relationships between auctions and other economic questions. I show how modern auction theory can illuminate such diverse phenomena as booms and busts in housing markets, financial crashes and trading "frenzies", political lobbying and negotiations, the differing costs of alternative legal systems, and the relative intensities of different forms of industrial competition. Thus the tools of auction theory help to explain many issues in economics—and every economist should learn about auctions.

OVERVIEW

This book can be used by a general reader, for a graduate course on auction theory, or—by picking more selectively—an advanced undergraduate or MBA course on auctions and auction design.

None of the writing is technical, except in the appendix to chapter 1. (Indeed there are barely any mathematical symbols, let alone equations, outside footnotes and appendices).

Part A introduces the basic theory, and surveys the existing literature. It includes exercises, and technical appendices (in chapter 1).

Part B shows that modern auction-theoretic tools and intuitions can provide extremely useful arguments and insights in a broad range of economic settings. Auction theory has turned out to be surprisingly powerful in places that are superficially unconnected with auctions—many economic contexts that do not at first sight look like auctions can be recast to use auction-theoretic techniques.

Part C argues that important insights also flow in the other direction—from other parts of economics to the analysis of auctions: in particular, the key issues in practical auction design are not so much those that have been addressed by recent advanced auction theory, but rather the traditional industrial-organization issues of collusion, entry-deterrence, etc. I give numerous examples. I then discuss economic policy-making more broadly, including the need to pay attention to political pressures and to the wider economic context, but illustrate these points using auction examples.

Part D describes and evaluates the world-record-setting 2000–2001 3G mobile-phone license auctions, as a case study for the earlier parts. I discuss the design *process*, as well as the designs and the overall successes of the different auctions. I also analyze why bidder strategies were a little different from those that would be suggested by the elementary theory described in Part A. I conclude by considering the merits of running auctions versus the alternatives.

USING THIS BOOK

The independent **general reader** may read the parts in whichever order interests him or her—each part is self-sufficient and can be read in isolation, even by those without any previous background in auction theory.

A **graduate course** on auctions (or a segment of a core microeconomics course) would dwell on Parts A and B, and cover Parts C and D more cursorily. It should include the exercises and the technical appendices to chapter 1, and could usefully be complemented by some additional readings from those discussed in chapter 1. (These further readings are reprinted in Klemperer, 2000a.)

Undergraduate lectures might cover the first half of Part A (and, perhaps, some of chapter 1's appendices), and Parts C and D.

An **MBA course** segment might focus on Parts C and D (except chapter 7).

Some suggested course outlines are at the end of the volume.

ACKNOWLEDGMENTS

Most of this material was first published in 2002–2003. The exception is chapter 1 which was first published in 1999; I have therefore added a short Afterword to that chapter to bring it up to date.

Since the papers were originally written as stand-alone contributions, there is inevitably a little repetition, but the overlaps should be obvious and cause the reader no problems.

The papers were originally published as follows:

Chapter 1 (except Afterword and Exercises). Auction Theory: A Guide to the Literature. *Journal of Economic Surveys* 1999, 13(3), 227–286.[1]

[1] Also reprinted in *The Current State of Economic Science*, S. Dahiya (ed.), 1999.

Chapter 2. Why Every Economist should Learn some Auction Theory. In Dewatripont, M., Hansen, L., and Turnovsky, S. (eds.), (2003) *Advances in Economics and Econometrics: Theory and Applications* vol. 1, pp. 25–55 (reprinted by permission of Cambridge University Press).[2]

Chapter 3. What Really Matters in Auction Design. *Journal of Economic Perspectives* 2002, 16(1), 169–189 (reprinted by permission of the American Economic Association).

Chapter 4. Using and Abusing Economic Theory. *Journal of the European Economic Association* 2003, 1(2–3), 272–300 (reprinted by permission of the European Economic Association).[3]

Chapter 5. How (Not) to Run Auctions. *European Economic Review* 2002, 46(4–5), 829–845 (reprinted by permission of Elsevier).[4]

Chapter 6. The Biggest Auction Ever. *Economic Journal* 2002, 112, C74–C96, with Ken Binmore (reprinted by permission of Blackwell Publishing, and the Royal Economic Society).

Chapter 7. Some Observations on the British 3G Telecom Auction. *ifo Studien* 2002, 48(1), 115–120, and Some Observations on the German 3G Telecom Auction. *ifo Studien* 2002, 48(1), 145–156 (reprinted by permission of the Ifo Institute).[5]

Chapter 8. The Wrong Culprit for Telecom Trouble. *Financial Times* 26 November 2002, 21.

Exercises. Oxford University MPhil in Economics Examination (reprinted by permission of Oxford University).

Collecting these papers together in a volume was inspired by the invitation to give the inaugural series of the Toulouse Lectures which were based on them. I am most grateful to Jacques Crémer, Jean-Jacques Laffont, and Jean Tirole for the invitation and for their hospitality during my visit, and to Richard Baggaley of Princeton University Press for his smooth running of the whole publication process.

I could not have written any of these papers without the benefit of the enormous amount I have learnt from my friends and colleagues. Many of these are thanked in the acknowledgments to the individual chapters, but Jeremy Bulow and Marco Pagnozzi deserve special thanks.

Finally, I was the principal auction theorist advising the UK Government on the design of its "3G" mobile-phone auction,[6] I am a Member of the UK

[2] Also Invited Lecture to Eighth World Congress of the Econometric Society, 2000.

[3] Also Alfred Marshall Lecture to European Economic Association, 2002, and reprinted in *Advances in Economics and Econometrics: Theory and Applications*, S. Hurn (ed.), forthcoming.

[4] Also reprinted in *Spectrum Auctions and Competition in Telecommunications*, G. Illing and Klüh, U. (eds.), MIT Press, 2004.

[5] Both papers also reprinted in *Spectrum Auctions and Competition in Telecommunications*, G. Illing and Klüh, U. (eds.), MIT Press, 2004.

[6] Ken Binmore led the team and supervised experiments testing the proposed designs.

Competition Commission, and I have advised several other Government agencies in the United Kingdom, United States, and European Union, but the views expressed in this book are mine alone. Furthermore, although some observers thought some of the behavior described below warranted regulatory investigation, I do not intend to suggest that any of it violates any applicable rules or laws.

Auctions: Theory and Practice

Introduction

Auction theory is one of economics' success stories. It is of both practical and theoretical importance: practical importance, because many of the world's most important markets are auction markets, and good auction theory has made the difference between successful auctions and disastrous ones; theoretical importance, because lessons from auction theory have led to important insights elsewhere in economics.

Auctions are not a new idea: the Babylonians auctioned wives, the ancient Greeks auctioned mine concessions and, in addition to their notorious slave auctions, the Romans auctioned everything from war booty to debtors' property. In the modern world, auctions are used to conduct a huge volume of economic transactions. Governments use them to sell treasury bills, foreign exchange, mineral rights including oil fields, and other assets such as firms to be privatized. Government contracts are typically awarded by procurement auctions, which are also often used by firms subcontracting work or buying services and raw materials. In these cases, of course, the auctioneer is seeking a low price rather than a high price. Houses, cars, agricultural produce and livestock, art and antiques are commonly sold by auction. Other economic transactions, for example takeover battles, are auctions by another name.

The range of items sold by auction has been greatly increased by e-commerce, and in the last decade or so there has also been an explosion of interest in using auctions to set up new markets, for example, for energy, transport, and pollution permits. Although many of these markets do not look like auctions to the layperson, they are best understood through auction theory. (For example, electricity markets are best described and analyzed as auctions of infinitely divisible quantities of identical goods.) The auctions of mobile phone licenses across the world are only the most famous of the new auction markets.

Not only are auctions an increasingly important part of the way the economy allocates resources, but also economists have increasingly realized the wider importance of auction theory: it has been the basis of much fundamental theoretical work not directly related to auctions. Many economic contexts that do not at first sight look like auctions can be re-cast to use auction-theoretic techniques, and a good understanding of auction theory is valuable in developing intuitions and insights that can inform the analysis of many mainstream economic questions.

This book considers the theory of auctions, practical auction design including case studies, and the application of auction theory to *other* areas of economics.

A. Auction Theory

Two basic designs of auction are most commonly used: the ascending auction, in which the price is raised successively until only one bidder remains and that bidder wins the object at the final price she bid; and the first-price sealed-bid auction, in which each bidder independently submits a single bid without seeing others' bids, the object is sold to the bidder who makes the highest bid, and the winner pays the amount she offered.

The key result in auction theory is the remarkable *Revenue Equivalence Theorem* which, subject to some reasonable-sounding conditions, tells us that the seller can expect equal profits on average from all the standard (and many non-standard) types of auctions, and that buyers are also indifferent among them all. William Vickrey's Nobel Prize was in large part awarded for his (1961, 1962) papers which developed some special cases of the theorem, and Riley and Samuelson (1981) and Myerson (1981) offer more general treatments.

Much of auction theory can be understood in terms of this theorem, and how its results are affected by relaxing its assumptions of a fixed number of "symmetric", risk-neutral bidders, who each want a single unit, have independent information, and bid independently. Myerson's (1981) paper shows how to derive optimal auctions (i.e., auctions that maximize the seller's expected revenue) when the assumption of symmetry fails. Maskin and Riley (1984) consider the case of risk-averse bidders, in which case the first-price sealed-bid auction is the most profitable of the standard auctions. Milgrom and Weber (1982a) analyzed auctions when the assumption of independent information is replaced by one of "affiliated" information, and showed that the most profitable standard auction is then the ascending auction. (Roughly, bidders' information is affiliated if when one bidder has more optimistic information about the value of the prize, it is more likely that other bidders' information will also be optimistic.) Models of auctions in which bidders bid for multiple units lead to less clear conclusions. For practical auction design, however, it is probably most important to remove the assumptions that the number of bidders is unaffected by the auction design, and that the bidders necessarily bid independently of each other; sealed-bid designs frequently (but not always) both attract a larger number of serious bidders and are better at discouraging collusion than are ascending designs (Klemperer, 1998, 1999b, 2000b).

Part A covers all these issues and a range of other topics including double auctions, royalties, incentive contracts, budget constraints, externalities between bidders, and the winner's curse. Appendices to chapter 1 contain technical details, some simple worked examples, and bibliographies. Exercises at first- and second-year graduate student level are at the end of this part; the solutions are at the end of the book.

B. APPLICATIONS TO *OTHER* AREAS OF ECONOMICS

There are close connections between auction theory and other areas of economics.

By carefully analyzing very simple trading models, auction theory is developing the fundamental building blocks for our understanding of more complex environments. It has been important in developing our understanding of other methods of price formation, including posted prices and negotiations in which both the buyer and seller are actively involved in determining the price.

There are especially close connections between the theories of auctions and perfect competition. Wilson (1977), Milgrom (1979), and others have developed conditions under which the sale price of an object whose value is actually the same to all bidders converges to this value as the number of bidders increases, even though each individual bidder has only partial information about this value. The fact that an auction can thus fully aggregate all of the economy's information helps to support some of our ideas about perfect competition and rational expectations equilibrium.

There is also a close analogy between the theory of optimal auctions and that of monopoly pricing; the analysis of optimal auctions is "essentially equivalent to the analysis of standard monopoly third-degree price discrimination" (Bulow and Roberts, 1989). Thus insights can be translated from monopoly theory to auction theory and vice versa.

Because auctions are such simple and well-defined economic institutions, they have become an important testing ground for economic theory, and especially game theory. So auctions are also the basis of flourishing new empirical and experimental literatures.

More recently, auction-theoretic tools have been used to provide useful arguments in a broader range of contexts—including many that do not, at first sight, look like auctions—starting with models of oligopolistic pricing, running through non-price means of allocation such as queues, wars of attrition, lobbying contests, other kinds of tournaments, and rationing, and extending to models in finance, law and economics, labor economics, political economy, etc.

Part B discusses the connections between auctions and other areas of economics, emphasizing these broader uses of auction theory. It aims to demonstrate that auction theory should be a part of every economist's armory.

C. Practical Auction Design

Although there are now many extremely successful auction markets—and economists have much to be proud of in their role in developing them— there have also been some notable fiascos. Certain auctions of TV franchises, companies, electricity, mobile-phone licenses, etc., have failed badly—even comically—providing useful illustrations of what really matters in practical auction design.

The most important point is that everything depends on the context. Auction design is *not* "one size fits all". A good auction needs to be tailored to the specific details of the situation, and must also reflect the wider economic circumstances.

Second, as stressed above, the critical issues are usually the bread-and-butter industrial-organization problems of encouraging entry and discouraging collusion. The more subtle points addressed by recent advanced auction theory are, more often than not, of lesser importance. So, for example, the Anglo-Dutch auction—a hybrid of the sealed-bid and ascending auctions—may often perform better than standard ascending auctions which are particularly vulnerable to collusive, predatory, and entry-deterring behavior.

Finally, when advising governments, auction designers (and economic policy-makers more generally) need to be sensitive to the dangers posed by political and administrative pressures, and make their proposals robust to changes that are likely to be imposed.

Part C discusses all these issues, using numerous examples. Chapter 3 focuses on practical auction design, while chapter 4 takes a broader perspective on the policy-making process, but illustrates its points using examples of auctions.

D. Case Study

The 2000–2001 "3G" mobile-phone license auctions not only raised one hundred billion dollars and attracted intense media scrutiny, they also provide an excellent illustration of our points about practical design. Even though the licenses sold were very similar in each of the nine west European auctions, the different auction designs resulted in revenues that varied from less than 20 dollars per capita in Switzerland to almost 600 dollars per capita in the United Kingdom.

Part D describes and evaluates the 3G auctions as a case study for the earlier parts. I describe the design, and overall success, of each of the auctions (chapter 5); discuss the design *process*, and give fuller details of the successful UK auction which I helped design (chapter 6); and analyze why bidder strategies were a little different from those suggested by elementary theory (chapter 7). Finally, I discuss the merits of running auctions versus the alternatives (chapter 8): although it is now fashionable to blame the 3G auctions for all the telecommunication industry's problems, there is absolutely no foundation for this. In spite of the design errors that were made, allocating the 3G licenses by auctions was clearly the correct policy.

PART A
_____

Introduction to the Theory

CHAPTER ONE

A Survey of Auction Theory*

This chapter provides an elementary, non-technical survey of auction theory, by introducing and describing some of the critical papers in the subject. (The most important of these are reproduced in a companion book, Klemperer, Paul (ed.) (2000a) The Economic Theory of Auctions. Cheltenham, UK: Edward Elgar.) We begin with the most fundamental concepts, and then introduce the basic analysis of optimal auctions, the revenue equivalence theorem, and marginal revenues. Subsequent sections address risk aversion, affiliation, asymmetries, entry, collusion, multi-unit auctions, double auctions, royalties, incentive contracts, and other topics. Appendices contain technical details, some simple worked examples, and bibliographies. An Afterword to bring the survey up to date, and Exercises, are at the end of the chapter.[1]

1.1 INTRODUCTION

Auction theory is important for practical, empirical, and theoretical reasons.

First, a huge volume of goods and services, property, and financial instruments, are sold through auctions, and many new auction markets are being designed, including, for example, for mobile-phone licenses, electricity, and pollution permits.[2] Parts C and D of this volume discuss auction design in practice.

Second, auctions provide a very valuable testing-ground for economic theory—especially of game theory with incomplete information—which has been increasingly exploited in recent years. Major empirical research efforts

* This chapter (without the Afterword and Exercises) was originally published under the title *Auction Theory: A Guide to the Literature*, in the *Journal of Economic Surveys* 1999, 13, 227–286. (It is also reprinted in Dahiya, S. (ed.) (1999) *The Current State of Economic Science*. India: Spellbound Publications.) I would like to thank my friends and colleagues, including Mark Armstrong, Chris Avery, Alan Beggs, Sushil Bikhchandani, Simon Board, Jeremy Bulow, Peter Cramton, Nils Henrik von der Fehr, Tim Harford, Jon Levin, Ulrike Malmendier, Flavio Menezes, Meg Meyer, Paul Milgrom, John Morgan, John Riley, Mark Satterthwaite, Stuart Sayer, Daniel Sgroi, Margaret Stevens, John Thanassoulis, Chris Wallace, Lucy White, Bob Wilson, and a referee for helpful advice.

[1] Other detailed treatments of the theory are in Krishna (2002) and Menezes and Monteiro (in preparation). For a more advanced analysis, see Milgrom (2004).

[2] See part D, McAfee and McMillan (1994, 1996), Klemperer (1998), and Milgrom (2004) for discussion of mobile-phone license auctions; Green and Newbery (1992), for example, discuss the use in the UK electricity market of the auction mechanism first analyzed in Klemperer and Meyer (1989); Klemperer et al. (forthcoming) discuss auctions for environmental improvements.

have focused on auctions for oil drilling rights, timber, and treasury bills,[3] and there has also been an upsurge of interest in experimental work on auctions.[4]

Finally, auction theory has been the basis of much fundamental theoretical work: it has been important in developing our understanding of other methods of price formation, most prominently posted prices (as, e.g., observed in most retail stores) and negotiations in which both the buyer and seller are actively involved in determining the price. There are close connections between auctions and competitive markets.[5] There is also a very close analogy between the theory of optimal auctions and the theory of monopoly pricing,[6] and auction theory can also help develop models of oligopolistic pricing.[7] Auction-theoretic models and techniques also apply to non-price means of allocation.[8] The connections between auction theory and other parts of economic theory are the topic of part B of this volume.

1.1.1 Plan of This Chapter

This chapter provides an elementary survey of auction theory, by introducing and describing some of the critical papers in the subject. The most important of these are reproduced in a companion book, *The Economic Theory of Auctions*,[9] for which this chapter was originally prepared.

For readers completely new to auction theory, the remainder of this section provides a brief resumé of the simplest concepts. The subsequent sections correspond to the sections into which *The Economic Theory of Auctions* is organized. Section 1.2 discusses the early literature, and section 1.3 introduces the more recent literature. Section 1.4 introduces the analysis of optimal auctions and auction theory's most fundamental result: the revenue equivalence theorem. It also describes how the concept of "marginal revenue" can inform auction theory. (Technical details are given in appendices.) Section 1.4 focuses on auction theory's basic model of a fixed set of symmetric, risk-neutral bidders with independent information who bid independently for a single object. Most of the remainder of this chapter is about the effects of relaxing one or more of these assumptions. Section 1.5 permits risk-aversion; section 1.6 allows for correlation or affiliation of bidders' information (with

---

[3] See Laffont (1997).

[4] See Kagel (1995).

[5] See section 1.8.3.

[6] See sections 1.4 and 2.4.

[7] Appendix B of Bulow and Klemperer (1998) provides one illustration. See also section 2.5.

[8] Queues and lobbying contests are examples of all-pay auction models; see, for example, section 2.2.3, Holt and Sherman (1982), and Riley (1989b). The war of attrition can also be modeled as a kind of all-pay auction; see sections 1.13.4 and 2.2.2, and Bulow and Klemperer (1999). Insights from auction theory can explain rationing; see sections 1.8.1 and 2.3.2, and Gilbert and Klemperer (2000).

[9] Klemperer (2000a).

technical details in an appendix); section 1.7 analyzes cases with asymmetric
bidders; section 1.8 considers bidders who have costs of entering an auction,
and addresses other issues pertaining to the number of bidders; section 1.9
asks what is known if there are possibilities for collusion among bidders; and
section 1.10 considers multi-unit auctions. Section 1.11 looks at auctions for
incentive contracts, and auctions in which contestants may bid on royalty rates
or quality levels in addition to prices. Section 1.12 reviews the literature on
double auctions, and section 1.13 briefly considers some other important
topics including budget constraints, externalities between bidders, jump
bidding, the war of attrition, and competing auctioneers. Section 1.14 is
about testing the theory, and section 1.15 concludes. Appendices 1.A, 1.B,
and 1.C provide technical details about the revenue equivalence theorem,
marginal revenues, and affiliation, respectively. Appendix 1.D provides
some simple worked examples illustrating these appendices. Appendix 1.E
provides a bibliography organized according to the sections of this chapter. An
Afterword to bring the survey up to date, and Exercises, are at the end of the
chapter.

1.1.2 The Standard Auction Types

Four basic types of auctions are widely used and analyzed: the ascending-bid
auction (also called the open, oral, or English auction), the descending-bid
auction (used in the sale of flowers in the Netherlands and so also called the
Dutch auction by economists), the first-price sealed-bid auction, and the
second-price sealed-bid auction (also called the Vickrey auction by economists).[10,11] In describing their rules we will focus for simplicity on the sale of a
single object.

In the ascending auction, the price is successively raised until only one
bidder remains, and that bidder wins the object at the final price. This auction
can be run by having the seller announce prices, or by having the bidders call
out prices themselves, or by having bids submitted electronically with the best
current bid posted. In the model most commonly used by auction theorists
(often called the Japanese auction), the price rises continuously while bidders
gradually quit the auction. Bidders observe when their competitors quit, and
once someone quits, she is not let back in. There is no possibility for one
bidder to preempt the process by making a large "jump bid". We will assume
this model of the ascending auction except where stated otherwise.[12]

[10] Confusingly, the second-price sealed-bid auction is sometimes called a Dutch auction by
investment bankers.
[11] Cassady's (1967) book provides a detailed, although now somewhat dated, account of many
of the contemporaneous auction institutions.
[12] Antiques and artwork are commonly sold using versions of the ascending auction, and houses
are sometimes sold this way, too. Bikhchandani and Riley (1991) discuss different types of
ascending auction. See also section 1.13.3.

The descending auction works in exactly the opposite way: the auctioneer starts at a very high price, and then lowers the price continuously. The first bidder who calls out that she will accept the current price wins the object at that price.[13]

In the first-price sealed-bid auction each bidder independently submits a single bid, without seeing others' bids, and the object is sold to the bidder who makes the highest bid. The winner pays her bid (i.e., the price is the highest or "first" price bid).[14]

In the second-price sealed-bid auction, also, each bidder independently submits a single bid, without seeing others' bids, and the object is sold to the bidder who makes the highest bid. However, the price she pays is the *second*-highest bidder's bid, or "second price". This auction is sometimes called a Vickrey auction after William Vickrey, who wrote the seminal (1961) paper on auctions.[15]

For reasons we will explain shortly, the ascending and descending auctions are sometimes referred to as open second-price and open first-price auctions, respectively.

1.1.3 The Basic Models of Auctions

A key feature of auctions is the presence of asymmetric information.[16] (With perfect information most auction models are relatively easy to solve.)

[13] For example, in Dutch flower auctions, the potential buyers all sit in a room at desks with buzzers connected to an electronic clock at the front of the room. The interior of the clock has information about what is being sold and the price at which the auction starts. Once the auction begins, a series of lights around the edge of the clock indicate to what percentage of the original asking price the good has fallen. As soon as one bidder buzzes in, she gets the flowers at the price indicated on the clock. (Except that, if there are several lots of the same flowers from the same seller available that morning, the buyer can choose to buy only some of the available lots, and the rest will be re-auctioned.) Fish are sold in a similar way in Israel, as is tobacco in Canada.

[14] First-price sealed-bid auctions are used in auctioning mineral rights in government-owned land; they are also sometimes used in the sales of artwork and real estate. This method is also often used in procurement (i.e., competing contractors submit prices and the *lowest* bidder wins and receives her price for fulfilling the contract). UK Treasury securities are sold through the multi-unit equivalent of the first-price auction (every winner pays her own bid), and US Treasury auctions used to be run this way too, though recently the US Treasury has also been using a multi-unit version of the second-price sealed-bid auction.

[15] This auction form is used for most auctions of stamps by mail, and is also used for other goods in some auctions on the internet (see Lucking-Reiley, 2000), but it is much less commonly used than the other standard forms (see Rothkopf, Teisberg, and Kahn, 1990 for some discussion why); it is commonly studied in part because of its attractive theoretical properties. A multi-unit version is sometimes used by governments when selling foreign exchange and by companies when buying back shares. Economists usually model the multi-unit version by assuming the price paid is the highest losing bid, since this has theoretical properties analogous to those of the single-unit second-price case. In practice the price paid is often that of the lowest winning bidder.

[16] The appropriate concept of equilibrium is therefore Bayesian–Nash equilibrium. That is, each player's strategy is a function of her own information, and maximizes her expected payoff given other players' strategies and given her beliefs about other players' information. See, for example, Gibbons (1992).

In the basic *private-value* model each bidder knows how much she values the object(s) for sale, but her value is private information to herself.

In the *pure common-value* model, by contrast, the actual value is the same for everyone, but bidders have different private information about what that value actually is. For example, the value of an oil lease depends on how much oil is under the ground, and bidders may have access to different geological "signals" about that amount. In this case a bidder would change her estimate of the value if she learnt another bidder's signal, in contrast to the private-value case in which her value would be unaffected by learning any other bidder's preferences or information.

A general model encompassing both these as special cases assumes each bidder receives a private information signal, but allows each bidder's value to be a general function of *all* the signals.[17] For example, your value for a painting may depend mostly on your own private information (how much you like it) but also somewhat on others' private information (how much they like it) because this affects the resale value and/or the prestige of owning it.

1.1.4 Bidding in the Standard Auctions

Consider first the descending auction. Note that although we described this as a dynamic game, each bidder's problem is essentially static. Each bidder must choose a price at which she will call out, conditional on no other bidder having yet called out; and the bidder who chooses the highest price wins the object at the price she calls out. Thus this game is strategically equivalent to the first-price sealed-bid auction,[18] and players' bidding functions are therefore exactly the same.[19] This is why the descending auction is sometimes referred to as an open first-price auction.

Now with private values, in the ascending auction, it is clearly a dominant strategy to stay in the bidding until the price reaches your value, that is, until you are just indifferent between winning and not winning. The next-to-last person will drop out when her value is reached, so the person with the highest

---

[17] That is, bidder i receives signal t_i and would have value $v_i(t_1, ..., t_n)$ if all bidders' signals were available to her. In the private-value model $v_i(t_1, ..., t_n)$ is a function only of t_i. In the pure common-value model $v_i(t_1, ..., t_n) = v_j(t_1, ..., t_n)$, for all $t_1, ..., t_n$. (If i's actual value $V_i(t_1, ..., t_n, s_1, ..., s_k)$ is also a function of other information $s_1, ..., s_k$, then of course $v_i(t_1, ..., t_n) = E\{V_i(t_1, ..., t_n, s_1, ..., s_k) \mid t_1, ..., t_n\}$ is just i's estimated value, but for most purposes it does not matter whether $v_i(t_1, ..., t_n)$ is an estimated or an actual value.)

[18] That is, the set of strategies available to a player is the same in the descending auction as in the first-price sealed-bid auction. Choosing any given bid yields the same payoffs in both games as a function of the other players' bids.

[19] To solve for the bidding strategies, the direct method is to examine a player's first-order condition in which she trades off her probability of winning (which increases with her bid) with her profit conditional on winning (which decreases with her bid). Note 121 illustrates the method. For the independent-signal case a faster and more elegant approach is to use the revenue equivalence theorem, see Appendix 1.A. Appendix 1.D gives examples.

value will win at a price equal to the value of the second-highest bidder. Furthermore, a little reflection shows that in a second-price sealed-bid private-values auction it is optimal for a player to bid her true value, whatever other players do.[20] In other words "truth telling" is a dominant strategy equilibrium (and so also a Nash equilibrium), so here, too, the person with the highest value will win at a price equal to the value of the second-highest bidder. This is why the ascending auction is sometimes referred to as an open second-price auction. However, this equivalence applies only for private values, or if there are just two bidders. With any common components to valuations and more than two bidders, players learn about their values from when other players quit an ascending auction and condition their behavior on this information.

A key feature of bidding in auctions with common-values components is the *winner's curse*: each bidder must recognize that she wins the object only when she has the highest signal (in symmetric equilibrium). Failure to take into account the bad news about others' signals that comes with any victory can lead to the winner paying more, on average, than the prize is worth, and this is said to happen often in practice. In equilibrium, bidders must adjust their bids downwards accordingly.

Appendix 1.D provides examples of equilibrium bidding strategies (and the winner's curse) in the standard auctions, in both private- and common-value contexts.

1.1.5 Terminology

Since the equivalence of descending and first-price sealed-bid auctions is completely general in single-unit auctions, and ascending and second-price sealed-bid auctions are also equivalent under many conditions (and have similar properties more broadly) we will often refer to the two kinds of auctions simply as *first-price* and *second-price*, respectively.

Also, we will refer to any model in which a bidder's value depends to some extent on other bidders' signals as a *common-value* model. However, note that some authors reserve the term "common-value" to refer only to the special case when all bidders' actual values are identical functions of the signals (what we

---

[20] To confirm this, consider bidding $v - x$ when your true value is v. If the highest bid other than yours is w, then if $v - x > w$ you win the auction and pay w, just as if you bid v. If $w > v$ you lose the auction and get nothing, just as if you bid v. But if $v > w > v - x$, bidding $v - x$ causes you to lose the auction and get nothing, whereas if you had bid v, you would have won the auction and paid w for a net surplus of $v - w$. So you never gain, and might lose, if you bid $v - x$.

Now consider bidding $v + x$ when your true value is v. If the highest bid other than yours is w, then if $v > w$ you win and pay w, just as if you bid v. If $w > v + x$ you lose and pay nothing, just as if you bid v. But if $v + x > w > v$, having bid $v + x$ causes you to "win" an auction you otherwise would have lost, and you have to pay $w > v$ so you get negative surplus. So bidding $v + x$ may hurt you compared with bidding v, but it never helps you.

called the pure common-value case). Also (and somewhat inconsistently) we will use the term *almost common values* to mean almost pure common values.

Finally, there is no formal distinction between normal auctions, in which the auctioneer is the seller and the bidders are buyers who have values for the object(s) sold, and procurement auctions, where the auctioneer is a buyer and the bidders are sellers who have costs of supplying the object(s) bought. To avoid confusion we will generally adopt the former perspective (that the auctioneer is the seller) even when discussing papers that are couched in terms of the latter perspective.

1.2 EARLY LITERATURE

Auctions have been used from time immemorial,[21] but they entered the economics literature relatively recently. Remarkably, the first treatment that recognized the game-theoretic aspects of the problem,[22] Vickrey (1961), also made enormous progress in analyzing it including developing some special cases of the celebrated *Revenue Equivalence Theorem* (see below). Vickrey's 1961 and 1962 papers were deservedly a major factor in his 1996 Nobel prize,[23] and the 1961 paper, especially, is still essential reading.

Other influential early work was performed by Shubik and his co-authors, and by Wilson and his student, Ortega Reichert.

Griesmer, Levitan, and Shubik (1967) analyze the equilibrium of a first-price auction in which contestants' valuations are drawn from uniform distributions with different supports, while Wilson (1969) introduced the (pure) common-value model and developed the first closed-form equilibrium analysis of the winner's curse.[24]

---

[21] Shubik (1983) provides an attractively written historical sketch going back to the Babylonian and Roman empires. Most famously, the whole Roman empire was sold by ascending auction in A.D. 193 by the Praetorian Guards; the winner, and therefore next Emperor, was Didius Julianus who reigned for just over two months before being overthrown and executed by Septimius Severus (an early and sad case of the winner's curse); see also notes 56, 106, and 108, and see Gibbon (1776), volume I, chapter V for an account.

[22] There are slightly earlier studies in the operations research literature, especially Friedman (1956), but these treat the problem decision-theoretically with bidders estimating opponents' bidding strategies based on a naive model of past behavior.

[23] He shared the prize with Jim Mirrlees whose 1971 paper, although couched in the context of the theory of optimal income taxation, developed techniques that were to prove critical to the later analysis of auctions. Vickrey (1976) makes additional contributions to auction theory, including sketching the "simultaneous ascending auction" later proposed by McAfee, Milgrom, and Wilson for the recent FCC auctions of radio spectrum licenses (see note 78).

[24] Rothkopf (1969) addresses a similar problem to Wilson's, but implicitly restricts bidders' strategies to multiples of their estimated values (see Rothkopf, 1980). Capen, Clapp, and Campbell (1971) is a well-known, more popular account of the winner's curse in practice that was immensely important in influencing bidding practice. Wilson (1967) is a precursor to Wilson (1969), but with a less natural equilibrium concept.

Ortega Reichert's (1968a) PhD thesis contains the seeds of much future work, but the time was perhaps not ripe for it, and it unfortunately never reached publication. It is a pleasure to be able to publish a small part of it in *The Economic Theory of Auctions*: the chapter we publish considers a sequence of two first-price auctions in which the correlation of players' values for the two objects means that a player's bid for the first object conveys information about her value for the second object, and hence about her likely second bid. (We also publish a short explanatory foreword to the chapter.[25]) This analysis of a signaling game was enormously influential in, for example, guiding Milgrom and Roberts' (1982) analysis of limit pricing.[26]

However, with the exception of Vickrey's first (1961) article, these are no longer papers for the beginner.

1.3 Introduction to the Recent Literature

The full flowering of auction theory came only at the end of the 1970s with critical contributions from Milgrom, in papers both on his own and with Weber; from Riley, in papers with Maskin and with Samuelson; and from Myerson, among others, in addition to more from Wilson. These and contemporaneous contributions rapidly moved the field close to its current frontier. A very readable introduction to the state of the field by the late 1980s is in McAfee and McMillan (1987a). Another helpful introductory article is Maskin and Riley (1985) which manages to convey many of the key ideas in a few pages by focusing on the case with just two possible types of each of just two bidders.[27,28]

1.4 The Basic Analysis of Optimal Auctions, Revenue Equivalence, and Marginal Revenues

Roughly simultaneously, Myerson (1981) and Riley and Samuelson (1981) showed that Vickrey's results about the equivalence in expected revenue of different auctions apply very generally:[29]

[25] See also the brief exposition of this work in Section 3.1 of Weber (1983) (see section 1.10.3 of this survey, and reprinted in the corresponding part of *The Economic Theory of Auctions*).

[26] Personal communication from Paul Milgrom.

[27] A caveat is that the effects of correlated types cannot properly be discussed with just two types, and this section of the paper is a little flawed and confusing. However Riley (1989a) has a nice discussion of correlation with just *three* possible types of each bidder. See also Appendix 1.C.

[28] Other valuable survey material includes Milgrom (1985, 1987, 1989), Weber (1985), Riley (1989b), Maskin (1992), Wilson (1992), Harstad and Rothkopf (1994), Rothkopf (1994), and Wolfstetter (1996).

[29] Ortega Reichert (1968a) and Holt (1980) made some earlier extensions of Vickrey's work. Harris and Raviv (1981) covers much of the same ground as Myerson and Riley and Samuelson.

Assume each of a given number of risk-neutral potential buyers of an object has a privately known signal independently drawn from a common, strictly increasing, atomless distribution. Then any auction mechanism in which (i) the object always goes to the buyer with the highest signal, and (ii) any bidder with the lowest-feasible signal expects zero surplus, yields the same expected revenue (and results in each bidder making the same expected payment as a function of her signal).[30]

Note that the result applies both to private-value models (in which a bidder's value depends only on her own signal), and to more general common-value models provided bidders' signals are independent.

Thus all the "standard" auctions, the ascending, the descending, the first-price sealed-bid, and the second-price sealed-bid, yield the same expected revenue under the stated conditions, as do many non-standard auctions such as an "all-pay" auction (in which every competitor pays her bid but only the highest bidder wins the object, as in a lobbying competition).[31]

This *Revenue Equivalence Theorem* result is so fundamental, so much of auction theory can be understood in terms of it, and at root the proof is so simple, that we offer an elementary derivation of it in Appendix 1.A. Any reader who is unfamiliar with the result, or who is under any misapprehension that it is a difficult one, is strongly urged to begin here.[32]

Riley and Samuelson's proof is less direct than that of Appendix 1.A, but is still a simpler read than Myerson's, and Riley and Samuelson give more illustrations. However, Myerson offers the most general treatment, and also develops the mathematics used to prove revenue equivalence a little further to show how to derive optimal auctions (i.e., auctions that maximize the seller's expected revenue) for a wide class of problems (see below).

Although this work was a remarkable achievement, there seemed to be little relationship to traditional price theory, which made the subject a difficult one for many economists. Bulow and Roberts (1989) greatly simplified the analysis of optimal auctions by showing that the problem is, in their own words, "essentially equivalent to the analysis of standard monopoly third-degree price discrimination. The auctions problem can therefore be understood by applying the usual logic of marginal revenue versus marginal cost."

---

[30] This is not the most general statement. See Appendix 1.A. To see the necessity of a strictly increasing or atomless distribution, see note 117. See Riley (1989a) for revenue equivalence results for discrete distributions.

[31] Other examples that can be modeled as all-pay auctions include queues (see Holt and Sherman (1982)), legal battles (see Baye, Kovenock, and De Vries (1997)), and markets with consumer switching costs in which firms compete for the prize of selling to new unattached consumers by lowering their prices to their old locked-in customers (see especially Appendix B of Bulow and Klemperer (1998) which explicitly uses the revenue equivalence theorem, and also Rosenthal (1980) and more generally, Klemperer (1995)). The war of attrition is also a kind of all-pay auction (see section 1.13.4) and Bulow and Klemperer (1999)).

[32] The appendix also gives an example of solving for bidding strategies in more complex auctions by using revenue equivalence with an ascending auction.

In particular, it is helpful to focus on bidders' "marginal revenues". Imagine a firm whose demand curve is constructed from an arbitrarily large number of bidders whose values are independently drawn from a bidder's value distribution. When bidders have independent private values, a bidder's "marginal revenue" is defined as the marginal revenue of this firm at the price that equals the bidder's actual value. Bulow and Roberts follow Myerson to show that under the assumptions of the revenue equivalence theorem *the expected revenue from an auction equals the expected marginal revenue of the winning bidder(s).*

Bulow and Klemperer (1996)[33] provide a simpler derivation of this result that also generalizes its application.[34] We give an elementary exposition of this material in Appendix 1.B.

So in an optimal auction the objects are allocated to the bidders with the highest marginal revenues, just as a price-discriminating monopolist sells to the buyers with the highest marginal revenues (by equalizing the lowest marginal revenues sold to across different markets). And just as a monopolist should not sell below the price where marginal revenue equals marginal cost, so an auctioneer should not sell below a reserve price set equal to the value of the bidder whose marginal revenue equals the value to the auctioneer of retaining the unit. (The marginal revenue should be set equal to zero if the auctioneer, or monopolist, is simply maximizing expected revenues.)

These principles indicate how to run an optimal auction in the general case.[35] Furthermore, when bidders are symmetric (i.e., when their signals are drawn from a common distribution), any "standard" auction sells to the bidder with the highest signal. Therefore, if bidders with higher signals have higher marginal revenues—in the private-value context this is just equivalent to the usual assumption that a monopolist's marginal revenue is downward sloping[36]—then the winning bidder has the highest marginal revenue. So under the assumptions of the revenue equivalence theorem, and if bidders with higher signals have higher marginal revenues, *all the standard auctions are optimal if the seller imposes the optimal reserve price.*

[33] Also discussed in section 1.8.2, and reprinted in the corresponding part of *The Economic Theory of Auctions.*

[34] Bulow and Klemperer show how the result extends with common values, non-independent private information, and risk-aversion, while Bulow and Roberts restrict attention to the risk-neutral, independent, private-value, framework. See Appendix 1.B.

The main thrust of Bulow and Klemperer's analysis is to develop a result about the value to an auctioneer of an additional bidder relative to the importance of constructing an optimal auction (see section 1.8.2).

[35] See Myerson (1981) and Bulow and Roberts (1989) for details.

[36] This amounts to the assumption that the monopolist's demand curve (or bidder's distribution function) is not too convex.

The assumption that bidders with higher signals have higher marginal revenues is more stringent in common-value contexts. See note 54.

Much of auction theory can be most easily understood by thinking in terms of marginal revenues and the relationship to the conditions for revenue equivalence; this chapter emphasizes this perspective.

1.5 RISK-AVERSION

It is easy to see how risk-aversion affects the revenue equivalence result: in a second-price (or an ascending) auction, risk-aversion has no effect on a bidder's optimal strategy which remains to bid (or bid up to) her actual value.[37] But in a first-price auction, a slight increase in a player's bid slightly increases her probability of winning at the cost of slightly reducing the value of winning, so would be desirable for a risk-averse bidder if the current bidding level were optimal for a risk-neutral bidder. So risk-aversion makes bidders bid more aggressively in first-price auctions. Therefore, since the standard auctions were revenue equivalent with risk-neutral bidders, a risk-neutral seller faced by risk-averse bidders prefers the first-price auction to second-price sealed-bid or ascending auctions.

What if the auctioneer is risk-averse but the buyers are risk-neutral? Observe that the winner pays a price set by the runner-up in a second-price or ascending auction and, by revenue equivalence, must bid the expectation of this price in a first-price auction. That is, conditional on the winner's actual information, the price is fixed in the first-price auction, and random but with the same mean in the second-price auction. So also unconditional on the winner's information, the price is riskier (but with the same mean) in the second-price auction. So a risk-averse seller prefers the first-price auction to the second-price sealed-bid auction and, for a similar reason, prefers the second-price sealed-bid auction to an ascending open auction.[38]

In another of the crucially important papers of the early 1980s, Maskin and Riley (1984) develop and generalize these results and then go on to consider the design of optimal auctions when the seller is risk-neutral and the buyers are risk-averse.[39]

However, although first-price auctions lead to higher prices with risk-averse buyers, this does not mean risk-averse buyers prefer second-price or ascending auctions since, as noted above, prices in the first-price auction are less risky. Matthews (1987) takes up the buyer's viewpoint; in fact, buyers are just indifferent with constant absolute risk aversion and tend to prefer the first-price auction if they have increasing absolute risk aversion or "affiliated

---

[37] In a sealed-bid second-price auction with common-value components, a bidder bids her expected utility conditional on being tied for highest bidder (see Appendices 1.C and 1.D).

[38] See Waehrer, Harstad, and Rothkopf (1998) for the fullest exposition of the case of a risk-averse auctioneer.

[39] Matthews (1983) has many similar results. Holt (1980) is an earlier treatment.

values" (see next section).[40] These results can be developed by generalizing the revenue equivalence result to a "utility equivalence" result that applies for risk-averse bidders.[41]

1.6 CORRELATION AND AFFILIATION

Another crucial assumption in the basic analysis of optimal auctions is that each bidder's private information is independent of competitors' private information. We now relax this assumption while reverting to the assumption of risk-neutrality.

Section 7 of Myerson's extraordinary (1981) paper provides a very simple and instructive example showing that if bidders' private information is correlated, then the seller can construct a mechanism that yields for herself the entire social surplus that would be feasible if bidders' information were fully public! The mechanism offers each bidder a schedule of bets among which she is required to choose if she is to participate. For any given private information, the best of these bets will yield her exactly zero surplus in expectation, and by choosing it she is revealing her type so that her surplus can be fully and efficiently extracted. We give an example in Appendix 1.C.

Crémer and McLean (1985) show that Myerson's result is very general, although it does seem to rely heavily on assumptions such as risk-neutrality of both the bidders and the seller, common knowledge of the distributions from which bidders' signals are drawn, the inability of bidders to collude, and the ability of the seller to credibly and costlessly communicate and enforce the auction's results (often including extracting large payments from losing bidders).[42]

Since the "optimal mechanisms" seem unrealistic in this environment, how do standard auctions compare? Milgrom and Weber's remarkable (1982a) paper addresses this question in the context of developing a general theory of auctions with affiliated information. (Very roughly, bidders' signals are *affiliated* if a high value of one bidder's signal makes high values of other bidders' signals more likely.[43]) Since this paper is both very important in the literature and quite challenging for many readers, we given an elementary exposition of the main results in Appendix 1.C, by starting from the revenue equivalence argument developed in Appendix 1.A.

---

[40] Matthews' paper is also important for its analysis of the case where the number of buyers is unknown. See section 1.8.4.

[41] See Robert, Laffont, and Loisel (1994).

[42] Crémer and McLean (1988), McAfee, McMillan, and Reny (1989), and McAfee and Reny (1992) show the result in even greater generality. Esö (1999) argues the result may not be too sensitive to bidder risk-aversion.

[43] See Appendix 1.C for a precise definition.

The main results are that ascending auctions lead to higher expected prices than sealed-bid second-price auctions, which in turn lead to higher expected prices than first-price auctions.[44] The intuition is that the winning bidder's surplus is due to her private information. The more the price paid depends on others' information (the price depends on all other bidders' information in an ascending auction with common-value elements, and on one other bidder's information in a second-price sealed-bid auction), the more closely the price is related to the winner's information, since information is affiliated. So the lower is the winner's information rent and hence her expected surplus, and so the higher is the expected price.

For the same reason, if the seller has access to any private source of information, her optimal policy is to pre-commit to revealing it honestly. The general principle that expected revenue is raised by linking the winner's payment to information that is affiliated with the winner's information, is known as the Linkage Principle.[45]

One of the more striking results of the basic analysis of optimal auctions is that if bidders have independent private values, the seller's reserve price is both independent of the number of bidders, and also well above the seller's cost. The reason is that the optimal reserve price is where marginal revenue equals the seller's cost, and a bidder's marginal revenue is independent of other bidders' marginal revenues when values are independent. However, if valuations are affiliated, more bidders implies more certainty about any one bidder's valuation conditional on other bidders' information, hence flatter marginal revenue curves, so a far higher proportion of bidders have marginal revenues in excess of the seller's cost.[46] So the reserve price must be set lower. Levin and Smith (1996a) show that the optimal reserve price converges to the seller's true value as the number of bidders grows.

1.7 ASYMMETRIES

Along with risk-neutrality, and independent private information, a third crucial assumption of the revenue equivalence theorem is that buyers' private

---

[44] Appendix 1.D gives an example.

[45] See also the discussion of Milgrom and Weber (2000) in section 1.10.3.

[46] More precisely, consider setting an optimal reserve price after seeing all but the highest valuation. Affiliation implies the highest value is likely to be close to the second-highest, so the demand curve formed by a continuum of bidders with valuations drawn from the highest bidder's value distribution conditional on all others' values is rather flat just above the second value. Thus the final part of the highest-bidder's marginal revenue curve, conditional on all that has been observed, is also rather flat around the second-highest valuation. So even if the reserve price could be set based on all this information, it would usually be set very low. Hence it will also be set very low if it must be set prior to the auction.

(Note that even with independent signals the reserve price should optimally be set after the auction if there are common-value components to valuations. See, for example, Bulow and Klemperer (1996) for how to set the optimal reserve price in this case.)

values or signals were drawn from a common distribution. We now discuss relaxing the symmetry assumption.[47]

1.7.1 Private Value Differences

Myerson (1981) and Bulow and Roberts (1989) showed that a revenue-maximizing auction allocates objects to the bidder(s) with the highest marginal revenue(s) rather than to those with the highest value(s). Recall from the standard theory of demand that a buyer on a given demand curve has a higher marginal revenue than any buyer with the same valuation on a demand curve that is higher everywhere due to being shifted out by a fixed amount horizontally. So a revenue-maximizing auctioneer typically discriminates in favor of selling to bidders whose values are drawn from lower distributions, that is, "weaker" bidders. McAfee and McMillan (1989) develop this point in a procurement context.[48]

Since in a first-price auction a bidder whose value is drawn from a weaker distribution bids more aggressively (closer to her actual value) than a bidder from a stronger distribution,[49] a first-price auction also discriminates in favor of selling to the weaker bidder, in contrast to a second-price (or ascending) auction which always sells to the bidder with the higher valuation (in a private-values model). So it is plausible that a first-price auction may be more profitable in expectation, even though less allocatively efficient, than a second-price auction, when all the assumptions for revenue equivalence except symmetry are satisfied.[50] This is in fact often, though not always, the case. The large variety of different possible kinds of asymmetries makes it difficult to develop general results, but Maskin and Riley (2000b) make large strides.[51] A very useful brief discussion in Maskin and Riley (1985) summarizes the situation as "roughly speaking, the sealed-bid auction generates more revenue than the open [second-price] auction when bidders have distributions with the same shape (but different supports), whereas the open auction dominates when,

---

[47] For results about the existence and uniqueness of equilibria in first-price auctions see Lebrun (1996), Maskin and Riley (2000a, forthcoming), Athey (2001), and Lizzeri and Persico (2000) (who consider a broader class of games). Some similar results can be developed following Bulow, Huang, and Klemperer (1995). Wilson (1998) derives explicitly the equilibrium of an ascending auction for a model with both private- and common-value components which allows asymmetries.

[48] See also Rothkopf, Harstad, and Fu (2003).

[49] In a first-price auction the first-order condition of a bidder with value v considering raising her bid, b, by a small amount Δb that would raise her probability of winning, p, by a small amount Δp sets $(v - b)\Delta p - p\Delta b = 0$. Weaker bidders have smaller probabilities of winning, p, and hence smaller "profit margins", $v - b$, when they do win.

[50] Maskin (1992) shows an ascending auction is efficient for a single good, even when valuations have common-value components, under a broad class of assumptions.

[51] The earliest analyses of asymmetric cases are in Vickrey (1961) and Griesmer, Levitan, and Shubik (1967). Marshall, Meurer, Richard, and Stromquist (1994), and Riley and Li (1997) solve additional cases by numerical methods.

across bidders, distributions have different shapes but approximately the same support."

Maskin and Riley (2000b) also show quite generally that "strong" buyers prefer the second-price auction, whereas "weak" buyers prefer the first-price auction. This may be important where attracting buyers to enter the auction is an important consideration; see below.

1.7.2 Almost-Common-Values

If valuations have common-value components the effects of asymmetries can be even more dramatic. If one player has a small advantage, for example, a slightly higher private value in a setting that is close to pure-common-values, that player will bid a little more aggressively. This strengthens the opponent's "winner's curse" (since winning against a more aggressive competitor is worse news about the actual value of a common value object), so the opponent will bid a little less aggressively in an ascending auction, so the first player's winner's curse is reduced and she can bid a little more aggressively still, and so on. Klemperer (1998) discusses a range of contexts in which, in consequence, an apparently small edge for one player translates into a very large competitive advantage in an ascending auction. The earliest specific example in the literature is Bikhchandani's (1988) demonstration that a small reputation advantage can allow a bidder to almost always win a pure-common-value auction, and that this reputational advantage may be very easy to sustain in a repeated context. Bulow, Huang, and Klemperer (1999) demonstrate that having a small toehold can be an enormous advantage in an otherwise pure-common-values takeover battle.[52]

The original stimulus for all this work is Milgrom (1981)[53] which analyzes equilibria in ascending auctions and shows that there is a vast multiplicity in the pure-common values case, ranging from the symmetric equilibrium to equilibria in which an arbitrarily chosen player always wins. Later work shows that adding some "grit" into the model, whether it be a small private-value component, a small reputation component, or a small ownership component, etc., selects one of these equilibria, but which equilibrium is selected depends on exactly how the pure-common-values model is perturbed.

---

[52] This analysis has been influential in competition policy. The UK Government recently blocked BSkyB (Rupert Murdoch's satellite television company) from acquiring Manchester United (England's most successful football club). An important reason was concern that by acquiring Manchester United, which receives the biggest share of the Premier League's television revenues (about 7 percent), BSkyB would be able to shut out other television companies when the contract for the league's broadcasting rights next comes up for auction (see *Economist*, March 20, 1999, p. 35; *Financial Times*, April 10, 1999, p. 22; and U.K. Monopolies and Mergers Commission, 1999).

[53] Also discussed in sections 1.7.3 and 1.8.3, and reprinted in *The Economic Theory of Auctions*.

Thus an apparently small change in the environment can greatly increase a player's chance of winning.

Since the winner of an "almost-common-value" ascending auction may therefore often have the lower signal, and so typically the lower marginal revenue, ascending auctions may be very unprofitable in this context.

By contrast, in a first-price auction a small change to the symmetric model generally results in a small change to the (unique) symmetric equilibrium, so the bidder with the higher signal hence, typically, higher marginal revenue continues to (almost always) win. Thus the first-price auction is almost optimal for a revenue-maximizing auctioneer, and is much more profitable than an ascending auction, provided bidders with higher signals have higher marginal revenues.[54]

The effects of almost-common-values in ascending auctions are most extreme where there are also entry or bidding costs (see section 1.8) in which case the disadvantaged bidder(s) may not enter at all, leaving the auctioneer to face a single bidder (see Klemperer, 1998).

1.7.3 Information Advantages

Another important form of asymmetry is that one player may have superior information. Here, again, Milgrom (1981)[55] is critically important, showing that in a pure-common-value setting a bidder with no private information makes no profits in equilibrium in a second-price auction. Milgrom and Weber (1982b) show the same result (and much more) in the first-price context. The latter paper builds in part on work published later in Engelbrecht-Wiggans, Milgrom, and Weber (1983).

---

[54] However, Bulow and Klemperer (2002) show that the assumption that bidders with higher signals have higher marginal revenues is not innocuous in the common-values context. In the private-values context the assumption is equivalent to the assumption of downward-sloping marginal revenue for a monopolist whose demand corresponds to the distribution of a bidder's signals; in common-value settings, bidders' values and hence marginal revenues depend on *others'* signals, and oligopolists' marginal revenues are not necessarily decreasing in *other* firms' outputs. In the pure-common-values (and almost-common-values) cases the assumption is related to the assumption of strategic substitutes (see Bulow and Klemperer, 2002; and also Bulow, Geanakoplos, and Klemperer, 1985a,b).

Bulow and Klemperer (2002) show that if in fact this assumption does not hold, then a number of standard presumptions are violated in the symmetric equilibrium of a pure-common-values ascending auction; for example, more bidders can lower expected profits (see note 63) selling more units can raise average price, and rationing (as in Initial Public Offerings) can raise expected price. Furthermore, even if the assumption on marginal revenue holds, these results arise in the almost-common values case.

[55] Also discussed in sections 1.7.2 and 1.8.3, and reprinted in *The Economic Theory of Auctions*.

1.8 ENTRY COSTS AND THE NUMBER OF BIDDERS

1.8.1 Endogenous Entry of Bidders

In practical auction design, persuading bidders to take the time and trouble to enter the contest is a major concern, so we now endogenize the number of bidders and ask how it depends on the selling mechanism chosen.[56] (See also the Afterword to this chapter and parts C and D.)

The first key result is that in a private-value setting that satisfies the revenue-equivalence assumptions except for the presence of entry costs, bidders make the socially correct decision about whether or not to enter any standard auction if the reserve price is set equal to the seller's valuation. To see this, note that the expected social value of the bidder being present is the probability she wins the auction times the difference between her value and the runner-up's value. But this is exactly the bidder's expected profit after entering a second-price auction, and so also, using revenue equivalence, in a very wide class of auctions including all standard auctions.

Furthermore, in a free-entry equilibrium in which ex-ante identical bidders enter to the point at which each expects zero profits net of the entry cost (and each finds out her private value subsequent to the entry decision[57]), the seller obtains the entire social surplus in expectation. So it also follows that running any standard auction with a reserve price equal to the seller's cost is revenue maximizing for the seller.[58]

These results can be found in, for example, Levin and Smith (1994)[59] in a model in which bidders simultaneously make symmetric mixed-strategy entry decisions so that their expected profits are exactly zero. The results apply whether or not bidders observe how many others have chosen to enter before bidding in the auction, since revenue equivalence applies across and between both cases.[60] The results also apply if entry is sequential but the number of

---

[56] The Praetorians, when auctioning the Empire (see note 21), seem to have stipulated that the winning bidder could not punish the losers. This provision may have encouraged entry to the auction, although it would presumably reduce revenue from any exogenously fixed number of bidders.

[57] See Menezes and Monteiro (2000) for the case in which bidders know their private values prior to the entry decision.

[58] But the seller can increase social surplus, and hence her own expected revenue, if she can run a series of auctions. For example, she might announce an auction with a reserve price and the proviso that if the reserve is not met there will be a subsequent auction. Then there will be additional entrants in the second round if the good is not sold in the first round, that is, in the states in which the first-round entrants turned out to have low valuations. This increases social efficiency and seller revenue. See Burguet and Sákovics (1996) and also McAfee and McMillan (1988).

[59] Earlier related literature includes Engelbrecht-Wiggans (1987) and McAfee and McMillan (1987c). Levin and Smith (1996b) consider the seller's preference between standard auction forms when buyers are risk-averse; the auctioneer typically, but not always, prefers first-price to second-price auctions when bidders have entry costs.

[60] See section 1.8.4 below.

firms is treated as a continuous variable so that entrants' expected profits are
exactly zero. In other cases the fact that the number of entrants must be an
integer means that the marginal entrant's expected profits may exceed zero,
but Engelbrecht-Wiggans (1993) shows that this makes very little difference:
the seller optimally adjusts the reserve price and/or sets an entry subsidy or fee
that sucks up all the entrants' surplus while altering the number of entrants by
at most one.[61,62]

In pure-common-value auctions, in marked contrast, the socially optimal
number of bidders is obviously just one. Furthermore, Matthews (1984) shows
that expected seller revenue can also be *decreasing* in the number of bidders in
non-pathological pure-common-value settings, and Bulow and Klemperer
(2002) provide intuition for why this is natural by using marginal-revenue
analysis.[63] So both socially and privately, entry fees and reservation prices are
much more desirable in common-value contexts. See Levin and Smith (1994)
and also Harstad (1990).

Where bidders are asymmetric ex-ante, an auctioneer may wish to run
an ex-post inefficient auction to attract weaker bidders to enter the contest.
Thus Gilbert and Klemperer (2000) show that committing to ration output
(i.e., selling at a fixed price at which demand exceeds supply) may be
more profitable than raising price to clear the market (i.e., running an
ascending auction that is ex-post efficient) because it attracts more buyers
into the market.[64,65]

Finally, bidders can influence the number of their rivals through their own
strategic behavior. In particular, Fishman (1988) demonstrates that it can be
profitable for a bidder to commit to a high bid (e.g., by making a preemptive

[61] The same result extends to affiliated private value auctions.

[62] Furthermore, Bulow and Klemperer (1996) show in the same setting that an additional bidder
is worth more than the ability to set an optimal reserve price against a given number of bidders. See
section 1.8.2.

[63] The point is that while the assumption that bidders with higher signals have higher marginal
revenues usually holds in private-value settings, it often does not hold in pure-common-value
settings. See note 54.

For a simple example consider the case where the common value equals the maximum of three
signals v_i, $i = 1, 2, 3$, each drawn independently from a uniform distribution on $[0, 1]$ and each known
by a different bidder. By selling to an uninformed bidder the seller makes $\frac{9}{12}$ ($= E\max\{v_1, v_2, v_3\}$).
Selling to a single informed bidder the maximum revenue equals $\frac{8}{12}$ ($= E\max\{v_2, v_3\}$) achieved by
setting a reservation price at this level (an informed bidder with signal 0 will just be willing to pay this
price). Selling to two informed bidders yields at most $\frac{7}{12}$ in expectation (by a slightly harder calculation). Selling to all three bidders yields at most $\frac{6}{12}$ in expectation (the expected second-highest signal).
(See exercise 8.)

[64] Or because it lowers the cost of persuading a given number of buyers to invest in participating
in the market. Possible examples include the rationing of microchips, and split-award defense
contracts.

Bulow and Klemperer (2002) provide another reason for rationing. See the previous paragraph.

[65] Similarly, Persico (2000b) shows that bidders have more incentive to collect information
prior to a first-price auction than prior to a second-price auction.

"jump" bid in a takeover battle) to deter potential rivals from incurring the cost required to enter the contest.[66]

1.8.2 The Value of Additional Bidders

Bulow and Klemperer (1996) show that when bidders are symmetric, an additional bidder is worth more to the seller in an ascending auction than the ability to set a reserve price, provided bidders with higher signals have higher marginal revenues. They then demonstrate that, very generally in a private-value auction, and also in a wide class of common-value settings,[67] a simple ascending auction with no reserve price and $N + 1$ symmetric bidders is more profitable than any auction that can realistically be run with N of these bidders.[68] So it is typically worthwhile for a seller to devote more resources to expanding the market than to collecting the information and performing the calculations required to figure out the best mechanism.

1.8.3 Information Aggregation with Large Numbers of Bidders

An important strand of the auction literature has been concerned with the properties of pure-common-value auctions as the number of bidders becomes large. The question is: does the sale price converge to the true value, thus fully aggregating all of the economy's information even though each bidder has only partial information? If it does, it is then attractive to think of an auction model as justifying some of our ideas about perfect competition.

Wilson (1977)'s important early contribution showed that the answer is "yes" for a first-price auction under his assumptions.[69] Milgrom (1981) obtained similar results for a second-price auction (or for a $(k + 1)$th price auction for k objects) in his remarkable paper that contains a range of other significant results and which we have already mentioned in sections 1.7.2 and 1.7.3.[70]

Matthews (1984) allows each bidder to acquire information at a cost. In his model, as the number of bidders becomes large the amount of information each obtains falls, but in such a way that the (first-price) sale price does not in general converge to the true value.

---

[66] Similarly, Daniel and Hirshleifer (1995) obtain jump bidding in an ascending auction when each successive bid is costly. See section 1.13.3.

[67] In common-value settings higher signals would not imply higher marginal revenues. See note 54.

[68] A Crémer and McLean (1985)-style mechanism is probably *not* a realistic one in a practical setting. See our discussion in section 1.6, and also Bulow and Klemperer (1996) and Lopomo (1998).

[69] Milgrom (1979) gives a precise characterization of the signal structures that imply Wilson's result.

[70] Pesendorfer and Swinkels (1997) show that the sale price converges to the true value in a $(k + 1)$th price auction for k objects under weaker assumptions than Wilson's, provided that the number of objects as well as the number of bidders becomes large.

1.8.4 Unknown Number of Bidders

Matthews (1987)[71] and McAfee and McMillan (1987b) consider auctions
when bidders with private values are uncertain about how many rivals they
are competing with,[72] and analyze how bidders' and the seller's preferences
between the number of bidders being known or unknown depend on the
nature of bidders' risk aversion and on whether bidders' signals are
affiliated, etc.[73]

Finally, it is not hard to see that under the usual assumptions (risk-neutrality, independent signals, symmetry, etc.), the standard argument for revenue
equivalence applies independent of whether the actual number of competitors
is revealed to bidders before they bid.[74]

1.9 COLLUSION

A crucial concern about auctions in practice is the ability of bidders to collude,
but the theoretical work on this issue is rather limited. (See, however, the
Afterword to this chapter and parts C and D.)

Robinson (1985) makes the simple but important point that a collusive
agreement may be easier to sustain in a second-price auction than in a first-
price auction. Assuming, for simplicity, no problems in coming to agreement
among all the bidders, or in sharing the rewards between them, and abstracting
from any concerns about detection, etc., the optimal agreement in a second-
price auction is for the designated winner to bid infinitely high while all the
other bidders bid zero, and no other bidder has any incentive to cheat on this
agreement. But to do as well in a first-price auction the bidders must agree that
the designated winner bid an arbitrarily small amount, while all the others bid
zero, and all the others then have a substantial incentive to cheat on the
agreement.[75]

An important question is whether the cartel can find a mechanism that
efficiently (and incentive-compatibly) designates the winner and divides the

---

[71] Also discussed in section 1.5, and reprinted in the corresponding part of *The Economic
Theory of Auctions*.

[72] In Piccione and Tan (1996) the number of bidders is known, but the number of bidders with
private information is uncertain. This paper also considers common-value settings.

[73] McAfee and McMillan (1987b) also consider optimal auctions for the case of risk-neutral
bidders.

[74] See Harstad, Levin, and Kagel (1990) for explicit bidding functions for the standard
auction forms when the assumptions for revenue equivalence apply. The revenue equivalence result is also a special case of results in Matthews (1987) and McAfee and McMillan
(1987b).

[75] Milgrom (1987) develops a similar intuition to argue that repeated second-price auctions are
more susceptible to collusion than repeated first-price auctions.

spoils by making appropriate side payments, when bidders have private information about their own values. McAfee and McMillan (1992)'s main result is
that this is possible and can be implemented by a simple pre-auction if all the
bidders in the auction are members of the cartel and they all have private
values drawn from the same distribution. This result is very closely related to
the demonstration in Cramton, Gibbons, and Klemperer (1987)[76] that a partnership (e.g., the gains from a cartel) can be efficiently divided up.

McAfee and McMillan also analyze cartels that contain only a subgroup of
the industry participants, and "weak cartels" that cannot make side payments
between members, and consider how a seller should respond to the existence
of a cartel.[77]

Although there are many fewer formal analyses of collusion than seem
merited by the issue's practical importance, Hendricks and Porter (1989) is
a very useful informal survey of the circumstances and mechanisms facilitating collusion. They focus especially on methods of detecting collusion.

1.10 Multi-unit Auctions

Most auction theory, and almost all of the work discussed this far, restricts
attention to the sale of a single indivisible unit. The literature on the sale of
multiple units is much less well developed, except for the case where bidders
demand only a single unit each. It is, however, the most active field of current
research in auction theory,[78] so this is probably the section of this survey that
will become obsolete most quickly. (See the Afterword to this chapter.)

1.10.1 Optimal Auctions

Maskin and Riley (1989) extend Myerson's (1981) analysis of optimal
auctions to the case in which buyers have downward-sloping demand-curves,

---

[76] Discussed in section 1.12.2, and reprinted in that part of *The Economic Theory of Auctions.*

[77] Graham and Marshall (1987) address similar issues and show how any subset of bidders can
achieve efficient collusion if an outside agent is available to achieve ex-post budget balancing (see
also Graham, Marshall, and Richard, 1990). Mailath and Zemsky (1991) show how to achieve
efficient collusion in second-price auctions, even among a subset of bidders who are not ex-ante
identical and without the need for an outside agent, but using a more complicated mechanism.
Hendricks, Porter, and Tan (1999) derive a necessary and sufficient condition for an efficient,
incentive-compatible cartel in a common-value setting.

[78] Much current work has been stimulated by the recent government auctions of radio spectrum
licenses (for mobile telephony, etc.), and emphasizes the problem of selling heterogenous goods
with complementarities between them, with common-value components to bidders' valuations,
and perhaps also externalities between bidders. For discussion of the spectrum sales see McAfee
and McMillan (1994, 1996), Klemperer (1998) (discussed in section 1.7.2, and reprinted in the
corresponding part of *The Economics of Auctions*) and especially, Milgrom (2004). Another large
body of important work has been stimulated by treasury auctions. See Bikhchandani and Huang
(1993) for a survey of treasury security markets.

independently drawn from a one-parameter distribution, for quantities of a homogeneous good.[79] They provide one of a number of expositions of revenue equivalence for the multi-unit case, when buyers each want no more than a single unit.

Palfrey (1983) analyzes a seller's (and buyers') preferences between bundling heterogeneous objects and selling them unbundled; he shows the seller's incentive to bundle diminishes as the number of bidders increases. Very little progress has been made since Palfrey's paper on the problem of determining the seller-optimal auction for selling heterogeneous objects, but this topic is the subject of active current research.[80]

1.10.2 Simultaneous Auctions

Wilson (1979), in another of his papers that was many years ahead of its time, first analyzed *share auctions*—auctions in which each bidder offers a schedule specifying a price for each possible fraction of the item (e.g., a certain volume of Treasury notes). He showed that in a uniform-price auction (when all the shares are sold at the (same) price that equates the supply and demand of shares) there are Nash equilibria that look very collusive, in that they support prices that may be much lower than if the item were sold as an indivisible unit. The intuition is that bidders can implicitly agree to divide up the item at a low price by each bidding extremely aggressively for smaller quantities than her equilibrium share so deterring the others from bidding for more.

This intuition suggests (at least) two ways of "undoing" the equilibrium. One way is to run a discriminatory auction in which bidders pay the price they bid for each share; bidding aggressively for small quantities is then very costly, so bidders submit flatter demand curves which induce greater price competition at the margin. See Back and Zender (1993), who argue that discriminatory auctions are therefore likely to be far more profitable for a seller.[81] Nevertheless, Anton and Yao (1992) show that implicit coordination is still possible in this kind of auction if bidders' values are non-linear in the volume purchased.[82]

A second way of undoing the low-price uniform-price equilibrium is to include some randomness in demands (e.g., from non-competitive bidders)

---

[79] As for Myerson (1981), the analysis can be interpreted through marginal revenues, though it is not presented this way.

[80] See, for example, Armstrong (2000) and Avery and Hendershott (2000), and Rothkopf, Pekeč, and Harstad (1998).

[81] The section of Wilson's paper on discriminatory auctions is a little misleading about the relationship with uniform-price auctions.

Maxwell (1983) is earlier work extending Wilson's paper.

[82] Anton and Yao also use a private-value framework in contrast to Back and Zender's and Wilson's common-value setting. See also Bernheim and Whinston (1986) and Anton and Yao (1989) for related models without incomplete information about costs or values.

or in the seller's supply. Klemperer and Meyer (1989) take this tack and show that sufficient supply uncertainty can reduce the multiplicity of uniform-price equilibria to a single equilibrium that is highly competitive if bidders' values are linear in their volumes purchased.[83] They pose their model in an oligopoly setting, or equivalently a procurement auction, and allow non-linear (but publicly-known) costs; the model closely corresponds to the actual operation of electricity-supply auction markets.[84]

Klemperer and Meyer's model allows downward-sloping demand (in the procurement context) hence the quantity is endogenous to the bids (even absent demand uncertainty). Hansen (1988) considers endogenous quantity in the winner-take-all context, and shows that not only does the auctioneer prefer a first-price to a second-price auction (in a context where revenue equivalence would hold if the quantity were fixed) but the first-price auction is also socially more efficient and may even be preferred by the bidders. The intuition is that in first- and second-price auctions the quantity traded depends on the prices bid by the winner and the runner-up, respectively. So the first-price auction is more productively efficient (the quantity traded reflects the winner's cost or value) and provides greater incentive for aggressive bidding (a more aggressive bid not only increases the probability of winning, but also increases the quantity traded contingent on winning).

1.10.3 Sequential Auctions

The analysis of auctions where units are sold sequentially is well developed for the important special case in which no buyer is interested in more than one unit. In this case, if the units are homogeneous, and under the other usual assumptions, revenue equivalence holds whether the units are sold sequentially or simultaneously (Weber, 1983; Maskin and Riley, 1989; Bulow and Klemperer, 1994).

Thus quite complex multi-unit auctions can be solved by using revenue equivalence to work out, at any point of the game, what players' strategies must be to yield them the same expected payoff as if all the remaining units were auctioned simultaneously in a simple ascending auction.

Bulow and Klemperer (1994) use the revenue equivalence theorem in this way to solve for the dynamic price-path of a model of a stock market or housing market; the model would be intractably hard to solve by the direct method of writing down the first-order conditions for equilibrium in a dynamic

---

[83] Back and Zender (1993) argue that realistic amounts of uncertainty may nevertheless leave a continuum of equilibria. See Nyborg (1997) for further discussion and other arguments against the low-price equilibrium. Other related recent work on simultaneous multi-unit auctions includes Daripa (1996a,b), Engelbrecht-Wiggans and Kahn (1998a,b), and Wang and Zender (2002).

[84] See, for example, the developments of Klemperer and Meyer's model in Bolle (1992), Green and Newbery (1992), and Green (1996).

program. The point of the paper is that rational, strategic, traders *should* be very sensitive to new information and so participate in rushes of trading activity (frenzies) that sometimes lead to crashes in the market price. However, it is the method rather than the specific application that deserves emphasis here.

A much simpler example is the sale of k units through k repetitions of a first-price auction, with only the winning bid announced at each stage, to bidders with independent private values. Here, revenue equivalence tells us that at each stage each bidder just bids the expected $(k + 1)$th highest value, conditional on being a winner and on the information revealed so far, since this is what she would pay if all the remaining units were auctioned simultaneously in a standard ascending auction. It is easy to see that this is a martingale, that is, the price neither rises nor falls over time, on average.

A large contribution of Milgrom and Weber's (2000) seminal paper is to consider a wider class of sequential auctions (including first-price auctions, both with and without price-announcements, second-price auctions, and English auctions) under more general assumptions. They show that with affiliation and/or common-value elements the price path drifts upwards. The intuition for the effect of affiliation is essentially that of the Linkage Principle (see section 1.6).[85] This paper has not previously been published, but it is a highly influential paper that it is gratifying to be able to publish at last in *The Economic Theory of Auctions*. Since it is unpolished, and the reader must beware of possible errors, we also publish a new foreword by the authors that explains the difficulties.

Milgrom and Weber's paper left a puzzle: contrary to the discussion above, it is more common to observe a *downward* drift in prices at auctions (see especially Ashenfelter, 1989). This discrepancy has spawned a small literature attempting to explain the "Declining Price Anomaly" (or "Afternoon Effect").[86] An early example is McAfee and Vincent (1993) who pursue the intuitive notion that risk-aversion might drive up early prices by providing an incentive to buy early. Actually, McAfee and Vincent's results are inconclusive; bidders use mixed strategies when risk-aversion is of the most plausible kind, so prices need not necessarily decline. Nevertheless, theirs is an impor-

---

[85] Note, however, that Perry and Reny (1998) show that the Linkage Principle need not hold if individuals can win more than one unit. The reason is that if (as in Milgrom and Weber's model) bidders desire at most one unit the underbidder is always a loser with pessimistic information, but in a multi-unit auction the underbidder for the marginal unit may already have won inframarginal units and have optimistic information.

[86] In fact Milgrom and Weber (2000) suggest a resolution of the "anomaly" themselves in their discussion of the 1981 sale of leases on RCA satellite-based telecommunications transponders. For other possible resolutions and analyses based on models in which no buyer demands more than one unit, see Bernhardt and Scoones (1994), Engelbrecht-Wiggans (1994), von der Fehr (1994), Gale and Hausch (1994), Beggs and Graddy (1997), and Ginsburg (1998). For analyses when bidders have multi-unit demand see several of the papers cited in note 88.

tant analysis and also provides an interesting example in which bidding functions that are monotonic in value do not exist.

Weber (1983) surveys many of the issues that arise in multi-object auctions, focusing primarily on sequential auctions. Unlike the previously mentioned papers in this subsection, he discusses the complex problems that arise when bidders desire multiple units; Ortega Reichert (1968b)[87] had already addressed some of these.[88,89]

1.10.4 Efficient Auctions

A main message of much of the current research on multi-unit auctions is that it is very hard to achieve efficient outcomes.[90] This is in contrast to the single-unit case, in which Maskin (1992) showed under a broad class of assumptions that an ascending auction is efficient if bidders' private signals are single-dimensional, even with asymmetries among bidders and common-value components to valuations.

A Vickrey auction is efficient in private-value multi-unit contexts,[91] and Dasgupta and Maskin (2000) and Perry and Reny (1998) show how to generalize the Vickrey mechanism to achieve efficiency in a wide variety of multi-unit contexts if each bidder's signal is one-dimensional. But Jehiel and Moldovanu (2001) obtain impossibility results showing that efficiency is not usually possible when each bidder's information signal is multidimensional, as is natural when there are multiple heterogeneous goods.

Ausubel (1998) and Ausubel and Cramton (1998a) emphasize the inefficiencies of standard auctions even in the sale of homogeneous objects. In particular, an ascending multi-unit auction (where the sale price equals the first price at which the number of units demanded falls to the supply available)

---

[87] Discussed in Weber's paper and in our section 1.2, and reprinted in the corresponding part of *The Economic Theory of Auctions.*

[88] Other nice papers analyzing sequential auctions when bidders have multi-unit demand include Robert's ($\approx$1995) very elegant, tractable example; Pitchik and Schotter's (1988), Pitchik's (1995), and Benoît and Krishna's (2001) analyses of budget-constrained bidders; Levin's (1996), Gale, Hausch, and Stegeman's (2000), and von der Fehr and Riis's (1999) models of procurement auctions where bidders have increasing or decreasing marginal costs of supply, or capacity constraints, and the related analyses of Black and de Meza (1992), and Gale and Stegeman (2001); Krishna's (1993) application to whether incumbents will outbid potential entrants for capacity; and Hausch's (1986) analysis of sequential versus simultaneous sales in a model with some similarities to Ortega Reichert's.

[89] McAfee and Vincent (1997) consider an auctioneer who cannot commit not to re-auction an object that fails to meet its reserve, so who might hold multiple auctions of a single unit.

[90] This is true even in the complete information case (see Bikhchandani, 1999).

[91] Although even in this context the Vickrey auction would be problematic for practical policy because high-valuers are often required to pay less than low-valuers (which seems odd to policy makers), because of the odd opportunities for collusive behavior, because of budget constraints, etc.

gives a large bidder an incentive to reduce her demand early in order to pay less for those units she does win.[92]

It is usually assumed that bidders' payments can depend only on the bids. But if the winner's value can be observed ex-post, even imperfectly, the seller can do better by making the winner's payment depend on this observation. This removes some of the winner's information rent, and can be interpreted as an application of the Linkage Principle.

Riley (1988) makes this point in a general context. As a practical application, the quantity of oil extracted may be a noisy signal of an oilfield's profitability; Riley shows that the seller's expected revenue can then be increased either by setting per-unit royalties that the winner must pay in addition to the fee bid, or by having bidders bid on the royalty rate they are willing to pay rather than on fixed fees.[93,94]

Similarly, Laffont and Tirole (1987) analyze a procurement auction in which the winner will subsequently invest in unobserved effort to reduce its cost. The auctioneer observes the final realized cost. Auctioning an incentive contract with a cost-sharing provision gets a better price for the auctioneer by reducing the difference between firms' valuations of winning, so reducing the winner's rent (just like a royalty), even though it weakens the incentives for effort to reduce costs. One of Laffont and Tirole's key results is a "separation property": the optimal contract, and hence the winner's final cost, is similar to that which would apply if there were only a single firm and so no bidding competition, while the auction awards the contract to the firm that announces the lowest expected cost.[95]

Che (1993) uses a version of Laffont and Tirole's model to analyze a multi-dimensional auction in which firms bid on both quality and price in a procurement auction. The auctioneer uses a scoring rule to evaluate the bids. It is no surprise that a revenue equivalence result applies, for example, between "first-score" and

---

[92] Of course, the same effect is present in other models, for example, Klemperer and Meyer (1989).

[93] In analyzing this application, he builds on work by Reece (1979).

[94] But note royalties can be very dangerous in some settings. Imagine a government awarding a monopoly license for a market with downward-sloping demand to the firm that will pay the highest royalty per unit sold. Then firms with identical, constant, marginal costs will bid the royalty up to the vertical intercept of demand less this marginal cost. Government revenue, firm profits, and consumer surplus will all be zero. Riley assumes constant per unit revenue from the oil, and decreasing marginal cost up to some output level about which the bidders have private information.

[95] The same result is obtained independently in similar models due to McAfee and McMillan (1987d) and Riordan and Sappington (1987). A precursor to this work is McAfee and McMillan (1986).

"second-score" auctions. Che also shows that it is optimal for the auctioneer to pre-commit to a scoring rule that under-rewards quality relative to her real (ex-post) preferences.[96] Note that although this is a very elegant model of multi-dimensional bidding, firms only differ according to a one-dimensional type.[97]

1.12 DOUBLE AUCTIONS, ETC.

1.12.1 Double Auctions

Standard auction theory assumes a single seller controls the trading mechanism, while many buyers submit bids. In a double auction, buyers and sellers are treated symmetrically with buyers submitting bids and sellers submitting asks. The double-auction literature thus provides a link to the bargaining literature. We emphasize here models that are closely related to simple, static, standard (one-sided) auctions.[98]

The seminal model is the k-double auction of Chatterjee and Samuelson (1983) in which a single buyer and single seller submit a bid b and ask s, respectively, and if the bid exceeds the ask a trade is consummated at the price $kb + (1 - k)s$, where $0 \leq k \leq 1$. Of course, both buyer and seller have incentive to misrepresent their true values, so trades that would be efficient are not necessarily made.

Wilson (1985) first studied the generalization to the multi-buyer/multi-seller case in which each agent can trade at most one indivisible unit and, given the bids and asks, the maximum number of feasible trades are made at a price a fraction k of the distance between the lowest and highest feasible market clearing prices. The key result is that a double auction is efficient, in the sense that with sufficiently many buyers and sellers there is no other trading rule for which, conditional on agents' values it is common knowledge that all agents would be better off in expectation.

Rustichini, Satterthwaite, and Williams (1994) pursue the question of the extent to which agents' equilibrium bids and asks misrepresent their actual values. The answer is that in large markets the maximum misrepresentation is small, and hence the extent of the inefficiency caused by strategic behavior is also small.[99]

Some intuition is provided by McAfee (1992) who considers the following simple mechanism: if N trades are feasible, let the $(N - 1)$ highest value

---

[96] In terms of the formal model, "quality" plays the role of the bidder's expected cost in Laffont and Tirole. Hence this result.

[97] See also Branco (1997) on multidimensional auctions.

[98] Furthermore, all the papers discussed in this section are independent private-value models. The assumption of private values, especially, seems important.

[99] Satterthwaite and Williams (1989a) and Williams (1991) had earlier obtained similar results for the special case $k = 1$ (the "buyer's bid double auction") which is much easier to handle because sellers all have a dominant strategy of no misrepresentation.

buyers buy at the Nth highest buyer's value while the $(N - 1)$ lowest value sellers sell at the Nth lowest seller's value. Now, just as in a second-price auction, all agents report their actual values as dominant strategies, and only the least valuable feasible trade is foregone, and the mechanism also makes money. The fact that this mechanism is obviously so efficient (and McAfee shows how a slightly more complicated scheme does even better) makes it less surprising that other double auction mechanisms are also very efficient.

1.12.2 Related Two-Sided Trading Mechanisms

Related important work includes Myerson and Satterthwaite's (1983) path-breaking general analysis of mechanism design for bilateral trading. They use techniques similar to those of Myerson (1981), and the reader is similarly urged to study the reinterpretation in terms of marginal revenues and marginal costs given in Bulow and Roberts (1989).[100] Myerson and Satterthwaite show that the symmetric version ($k = \frac{1}{2}$) of Chatterjee and Samuelson's two-player double auction is in fact an optimal mechanism, in that it maximizes the expected gains from trade, in the case that the agents' values are independently drawn from identical uniform distributions.[101]

This paper also demonstrates that ex-post efficiency cannot be achieved in bargaining between a seller who initially owns the asset and a buyer with no prior ownership, when there is private information about valuations. However, Cramton, Gibbons, and Klemperer (1987) show that ex-post efficiency can be guaranteed (i.e., is consistent with incentive compatibility and individual rationality) when the asset to be traded is jointly owned: the reason is that traders' incentives to misrepresent their values are reduced by their uncertainty about whether they will be buyers or sellers. Cramton, Gibbons, and Klemperer exhibit one bidding game that achieves efficiency; revenue equivalence means that other auction forms can achieve the same outcome.[102] This paper explains why ex-post efficient collusion in an auction (i.e., efficiently dividing the joint spoils by designating a winner and making appropriate side payments) is possible (see section 1.9).

1.13. OTHER TOPICS

This section considers some other important topics, each of which is represented by a paper in *The Economic Theory of Auctions*.

---

[100] These two papers are both discussed in section 1.4 and reprinted in the corresponding part of *The Economic Theory of Auctions*.

[101] But this result depends critically on the distributional assumptions, and also assumes agents play the linear equilibrium constructed by Chatterjee and Samuelson. There are also non-linear equilibria (see Leininger, Linhart, and Radner, 1989; Satterthwaite and Williams, 1989b).

[102] This paper, too, can be understood along the same lines that Bulow and Roberts explain Myerson and Satterthwaite.

1.13.1 Budget Constraints

An important reason why revenue equivalence may fail in practice is that bidders may face budget constraints. To see why, consider the standard model in which revenue equivalence applies and bidders have independent private values v_i, but let bidder i have budget constraint b_i. Then in a second-price auction i bids exactly as if she had value $x_i = \min(b_i, v_i)$ but no budget constraint, so by the revenue equivalence theorem[103] the expected revenue equals that from a first-price auction in which bidders have values x_i and no budget constraints, or equivalently a first-price auction in which bidders have values x_i and budget constraints x_i. It is intuitive that this is less expected revenue than from a first-price auction in which bidders have values v_i ($\geq x_i$) and budget constraints b_i ($\geq x_i$). So first-price auctions are more profitable than second-price auctions. This and similar results are obtained in Che and Gale (1998).

It is also intuitive that auction forms that take payments from losers, such as lotteries and "all-pay" auctions, can be more profitable still in the presence of budget constraints.[104] Budget constraints are also very important in sequential multi-unit auctions, where they provide incentives to, for example, try to reduce opponents' budgets in early sales in order to lower subsequent sale prices. This is the subject of an important paper in the literature on experimental auctions, Pitchik and Schotter (1988), and is also an area of active research.[105]

1.13.2 Externalities between Bidders

Jehiel and Moldovanu (1996) make an important extension to the theory by incorporating the possibility that a potential buyer cares who buys the object for sale in the event that she does not. This might be the case, for example, when a patent is auctioned to oligopolistic competitors, or when selling nuclear weapons.[106] Jehiel and Moldovanu's paper raises many of the issues, including demonstrating in the context of first-price auctions with complete information that there may be multiple equilibria, and hence that a potential bidder may do better to avoid an auction rather than show up and risk galvanizing an enemy to win. Jehiel, Moldovanu, and Stacchetti (1996) address the issue of constructing optimal mechanisms, and

---

[103] We assume the b_i are independently drawn from a strictly increasing atomless distribution, so that the x_i correspond to independent draws from a strictly increasing atomless distribution.

[104] See Che and Gale (1996).

[105] See Pitchik (1995), Benoît and Krishna (2001), and Harford (1998).

Budget constraints also affect the risk that a successful bidder may go bankrupt, or otherwise fail to honor the sale contract. See Board (1999), Hansen and Lott (1991), Spulber (1990), Waehrer (1995), and Zheng (2001).

[106] Or an empire. See note 21.

Caillaud and Jehiel (1998) show that externalities between bidders tend to make collusion harder.[107]

1.13.3 Jump Bidding

An ascending auction is usually modeled as a continuous process in which each successive bid is an arbitrarily small increment above the previous bid. However, actual behavior in, for example, takeover battles, often involves "jump bidding" in which a bidder raises the price very substantially with a single bid.[108]

To understand why this might happen, consider a standard independent private-value English auction with two symmetric players. The following behavior is an equilibrium: one player bids the price she would bid in a *first*-price sealed-bid auction; the second player than infers the first player's actual value and bids that actual value if her own value is higher, but quits the auction otherwise.[109] So the player with the actual higher value wins, but the first player pays the first-price auction price when she wins, while the second player pays the second-highest valuation when she wins. Since the higher-value bidder always wins, the outcome is revenue-equivalent to that of the standard continuously ascending model in which the winner always pays the second-highest valuation. And since the first bidder may fear that the second may misunderstand the equilibrium and bid up the price when she will anyway lose, it is not the most natural equilibrium in the simple independent private-value model. But with affiliation, bidders prefer first-price sealed-bid auctions to continuous ascending auctions, as shown in Milgrom and Weber (1982a),[110] so the first-price features of this equilibrium are attractive to bidders, and Avery (1998) demonstrates that we may therefore expect a "jumping" equilibrium to be played.

If there are costs to making each bid, then jump bidding arises for similar reasons, even with independent private values, see Daniel and Hirshleifer (1995).

1.13.4 The War of Attrition

The War of Attrition is no more than a special kind of auction in which all the bidders pay, and keep on paying at some specified rate, until they quit compet-

---

[107] In a related vein, Fullerton and McAfee (1999) examine bidders who are concerned about the risk of entering an industry against stronger rivals.

[108] The auction of the Empire (see note 21) was settled by a final jump bid from 5,000 drachms to 6,250 drachms, though in this case bidders' strategies were probably not optimal ex-ante (and certainly not ex-post).

[109] To my knowledge Daniel and Hirshleifer were the first to note that this kind of jump bidding is an equilibrium of the basic model even absent affiliation or bidding costs.

[110] Discussed in section 1.6 and reprinted in the corresponding part of *The Economic Theory of Auctions*.

ing for the prize. (It is irrelevant to the analysis that in most practical contexts the payments are social waste, rather than collected by an auctioneer.) Important early contributions were made by Riley (1980), Bliss and Nalebuff (1984), and Fudenberg and Tirole (1986), among others. Bulow and Klemperer (1999) extends the analysis to the many-player case, and makes the auction-theoretic underpinnings most explicit, including several appeals to revenue equivalence arguments.[111,112]

1.13.5 Competing Auctioneers

McAfee (1993) examines a model in which many sellers compete for buyers. In equilibrium, in an infinitely large market, each seller holds an efficient auction including setting an efficient reserve price. Thus McAfee and ensuing papers endogenize the use of auctions, and so address the question of when we should expect auctions to arise.[113]

1.14. TESTING THE THEORY

This chapter is concerned with the theory of auctions, but its companion book, *The Economic Theory of Auctions*, concludes with recent surveys of the empirical evidence, Laffont (1997),[114] and of the experimental evidence, Kagel (1995).

1.15. CONCLUSION

Auction theory has been among the most successful branches of economics in recent years. The theory has developed rapidly, and is increasingly being looked to for assistance in practical applications. Testing auction-theoretic models is seen as one of the brightest spots in applied economics. Much

[111] Krishna and Morgan (1997) analyze an open-loop War of Attrition (i.e., bidders cannot revise their strategies based on others' drop-out times) and also analyze the closely related All-Pay Auction.

[112] See section 2.2.2. Many other models of tournaments, lobbying, political contests, R&D races, etc., can most easily be understood as auctions (see chapter 2).

[113] See Peters and Severinov (1997) and Burguet and Sákovics (1999) for further developments along McAfee's lines. In related veins, Manelli and Vincent (1995) study when a procurement auction is more desirable than sequential negotiation, if potential suppliers are privately informed about their goods' qualities; and Bulow and Klemperer (1996) show a standard auction with a reserve price at the auctioneer's value is more profitable than any negotiating mechanism (or optimal auction) if the standard auction attracts at least one more participant (see section 1.8.2).

[114] A good alternative is Hendricks and Paarsch (1995), while Porter (1995) and Laffont and Vuong (1996) offer valuable surveys covering a more limited range. Among the outstanding research articles are Hendricks and Porter (1988) and Laffont, Ossard, and Vuong (1995).

research remains to be done, especially perhaps on multi-unit auctions, and much research is currently being done. But the foundations of the subject, as presented in many of the papers described here, seem secure.

APPENDIX 1.A: THE REVENUE EQUIVALENCE THEOREM

For simplicity, we focus on the basic "independent private values" model, in which n bidders compete for a single unit. Bidder i values the unit at v_i, which is private information to her, but it is common knowledge that each v_i is independently drawn from the same continuous distribution $F(v)$ on $[\underline{v}, \overline{v}]$ (so $F(\underline{v}) = 0$, $F(\overline{v}) = 1$) with density $f(v)$. All bidders are risk-neutral.

Consider *any* mechanism (any single-stage or multi-stage game) for allocating the unit among the n bidders. For this mechanism, and for a given bidder i, let $S_i(v)$ be the expected surplus that bidder i will obtain in equilibrium from participating in the mechanism, as a function of her type, which we now denote by v, rather than v_i, for notational convenience. Let $P_i(v)$ be her probability of receiving the object in the equilibrium. So $S_i(v) = vP_i(v) - E(\text{payment by type } v \text{ of player } i)$.

The following equation is the key:

$$S_i(v) \geq S_i(\tilde{v}) + (v - \tilde{v})P_i(\tilde{v}). \tag{1}$$

The right-hand side is the surplus that player i would obtain if she had type v but deviated from equilibrium behavior, and instead followed the strategy that type $\tilde{v}$ of player i is supposed to follow in the equilibrium of the game induced by the mechanism. That is, if type v exactly mimics what type $\tilde{v}$ would do, then v makes the same payments and wins the object as often as $\tilde{v}$ would. So v gets the same utility that $\tilde{v}$ would get ($S_i(\tilde{v})$), except that in states in which $\tilde{v}$ would win the object (which happens with probability $P_i(\tilde{v})$) type v values the object at $(v - \tilde{v})$ more than $\tilde{v}$ does, and so v obtains an extra $(v - \tilde{v})P_i(\tilde{v})$ more surplus in all. In an equilibrium, v must prefer not to deviate from equilibrium behavior, so the left-hand side must (weakly) exceed the right-hand side.

So, since type v must not want to mimic type $v + dv$, we have

$$S_i(v) \geq S_i(v + dv) + (-dv)P_i(v + dv) \tag{2}$$

(this is just (1) with $\tilde{v}$ substituted by $v + dv$), and since $v + dv$ must not want to mimic type v we have

$$S_i(v + dv) \geq S_i(v) + (dv)P_i(v). \tag{3}$$

Reorganizing (2) and (3) yields

$$P_i(v + dv) \geq \frac{S_i(v + dv) - S_i(v)}{dv} \geq P_i(v)$$

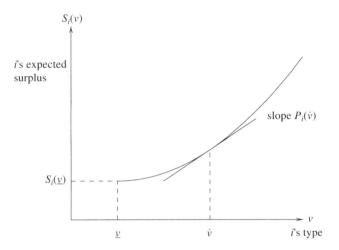

Figure 1.1   Bidder i's expected surplus as a function of her type.

and taking the limit as $dv \to 0$ we obtain[115]

$$\frac{dS_i}{dv} = P_i(v). \tag{4}$$

Integrating up,

$$S_i(v) = S_i(\underline{v}) + \int_{x=\underline{v}}^{v} P_i(x)dx. \tag{5}$$

Equation (5) gives us a picture like Figure 1.1.

At any type $\hat{v}$ the slope of the surplus function is $P_i(\hat{v})$, so if we know where the surplus function starts (i.e., know $S_i(\underline{v})$) we know the entire picture.

Now consider any two mechanisms which have the same $S_i(\underline{v})$ and the same $P_i(v)$ functions for all v and for every player i. They have the same $S_i(v)$ functions. So any given type, v, of player i makes the same expected payment in each of the two mechanisms (since $S_i(v) = vP_i(v) - E$(payment by type v of player i), since the bidder is risk-neutral). This means i's expected payment averaged

[115] An alternative way of obtaining this equation is to write $S_i(v) = T(v, \tilde{v}(v))$ equals v's surplus when she behaves optimally as type $\tilde{v}(v)$. (In fact, $\tilde{v}(v) = v$.) Then the envelope theorem implies

$$\frac{dS_i}{dv} = \frac{dT}{dv} = \frac{\partial T}{\partial v}.$$

(That is,

$$\frac{dT}{dv} = \frac{\partial T}{\partial v} + \frac{\partial T}{\partial \tilde{v}}\frac{d\tilde{v}}{dv}$$

but $\partial T/\partial \tilde{v} = 0$ when $\tilde{v}$ is chosen optimally.)

But $\partial T/\partial v = P_i(v)$ since if the bidder's behavior is unchanged, the incremental utility from a value dv higher is $P_i(v)dv$.

across her different possible types, v, is also the same for both mechanisms. Since this is true for all bidders, i, the mechanisms yield the same expected revenue for the auctioneer.[116,117]

This is the Revenue Equivalence Theorem. There are many different statements of it, but they all essentially give the results of the preceding paragraph in a more or less special form.

In particular any mechanism which always gives the object to the highest-value bidder in equilibrium (all the standard auction forms do this) has $P_i(v) = (F(v))^{n-1}$ (since a bidder's probability of winning is just the probability that all the other $(n-1)$ bidders have lower values then she does), and many mechanisms (including all the standard ones) give a bidder of the lowest feasible type no chance of any surplus, that is, $S_i(\underline{v}) = 0$, so all these mechanisms will yield the same expected payment by each bidder and the same expected revenue for the auctioneer.

Notice that nothing about this argument (except the actual value of $P_i(v)$) relied on there being only a single object. Thus the theorem extends immediately to the case of $k > 1$ indivisible objects being sold, provided bidders want no more than one object each; all mechanisms that give the objects to the k highest-value bidders are revenue-equivalent. So we have:

Revenue Equivalence Theorem (Private-Value Case). *Assume each of n risk-neutral potential buyers has a privately known value independently drawn from a common distribution $F(v)$ that is strictly increasing and atomless on $[\underline{v}, \overline{v}]$. Suppose that no buyer wants more than one of the k available identical indivisible objects. Then any auction mechanism in which (i) the objects always go to the k buyers with the highest values, and (ii) any bidder with value $\underline{v}$ expects zero surplus, yields the same expected revenue, and results in a buyer with value v making the same expected payment.*

[116] Some readers may wish to think of this analysis in terms of the Revelation Principle (see Myerson, 1979; Dasgupta, Hammond, and Maskin, 1979; Harris and Townsend, 1981) that says that we can always restrict attention to direct revelation mechanisms that satisfy incentive compatibility. That is, any mechanism is equivalent to another mechanism in which agents report their types, v, and wish to do so truthfully. Here we have analyzed *any* auction by focusing attention on the equivalent truthful direct revelation mechanism. In our problem the incentive compatibility (truth-telling) constraints, (1), completely pin down the expected payments that must be made to each type of agent once $P_i(v)$ and $S_i(\underline{v})$ have been specified.

[117] Note that this argument assumes that the distribution of types of bidder, v, has positive density everywhere on $[\underline{v}, \overline{v}]$ so that $dS_i(v)/dv$ is defined everywhere on the range, and hence $S_i(v)$ is completely determined by $S_i(\underline{v})$ and $P_i(v)$.

  For example, assume instead that there are just two types, $v = 0$ and $v = 1$, and each of two bidders is equally likely to be of either type (independent of the other's type) and the seller begins by simultaneously offering both bidders a price α; if just one accepts then the trade is made at price α, if both accept then the unit is allocated by lottery at price α, if neither accepts then the unit is allocated by lottery at price 0. Then a "high" type prefers to accept so $S_i(0) = 0$, $P_i(0) = \frac{1}{4}$, and $P_i(1) = \frac{3}{4}$, for any $\alpha \in (0, \frac{2}{3})$, but the seller's expected revenue is strictly increasing in α, so revenue equivalence fails. See also Harris and Raviv (1981), or closely study Maskin and Riley (1985). (See exercise 2.)

It is not hard to extend the result to the general (common- and/or private-value) case, in which each buyer, i, independently receives a *signal* t_i drawn from $[\underline{t}, \overline{t}]$ and each bidder's value $V_i(t_1, \ldots, t_n)$ depends on all the signals.[118] A more general statement of the theorem is then exactly the statement above, but with "signal" substituted for "value", and t, $\underline{t}$, and $\overline{t}$ substituted for v, $\underline{v}$, and $\overline{v}$, throughout.

Application to Computing Bidding Strategies

Again we focus, for simplicity, on the single-object private-value case.

One of the mechanisms satisfying the revenue equivalence theorem is the ascending auction, in which the expected payment of a bidder of type v is just $P_i(v)$ times the expectation of the highest of the remaining $(n - 1)$ values conditional on all these values being below v. Since the density of the highest of $(n - 1)$ values is $(n - 1)f(v)(F(v))^{n-2}$, this last expectation can be written as

$$\frac{\int_{x=\underline{v}}^{v} x(n - 1)f(x)(F(x))^{n-2}dx}{\int_{x=\underline{v}}^{v}(n - 1)f(x)(F(x))^{n-2}dx}$$

which, after integrating the numerator by parts,[119] yields

$$v - \frac{\int_{x=\underline{v}}^{v}(F(x))^{n-1}dx}{(F(v))^{n-1}}.$$

Since in a first-price sealed-bid auction, v's expected payments are $P_i(v)$ times her bid, it follows that v bids according to

$$b(v) = v - \frac{\int_{x=\underline{v}}^{v}(F(x))^{n-1}dx}{(F(v))^{n-1}}$$

in a first-price auction.

In an "all-pay" auction in which every competitor always pays her bid (but only the highest-payer wins the object), it likewise follows that v must bid

$$b(v) = (F(v))^{n-1}v - \int_{x=\underline{v}}^{v}(F(x))^{n-1}dx.$$

[118] See, for example, Lemma 3 of Bulow and Klemperer (1996) (reprinted in *The Economic Theory of Auctions*).

[119] The denominator integrates to $(F(v))^{n-1}$, and the numerator

$$\int_{x=\underline{v}}^{v} x[(n - 1)f(x)(F(x))^{n-2}]dx = \int_{x=\underline{v}}^{v} x d(F(x)^{n-1}) = [x \cdot (F(x))^{n-1}]_{\underline{v}}^{v} - \int_{x=\underline{v}}^{v} 1 \cdot (F(x))^{n-1}dx$$

which yields the result.

Computing the bidding strategies this way is somewhat easier than solving for them directly in these cases.[120,121]

In other cases, see, for example, Bulow and Klemperer (1994),[122] it is very much easier.[123]

APPENDIX 1.B: MARGINAL REVENUES

This appendix develops the basics of the "marginal revenue" approach to auctions.

We begin by following Bulow and Klemperer (1996)[124] to show, very generally, that the expected revenue from an ascending auction equals the expected marginal revenue of the winning bidder.

Figure 1.2 plots value, v, against $1 - F(v)$ for bidder i. We can interpret this as a "demand curve" because bidder i's value exceeds any v with probability $1 - F(v)$, so if a monopolist faced the single bidder, i, and set a take-it-or-leave-it offer of price $\hat{v}$, the monopolist would make a sale with probability $1 - F(\hat{v})$, that is, the monopolist's expected quantity of sales would be $q(\hat{v}) = 1 - F(\hat{v})$.

Figure 1.2 also shows a "marginal revenue curve", $MR(v)$, constructed from

[120] Appendix 1.D illustrates for the case in which $F(\cdot)$ is uniform.

[121] To solve directly for the first-price equilibrium bidding strategies, we look for a symmetric Nash equilibrium in which a bidder with value v chooses the bid $b(v)$, and assume (as can be proved, see, e.g., Example 6.5 of Fudenberg and Tirole (1991)) that b is a continuous strictly increasing function of v. Imagine player i with value v deviates and chooses the bid $\bar{b}$. Let $\bar{v}$ be the type of bidder she would just tie with, that is, let $b(\bar{v}) = \bar{b}$. Mimicking $\bar{v}$ would beat all the other $(n-1)$ bidders with probability $(F(\bar{v}))^{n-1}$ and so yield expected surplus to player i of $T(v, \bar{v}) = (v - b(\bar{v}))(F(\bar{v}))^{n-1}$.

Choosing the best bid to make is equivalent to choosing the best $\bar{v}$ to mimic, which we can do by looking at the first-order condition

$$\frac{\partial T(v, \bar{v})}{\partial \bar{v}} = -b'(\bar{v})(F(\bar{v}))^{n-1} + (v - b(\bar{v}))(n-1)(F(\bar{v}))^{n-2}f(\bar{v}).$$

For the bidding function $b(v)$ to be an equilibrium, i's best response to all others bidding according to this function must be to do likewise, that is, her optimal choice of $\bar{b}$ is $b(v)$ and of $\bar{v}$ is v. So

$$\frac{\partial T}{\partial \bar{v}}(v, \bar{v}) = 0 \quad \text{at } \bar{v} = v \quad \Rightarrow \quad b'(v) = (v - b(v))(n-1)\frac{f(v)}{F(v)}.$$

This differential equation can be solved for the equilibrium, using the boundary condition $b(\underline{v}) = \underline{v}$ (it is obvious type $\underline{v}$ will not bid more than $\underline{v}$, and we assume the auctioneer will not accept lower bids than $\underline{v}$).

[122] Described in section 1.10.3 and reprinted in the corresponding part of *The Economic Theory of Auctions*.

[123] For examples of using the revenue equivalence theorem to solve an oligopoly pricing problem, see Appendix B of Bulow and Klemperer (1998) and section 2.5.

[124] Also discussed in section 1.8.2, and reprinted in the corresponding part of *The Economic Theory of Auctions*.

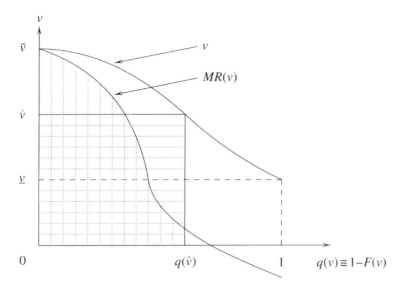

Figure 1.2 "Demand" and "marginal revenue" curves for bidder with value v drawn from $F(v)$.

the demand curve in exactly the usual way.[125] Note that at "price" $\hat{v}$ the monopolist's expected revenues can be computed either as the horizontally shaded rectangle $\hat{v} \cdot [1 - F(\hat{v})]$, or as the vertically shaded area under the "marginal revenue" curve $MR(v)$ up to "quantity" $1 - F(\hat{v})$. That is, just as in standard monopoly theory, the monopolist's revenues can be computed either as price times quantity, or as the sum of the marginal revenues of all the units sold. (Mathematically, we can write $\hat{v} \cdot [q(\hat{v})] = \int_{q=0}^{q(\hat{v})} MR(v(q))dq$.[126])

Now imagine bidder i is the winner of the ascending auction. Let $\hat{v}$ be the actual value of the second-highest bidder. So the actual price in the auction equals $\hat{v}$. But the result of the previous paragraph tells us that $\hat{v}$ equals the

[125] That is, "revenue" = "price" times "quantity" = $v \cdot q(v)$, so

$$MR(v) = \frac{d}{dq}[v \cdot q(v)] = v + \frac{q}{dq/dv} = v - \frac{1 - F(v)}{f(v)}.$$

[126] We can confirm

$$\int_{q=0}^{q(\hat{v})} MR(v(q))dq = \int_{v=\hat{v}}^{\bar{v}} MR(v)f(v)dv$$

(changing variables $q \to [1 - F(v)]$, $dq \to [-f(v)dv]$, reversing limits to cancel the minus sign and defining $q(\bar{v}) = 0$ as in Appendix 1.A) which equals

$$\int_{v=\hat{v}}^{\bar{v}} (vf(v) - 1 + F(v))dv = [vF(v) - v]_{v=\hat{v}}^{\bar{v}} = \hat{v} - \hat{v}F(\hat{v})$$

as claimed.

average level of the marginal revenue curve between 0 and $q(\hat{v})$. Mathematically, we have

$$\hat{v} = \frac{1}{q(\hat{v})} \int_{q=0}^{q(\hat{v})} MR(v(q))dq.$$

That is, $\hat{v}$ equals the average value of i's marginal revenue, conditional on i's value exceeding $\hat{v}$. But what we know about i's value is just that it exceeds $\hat{v}$, because i won the auction. So for any actual second-highest value $\hat{v}$, the price, and hence the actual revenue, equals the expected marginal revenue of the winner. *So the expected revenue from an ascending auction equals the expected marginal revenue of the winning bidder.*

Observe that the result is very general for ascending auctions. Nothing in the argument relies on bidders' private values being independent, nor on bidders being risk-neutral, nor on their values being drawn from a common distribution. It is also not hard to check that the argument extends directly to the general (common- and/or private-value) case. (See Bulow and Klemperer (1996) for full details.)

Obviously the result also extends to any auction that is revenue equivalent to the ascending auction. Noting the conditions for revenue equivalence (see Appendix 1.A) it follows that[127] *if the bidders are risk-neutral and their information signals are independent, the expected revenue from any standard auction equals the expected marginal revenue of the winning bidder.*

Alternative, Algebraic Proof

For the risk-neutral, independent, symmetric, private-value case we can alternatively obtain the result using the results (and notation) of Appendix 1.A:[128] Bidder i's expected payment to the auctioneer equals i's expected gross value received from the auction, $vP_i(v)$, less her expected surplus, $S_i(v)$. So the auctioneer's expected receipts from i are

$$\int_{v=\underline{v}}^{\bar{v}} (vP_i(v) - S_i(v))f(v)dv.$$

Substituting for $S_i(v)$ using equation (5) from Appendix 1.A yields

$$\int_{v=\underline{v}}^{\bar{v}} vP_i(v)f(v)dv - \int_{v=\underline{v}}^{\bar{v}} f(v) \int_{x=\underline{v}}^{v} P_i(x)dxdv - \int_{v=\underline{v}}^{\bar{v}} S_i(\underline{v})f(v)dv,$$

---

[127] It is not hard to check that bidders can be asymmetric, that is, their signals can be drawn from different distributions.

[128] This approach is the one taken by Bulow and Roberts (1989), who themselves follow Myerson (1981).

and integrating the second term by parts[129] yields

$$\int_{v=\underline{v}}^{\bar{v}} P_i(v)f(v)\left[v - \frac{1 - F(v)}{f(v)}\right]dv - S_i(\underline{v}).$$

Define bidder i's "marginal revenue" if she has value v to be

$$MR_i(v) = \left[v - \frac{1 - F(v)}{f(v)}\right];$$

following the discussion of figure 1.2, above, this corresponds to thinking of v as "price", p, and of $1 - F(v)$ as "quantity", q, hence

$$\text{marginal revenue} = \frac{d(pq)}{dq} = p + \frac{q}{dq/dp} = v + \frac{1 - F(v)}{-f(v)}.$$

Then, assuming $S_i(\underline{v}) = 0$, as is the case for any standard mechanism (see Appendix 1.A), the auctioneer's receipts from all n bidders are

$$\sum_{i=1}^{n} \int_{v=\underline{v}}^{\bar{v}} P_i(v)f(v)MR_i(v)dv = \sum_{i=1}^{n} E_{v_i}[P_i(v_i)MR_i(v_i)]$$

in which, for convenience, we changed the dummy variable from v to v_i in the last expression. This expression equals the expected marginal revenue of the winning bidder. To see this, it is helpful to write $\tilde{P}_i(v_1, \ldots, v_n)$ as the probability that i wins as a function of *all* bidders' signals (i.e., $\tilde{P}_i(v_1, \ldots, v_n) = 1$ if i is the winner, $\tilde{P}_i(v_1, \ldots, v_n) = 0$ otherwise). Then

$$P_i(v_i) = E_{v_1, \ldots, v_{i-1}, v_{i+1}, \ldots, v_n}[\tilde{P}_i(v_1, \ldots, v_n)]$$

so expected total receipts can be written

$$E_{v_1, \ldots, v_n}\left[\sum_{i=1}^{n} MR_i(v_i)\tilde{P}_i(v_1, \ldots, v_n)\right]$$

which equals the expected marginal revenue of the winning bidder, since the term in square brackets is exactly the marginal revenue of the winner. If there is no sale for some realization of $v_1, \ldots, v_n$, then the term in square brackets equals zero, so it is as if there was a winner with marginal revenue equal to zero.

So an auction that always sells to the bidder with the highest marginal revenue, except makes no sale if no bidder's marginal revenue exceeds zero, will maximize expected revenues. But with symmetric bidders, any standard auction will sell to the highest-value bidder. So if higher values imply higher marginal revenues, then any standard auction together with reserve price p_r such that $MR(p_r) = 0$

---

[129] That is,

$$\int_{v=\underline{v}}^{\bar{v}} f(v) \int_{x=\underline{v}}^{v} P_i(x)dxdv = \left[F(v) \int_{x=\underline{v}}^{v} P_i(x)dx\right]_{v=\underline{v}}^{\bar{v}} - \int_{v=\underline{v}}^{\bar{v}} F(v)P_i(v)dv = \int_{v=\underline{v}}^{\bar{v}} (1 - F(v))P_i(v)dv.$$

(to prevent any sale if all bidders have values below p_r, hence negative marginal revenues) maximizes the auctioneer's expected revenues.[130]

Note also that this approach generalizes easily to bidders drawn from different distributions, and to the general (common- and/or private-value) case, but the risk-neutrality and independence assumptions are important, as they are for the revenue equivalence theorem.

APPENDIX 1.C: AFFILIATED SIGNALS

This appendix analyzes the relative profitabilities of the standard auction forms when bidders' signals are *affiliated*, illustrates how an optimal mechanism can extract the entire social surplus in this case, and provides a formal definition of affiliation.[131]

Loosely, two signals are affiliated if a higher value of one signal makes a higher value of the other signal more likely, *and* this is true on every subspace of the variables' domain. Thus affiliation is stronger than correlation which is just a global summary statistic; affiliation can be thought of as requiring local positive correlation everywhere.

Milgrom and Weber found that when signals are affiliated, the second-price open (i.e., ascending) auction raises more expected revenue than the second-price sealed-bid auction, which in turn beats the first-price auction (assuming risk-neutral bidders, whose signals are drawn from symmetric distributions, and whose value functions are symmetric functions of the signals). Why?

Begin with independent-private-value first-price auctions. Recall the intuition for equation (4) from Appendix 1.A,

$$\frac{dS_i(v)}{dv} = P_i(v),$$

that if a player has a value of $v + dv$ instead of v, she can emulate the strategy of a player with value v and win just as often, at the same cost, but earning an extra dv in the probability $P_i(v)$ event she wins.

Now consider affiliation. A player with a value of $v + dv$ who makes the same bid as a player with a value of v will pay the same price as a player with a value of v when she wins, but because of affiliation she will expect to win a bit less often. That is, her higher signal makes her think her competitors are also likely to have higher signals, which is bad for her expected profits.

But things are even worse in a second-price affiliated private-values auction for

---

[130] Appendix 1.D illustrates for the case of uniform $F(\cdot)$.

See Myerson (1981) and Bulow and Roberts (1989) for the design of revenue-maximizing auctions when bidders are asymmetric or when higher values do not always imply higher marginal revenues.

[131] The first part of this appendix is based on notes written by Jeremy Bulow.

Appendix 1.D provides examples that illustrate the results.

the buyer. Not only does her probability of winning diminish, as in the first-price auction, but her costs per victory are higher. This is because affiliation implies that contingent on her winning the auction, the higher her value the higher the expected second-highest value which is the price she has to pay. Because the person with the highest value will win in either type of auction they are both equally efficient, and therefore the higher consumer surplus in the first-price auction implies higher seller revenue in the second-price auction. [132]

How about second-price sealed-bid auctions versus ascending auctions? Sticking to private values, these two auction types will still be identical: the highest-valued bidder will always pay the second value. Also, with only two bidders there is no difference between sealed and open bids even with a common-value element and affiliation. In the open auction the player drops out when the price reaches her value for the good conditional on the other bidder having the same signal as her; [133] in the sealed-bid version a player bids her value conditional on the other player having the same signal. [134]

If there are more than two bidders in a setting with affiliation and common values, then the ascending auction beats the sealed-bid auction: Assume there are three potential bidders in a second-price sealed-bid auction, each of whom reveals her signal to a trusted fourth party. The fourth party then tells the two most optimistic bidders that they are among the top two, but does not reveal the third bidder's signal. The first two will bid exactly as they would have without the information that they are in the top two, since their bids are only relevant in this case anyway. How will each bidder determine her bid? The marginal case in which it would be worthwhile for a bidder to win the auction is the case where she is tied for having the most optimistic signal. The second-highest actual bidder, whose bid determines the price, will bid the expectation of the asset's value, assuming that she is tied for the most optimistic assessment, and assuming there is a third observation with the distribution to be expected if, in fact, the second bidder *is* tied for the most optimistic signal. [135]

---

[132] To fill out this argument a little more, assume that in equilibrium there is some value for which the expected surplus (and therefore expected purchase price) is the same for a buyer in either type of auction. This will be true for the lowest-possible buyer value, for example, since that type of buyer obviously never wins the auction. Then by the argument in the text, the derivative of surplus with respect to value will be greater in the first-price auction than in the second-price auction. So the surplus in the first-price auction begins to grow faster, at least for a while, in the second-price auction. And if the surpluses ever came together again, the first-price surplus would have to forge ahead again. So on average across all possible bidder values, buyers will get more surplus in first-price auctions and sellers must therefore make more money in second-price auctions.

[133] To see why, check that if the other player is bidding this way then this player would lose money if she were to find herself a winner at a higher price (assuming higher signals imply higher values) but quitting at a lower price forgoes an opportunity to make money if the other player quits first. See Appendix 1.D for an example.

[134] The argument that the games are strategically equivalent is similar to the one for first-price and descending auctions.

[135] See Appendix 1.D for more discussion and examples.

However, the seller knows that contingent on the second bidder observing any given signal and there existing a first bidder with a more optimistic observation, the true distribution of this unknown third signal is a more optimistic one than the second bidder will use. (For example, given that the top two bidders have values of 30 and 40, the expectation of the third signal is higher than the expectation that the second bidder will use in a sealed-bid auction, which conditions on the top two values being 30 and 30.) Thus, the seller will do better on average to allow the bidder to make her offer contingent on the observation of the third bidder, as in the open auction where the third bidder's observation can be inferred from the price at which she drops out.

So, with affiliation, common-value elements, and more than two symmetric, risk-neutral, bidders, the first-price auction earns less revenue on average than the second-price sealed-bid auction which earns less than the ascending auction. With private values and/or only two bidders, the first-price auction still earns the least money but the other two types are tied.

Appendix 1.D provides some simple examples that illustrate these results.

Finally, we use a simple example to illustrate how an optimal mechanism can extract the entire social surplus from risk-neutral bidders whose signals are not independent. Let each of two bidders $i = 1, 2$ receive a private signal t_i which is either "high" or "low". Conditional on a bidder's signal, the other bidder receives the same signal with probability $\frac{2}{3}$ and receives the other possible signal with probability $\frac{1}{3}$. Bidder i's actual value is $v_i(t_1, t_2)$. Now consider the following selling mechanism: (i) ask each bidder to report her signal; call these reports $\tilde{t}_1$ and $\tilde{t}_2$ respectively; (ii) if $\tilde{t}_1 = \tilde{t}_2$, pay each bidder an amount V; (iii) if $\tilde{t}_1 \neq \tilde{t}_2$, require each bidder to pay $2V$ to the seller; and (iv) give the object to the bidder i with the highest value $v_i(\tilde{t}_1, \tilde{t}_2)$ at price $v_i(\tilde{t}_1, \tilde{t}_2)$. If V is sufficiently large, it is a Nash equilibrium for each bidder to "tell the truth", that is, report $\tilde{t}_i = t_i$ at stage 1, since if the other behaves this way, parts (ii) and (iii) of the mechanism then yield $\frac{2}{3}(V) + \frac{1}{3}(-2V) = 0$ to a truth-teller but yield $\frac{1}{3}(V) + \frac{2}{3}(-2V) = -V$ to a deviator. That is, the seller has essentially forced each bidder to make a bet on the other's signal, and the bidders can avoid losing money on these bets only by using their private information. But once all their private information has thus been revealed, the seller can extract the entire social surplus in part (iv) of the mechanism.[136]

Formal Definition of Affiliation

Formally, but still restricting for simplicity to the case of two bidders, signals t_1 and t_2 are affiliated if for all $t_1' > t_1''$ and $t_2' > t_2''$,

---

[136] This simple mechanism suffers from additional equilibria that are not truth-telling—for example, for large V it is also an equilibrium for both bidders to always report "low"—but more complex mechanisms can be designed in which honesty is the unique equilibrium (see Myerson, 1981).

$$f(t_1', t_2')f(t_1'', t_2'') \geq f(t_1', t_2'')f(t_1'', t_2') \tag{6}$$

in which t_i' and t_i'' are different possible realizations of the signals t_i, $i = 1, 2$, and $f(t_1, t_2)$ is the joint density function of the signals. Since, by the definition of conditional probability, $f(t_1, t_2) = g(t_1 \mid t_2)h(t_2)$, in which $g(t_1 \mid t_2)$ and $h(t_2)$ are the conditional density of t_1 given t_2, and the unconditional density of t_2, respectively, it follows that (6) holds if and only if

$$\frac{g(t_1' \mid t_2')}{g(t_1'' \mid t_2')} \geq \frac{g(t_1' \mid t_2'')}{g(t_1'' \mid t_2'')} \tag{7}$$

which is also known as the Monotone Likelihood Ratio Property, that is, higher values of t_1 become relatively more likely as t_2 increases. An implication of (7) is that[137]

$$G(t_1 \mid t_2') \leq G(t_1 \mid t_2'')$$

in which $G(t_1 \mid t_2)$ is the conditional distribution of t_1 given t_2. In words, the distribution of t_1 conditional on t_2' first-order stochastically dominates the distribution of t_1 conditional on t_2'', if $t_2' > t_2''$. The implications of affiliation that are probably used most frequently in auction-theory proofs are that[138]

$$\frac{\partial}{\partial t_2}\left(\frac{g(t_1 \mid t_2)}{1 - G(t_1 \mid t_2)}\right) \leq 0$$

(in words, the hazard rate of t_1 is everywhere decreasing in t_2), and

$$\frac{\partial}{\partial t_2}\left(\frac{g(t_1 \mid t_2)}{G(t_1 \mid t_2)}\right) \geq 0$$

(the hazard rate of the decumulative density of t_1 is increasing in t_2, that is, the probability density of $t = t_1$, conditional on $t \leq t_1$, is increasing in t_2).

In the case of independent signals, affiliation holds weakly.

APPENDIX 1.D: EXAMPLES USING THE UNIFORM DISTRIBUTION

This appendix uses the uniform distribution to develop some simple examples of bidding in the standard auctions, and illustrates the material in the preceding appendices.

The uniform distribution $(F(v) = (v - \underline{v})/(\bar{v} - \underline{v}), f(v) = (1/(\bar{v} - \underline{v}))$ is often particularly easy to work with in auction theory. The following fact is

---

[137] To obtain this, integrate first over $t_1' > t_1$, then multiply through by $g(t_1'' \mid t_2')g(t_1'' \mid t_2'')$, then integrate over $t_1'' < t_1'$ to yield an expression which implies this one.

[138] To obtain the next expression integrate (7) over $t_1' > t_1''$, and substitute t_1 for t_1''. To obtain the second expression, multiply (7) by $g(t_1'' \mid t_2')g(t_1'' \mid t_2'')$, then integrate over $t_1'' < t_1'$ and substitute t_1 for t_1'.

very helpful: the expected kth highest value among n values independently drawn from the uniform distribution on $[\underline{v}, \overline{v}]$ is

$$\underline{v} + \left(\frac{n + 1 - k}{n + 1} \right)(\overline{v} - \underline{v}).$$

Bidding with Independent Private Values, Revenue Equivalence, and Marginal Revenues

Begin with risk-neutral bidders $i = 1, \ldots, n$ each of whom has a private value v_i independently drawn from $[\underline{v}, \overline{v}]$.

Then in a second-price (or ascending) auction, everyone bids (or bids up to) her true value, so the seller's expected revenue is the expected second-highest value of the n values which, using the fact given above, equals

$$\underline{v} + \left(\frac{n - 1}{n + 1} \right)(\overline{v} - \underline{v})$$

In a first-price auction, by revenue equivalence, i bids her expected payment conditional on winning an ascending auction. Conditional on v_i being the highest value, the other $n - 1$ values are uniformly distributed on $[\underline{v}, v_i]$ so, using the fact about the uniform distribution, the expected value of the highest of these—which is what i would expect to pay conditional on winning—is

$$\underline{v} + \left(\frac{n - 1}{n} \right)(v_i - \underline{v})$$

so this will be i's bid.

Alternatively, we can derive i's equilibrium bidding strategy using the direct approach, and thus confirm revenue equivalence.[139]

Note that the proportion of buyers with valuations above any price v is linear in v, that is,

$$q(v) \equiv 1 - F(v) = \frac{\overline{v} - v}{\overline{v} - \underline{v}}$$

Therefore $v = \overline{v} - (\overline{v} - \underline{v})q$, so the uniform distribution corresponds to linear demand (since v plays the role of price). It follows that the marginal revenue curve is just linear and twice as steep as the demand curve, that is,

$$MR(q(v)) = \overline{v} - 2(\overline{v} - \underline{v})q$$

---

[139] The differential equation for i's first-price bidding strategy, $b(v_i)$, obtained using the direct approach, is $b'(v_i) = (v_i - b(v_i))(n - 1)[f(v_i)/F(v_i)]$ (see note 121).

For the uniform distribution, this yields $b'(v_i) = (v_i - b(v_i))(n - 1)[1/(v_i - \underline{v})]$ which is solved by $b(v_i) = \underline{v} + [(n - 1)/n](v_i - \underline{v})$.

Since the highest-value bidder will determine the price, the seller's expected revenue will be $E\{\underline{v} + [(n - 1)/n](\max_{i=1,\ldots,n} v_i - \underline{v})\}$, so using our result that $E\{\max_{i=1,\ldots,n} v_i\} = \underline{v} + [n/(n + 1)](\overline{v} - \underline{v})$ yields that the expected revenue is $\underline{v} + [(n - 1)/(n + 1)](\overline{v} - \underline{v})$, confirming revenue equivalence with the second-price auction forms.

which implies[140]

$$MR(v) = \bar{v} - 2(\bar{v} - \underline{v})\left(\frac{\bar{v} - v}{\bar{v} - \underline{v}}\right) = 2v - \bar{v}.$$

Since

$$E\left\{\max_{i=1,\dots,n} v_i\right\} = \underline{v} + \left(\frac{n}{n+1}\right)(\bar{v} - \underline{v}),$$

the expected marginal revenue of the highest bidder equals

$$\underline{v} + \left(\frac{n-1}{n+1}\right)(\bar{v} - \underline{v}),$$

which confirms our earlier result that this is the expected revenue from any standard auction (without a reserve price).

Furthermore, since the marginal revenue curve is downward sloping, an optimal (i.e., expected-revenue maximizing) auction is any standard auction together with a reserve price, $p_r = \frac{1}{2}\bar{v}$ (so that $MR(p_r) = 0$), below which no sale will be made.

Bidding with Common Values, and the Winner's Curse

Now let the bidders have signals t_i, and $v_i = \alpha t_i + \beta \sum_{j \neq i} t_j$. (So $\beta = 0$ is the private values case, and $\alpha = \beta$ is pure common values; we assume $\alpha \geq \beta$.) Let $t_{(j)}$ be the actual jth highest signal.

In the symmetric equilibrium of an ascending auction each player quits where she would just be indifferent about finding herself a winner. So the first quit is at price $(\alpha + (n-1)\beta)t_{(n)}$, since that would be the actual value to all if all bidders had this signal; the remaining bidders all observe this and the next quit is at $\beta t_{(n)} + (\alpha + (n-2)\beta)t_{(n-1)}$ since this would be the current quitter's value if all the other remaining bidders were to quit with her; the other bidders all observe this and infer the next lowest signal, etc. The final quit, and so actual sale price is at

$$\hat{p} = \beta \sum_{j=3}^{n} t_{(j)} + (\alpha + \beta)t_{(2)}.$$

To check this is the equilibrium, note, for example, that if the player with the second-highest signal, $t_{(2)}$, waited to quit and found herself a winner at a price $\hat{p} + (\alpha + \beta)\varepsilon$ she would then infer $t_{(1)} = t_{(2)} + \varepsilon$ (since the final opponent is bidding symmetrically to her equilibrium behavior) hence that the value of the object to her was just $\hat{p} + \beta\varepsilon$, so she had lost money. But when

---

[140] Obviously, we can also obtain this equation by using the definition,

$$MR(v) = v - \frac{1 - F(v)}{f(v)},$$

from Appendix 1.B.

the price reached $\hat{p} - (\alpha + \beta)\varepsilon$, she could infer that her final opponent's signal is at least $t_{(2)} - \varepsilon$ hence that the value of the object to her was at least $\hat{p} - \beta\varepsilon$, so quitting early would have given up the opportunity of making some money (in the states in which the final opponent would have quit close to this price).[141]

Note that when the player with the second-highest signal quits, she knows (assuming equilibrium behavior) that the remaining signal is (weakly) higher than hers. So she is sure the actual value of the object to her cannot be less than the price at which she is quitting, and that the expected value is higher. This illustrates the *winner's curse*. The point is that what is relevant to her is *not* the expected value of the object, but rather its expected value conditional on her

---

[141] The principle for solving the case where bidders' value functions are asymmetric is similar, and clarifies the argument. Assume just two bidders, for simplicity, with signals t_i, t_j and values $v_i(t_i, t_j)$ and $v_j(t_i, t_j)$. Assume that in equilibrium t_i quits at the same time as an opponent of type $t_j = w_i(t_i)$, in which $w_i(\cdot)$ is a strictly increasing function. So

$$b_i(t_i) = b_j(w_i(t_i)), \qquad (*)$$

and t_i will beat all opponents with types $t_j < w_i(t_i)$, and lose to all higher types.

Now if t_i deviated from her equilibrium strategy and waited a tiny bit longer to quit, she would win against all $t_j \leq w_i(t_i)$ at the same prices as before, and she would also win against a few additional types of j with signals of (slightly above) $w_i(t_i)$, at a price of (slightly above) $b_i(t_i)$. Her value of winning in these additional cases would be (slightly above) $v_i(t_i, w_i(t_i))$, so if $b_i(t_i)$ were (strictly) less than $v_i(t_i, w_i(t_i))$, then deviating to win against a few additional types would be profitable. So $b_i(t_i) \geq v_i(t_i, w_i(t_i))$.

Similarly, if t_i were to quit a tiny bit earlier than her equilibrium quitting price, it would make no difference except that she would lose against a few types with signals (slightly below) $w_i(t_i)$ at prices of (slightly below) $b_i(t_i)$, and type t_i would wish to do this unless $b_i(t_i) \leq v_i(t_i, w_i(t_i))$.
So

$$b_i(t_i) = v_i(t_i, w_i(t_i)). \qquad (**)$$

That is, t_i bids up to the value at which she would make no money if she were to find herself the winner.
Similarly

$$b_j(t_j) = v_j(w_j(t_j), t_j).$$

Substituting the value $t_j = w_i(t_i)$ into this equation yields

$$b_j(w_i(t_i)) = v_j(w_j(w_i(t_i)), w_i(t_i)).$$

But $b_j(w_i(t_i)) = b_i(t_i)$ by (*). And by definition $w_j(w_i(t_i)) = t_i$ (i.e., if t_i quits at the same time as $w_i(t_i)$, then the type that quits at the same time as $w_i(t_i)$—this type is $w_j(w_i(t_i))$— is t_i). So

$$b_i(t_i) = v_j(t_i, w_i(t_i)).$$

Comparing with (**) we have

$$v_i(t_i, w_i(t_i)) = v_j(t_i, w_i(t_i)).$$

That is, players have the same values when they have types that quit at the same time.

So to find the bidding strategies we solve this last equation for the function $w_i(t_i)$, and then substitute this function back into (**) to yield i's bidding function. (Note that this procedure does not necessarily yield an equilibrium, although it does so in natural two-bidder or symmetric examples, see Maskin, 1992.)

winning it.[142] Only when she wins the object does she care about its value, so she quits exactly at its value conditional on her winning. Exactly the same effect—that winning the auction is bad news about opponents' signals, so bids must be adjusted down to allow for the "winner's curse"—arises in the other auction types.

Note that the ascending auction equilibrium does not depend on the bidders' signals being independent or on their distributions (which can be different for different bidders), or on the bidders being risk-neutral. However, these properties do not extend to the other standard auctions. So henceforth assume the signals are independent and uniform on $[0, \bar{t}]$, and the bidders are risk-neutral.

In a *second-price sealed-bid* auction the logic is similar to that for the ascending auction. Bidder i with signal t_i is willing to pay anything up to her expected value conditional on her winning the object but being just tied with one other with the same signal. The difference is that the bidder does not see the other $n - 2$ opponents' bids, so estimates their signals at $\frac{1}{2} t_i$ (since conditional on them being below t_i, they are uniformly distributed below t_i). So i bids $\beta(n - 2)\frac{1}{2} t_i + (\alpha + \beta) t_i = (\alpha + \frac{1}{2} n\beta) t_i$.[143]

The simplest way to solve for *first-price* bidding strategies is to use revenue equivalence.[144] Conditional on winning the second-price auction, a bidder with signal t_i expects to pay $(\alpha + \frac{1}{2} n\beta)\hat{t}$ in which $\hat{t}$ is the expected highest of $n - 1$ signals uniformly distributed on $[0, t_i]$, that is,

$$\hat{t} = \left(\frac{n - 1}{n} \right) t_i.$$

So i bids this expected payment, that is,

$$\left(\frac{n - 1}{n} \right) \left(\alpha + \frac{1}{2} n\beta \right) t_i.$$

Bidding with Affiliated Signals, and Revenue Rankings

A tractable example of affiliated information that illustrates the revenue-ranking results derived in Appendix 1.C (and is also useful for developing other examples[145]) has risk-neutral bidders $i = 1, ..., n$ each of whom receives a signal t_i that is independently drawn from a uniform distribution on $[v - \frac{1}{2}, v + \frac{1}{2}]$ where v is the (pure) common value of a single object for sale. Assume a "diffuse prior" for v, that is, all values of v are equally likely. (More formally we can let v be uniformly distributed on $[-M, +M]$ and take the limit as $M \to \infty$.) So a higher value of t_i makes a higher value of v more likely, and hence higher values of the other signals more likely,

---

[142] This statement assumes risk-neutrality, but the point we are making obviously does not.

[143] We can also confirm this is the equilibrium either by revenue equivalence with the ascending auction, or by a similar argument to that for the ascending auction—the only effect on i of i bidding a small amount $(\alpha + \beta)\varepsilon$ more is if i moves from coming second to winning, etc.

[144] An alternative is the direct method, see note 121.

[145] Most examples of affiliated information are very hard to work with.

and it can be checked that this example satisfies the formal definition of affiliation.

Let the *j*th highest actual signal be $t_{(j)}$, and observe that conditional on *all* the signals $t_1, ..., t_n$, the expected value of v equals $\frac{1}{2}(t_{(1)} + t_{(n)})$ (since any value of $v \in [t_{(1)} - \frac{1}{2}, t_{(n)} + \frac{1}{2}]$ is equally probable).

We now compute the symmetric equilibria of the standard auction types.

In an *ascending auction*, the first quit will be at price $t_{(n)}$ (since that is where the lowest-signal bidder would be indifferent about winning were everyone else to quit simultaneously with her), and every other bidder i will then infer $t_{(n)}$ and quit at $\frac{1}{2}(t_{(n)} + t_i)$ (since that is where each i would be just indifferent about finding herself the winner). The price paid by the winner will therefore be $\frac{1}{2}(t_{(n)} + t_{(2)})$ which, using our result about the uniform distribution, on average equals

$$\tfrac{1}{2}\left(\left[v - \tfrac{1}{2} + \left(\frac{1}{n+1}\right)\right] + \left[v - \tfrac{1}{2} + \left(\frac{n-1}{n+1}\right)\right]\right) = v - \tfrac{1}{2}\left(\frac{1}{n+1}\right)$$

In a *sealed-bid second-price auction*, each bidder i bids her expected value, conditional on being tied for winner with one other bidder (see previous subsection). That is, i bids thinking of herself as being the highest of $n - 1$ bidders uniformly drawn from $[v - \frac{1}{2}, v + \frac{1}{2}]$ and tied with one other, so on average, in this case,

$$t_i = \left[v - \tfrac{1}{2} + \left(\frac{n-1}{n}\right)\right]$$

so i's estimate of v in this case, and hence her bid, equals

$$t_i + \tfrac{1}{2} - \left(\frac{n-1}{n}\right).$$

On average, the second-highest bidder of n bidders actually has signal

$$t_{(2)} = \left[v - \tfrac{1}{2} + \left(\frac{n-1}{n+1}\right)\right]$$

so bids

$$\left[v - \tfrac{1}{2} + \left(\frac{n-1}{n+1}\right)\right] + \left[\tfrac{1}{2} - \left(\frac{n-1}{n}\right)\right].$$

So the expected revenue from this auction equals

$$v - \left(\frac{n-1}{n}\right)\left(\frac{1}{n+1}\right).$$

In a *first-price auction*, likewise, each bidder i bids $t_i - x$ for some x; this is because of our "diffuse prior" assumption which means that i's signal gives her no information about whether she is high or low relative to others' signals or the "truth", and so should not affect how close she bids to her signal. Let $t_i = v - \frac{1}{2} + T_i$. In equilibrium i will have the highest signal, and so win the auction, with probability T_i^{n-1}, and will earn $v - (t_i - x) = x + \frac{1}{2} - T_i$ when she wins. So if, instead, i had deviated from the symmetric equilibrium by bidding a small amount ε more, as if she had signal $t_i + \varepsilon$, she would win $x + \frac{1}{2} - T_i(-\varepsilon)$ with additional probability $(T_i + \varepsilon)^{n-1} - (T_i)^{n-1} \approx (n-1)\varepsilon T_i^{n-2}$, for small ε, but pay an additional ε in the T_i^{n-1} cases in which she would have won anyway. In equilibrium i must be just indifferent about the small deviation so, since she knows only that T_i is uniformly distributed on $[0, 1]$,

$$\int_{T_i=0}^{1} \left[(n-1)\varepsilon T_i^{n-2}(x + \tfrac{1}{2} - T_i) - \varepsilon T_i^{n-1} \right] dT_i = 0$$

(we are omitting terms in ε^2 and higher orders of ε)

$$\Rightarrow \left[\varepsilon T_i^{n-1}\left(x + \tfrac{1}{2}\right) - (n-1)\varepsilon \frac{T_i^n}{n} - \varepsilon \frac{T_i^n}{n} \right]_{T_i=0}^{1} = 0 \quad \Rightarrow \quad x = \tfrac{1}{2}.$$

So i bids $t_i - \frac{1}{2}$, and the price is set by the bidder with the highest signal, $t_{(1)}$, which equals

$$v - \tfrac{1}{2} + \left(\frac{n}{n+1} \right)$$

on average. So the expected revenue from the auction is

$$v - \left(\frac{1}{n+1} \right).$$

These results confirm the Milgrom and Weber revenue rankings of the standard auctions.

Finally, since signals are affiliated an optimal auction can extract all the surplus for the auctioneer (see section 1.6 and Appendix 1.C). Here it suffices to ask each bidder to declare t_i, allocate the good to the high bidder (say) at the "fair" price $\frac{1}{2}[t_{(1)} + t_{(n)}]$, and ensure truth-telling behavior by imposing large fines on all the bidders if $t_{(1)} - t_{(n)} > 1$.

Appendix 1.E: Bibliography

Sections 1.2–1.14 of this bibliography correspond to those sections of this chapter. Articles marked (*) are reproduced in *The Economic Theory of Auctions* (see section 1.18 below).

1.1 Survey and Guide to the Literature

Klemperer (*1999a).

1.2 Early Literature

Vickrey (*1961); Vickrey (*1962); Griesmer, Levitan, and Shubik (*1967); Ortega Reichert (*1968a); Wilson (*1969); Friedman (1956); Wilson (1967); Rothkopf (1969, see also 1980); Capen, Clapp, and Campbell (1971); Vickrey (1976).

1.3 Introduction to the Recent Literature

McAfee and McMillan (*1987a); Maskin and Riley (*1985); Riley (1989a).

1.4. The Basic Analysis of Optimal Auctions, Revenue Equivalence, and Marginal Revenues

Myerson (*1981); Riley and Samuelson (*1981); Bulow and Roberts (*1989); Vickrey (*1961); Vickrey (*1962); Bulow and Klemperer (*1996); Harris and Raviv (1981).

1.5. Risk-Aversion

Maskin and Riley (*1984); Matthews (*1987); Matthews (1983); Waehrer, Harstad, and Rothkopf (1998).

1.6. Correlation and Affiliation

Milgrom and Weber (*1982a); Crémer and McLean (*1985); Levin and Smith (*1996a); Crémer and McLean (1988); McAfee, McMillan and Reny (1989); McAfee and Reny (1992); Perry and Reny (1999).

1.7 Asymmetries

1.7.1 Private Value Differences
McAfee and McMillan (*1989); Maskin and Riley (*2000b, *1985); Griesmer, Levitan, and Shubik (*1967); Marshall, Meurer, Richard, and Stromquist (1994); Rothkopf, Harstad, and Fu (2003).

1.7.2 Almost-Common-Values
Bikhchandani (*1988); Klemperer (*1998); Bulow, Huang, and Klemperer (1999); Bulow and Klemperer (2002).

1.7.3 Information Advantages
Milgrom and Weber (*1982b); Milgrom (*1981); Engelbrecht-Wiggans, Milgrom, and Weber (1983).

1.8. Entry Costs and the Number of Bidders

1.8.1 Endogenous Entry of Bidders
Levin and Smith (*1994); Engelbrecht-Wiggans (*1993); Matthews (*1984); Fishman (*1988); Engelbrecht-Wiggans (1987); McAfee and McMillan (1987c); McAfee and McMillan (1988); Harstad (1990); Menezes and Monteiro (2000); Persico (2000b); Gilbert and Klemperer (2000).

1.8.2 The Value of Additional Bidders
Bulow and Klemperer (*1996).

1.8.3 Information Aggregation with Large Numbers of Bidders
Wilson (*1977); Milgrom (*1981); Milgrom (1979); Pesendorfer and Swinkels (1997).

1.8.4 Unknown Number of Bidders
Matthews (*1987); McAfee and McMillan (1987b); Harstad, Kagel, and Levin (1990); Levin and Smith (1996b); Piccione and Tan (1996).

1.9 Collusion

Robinson (*1985); McAfee and McMillan (*1992); Hendricks and Porter (*1989); Graham and Marshall (1987); Graham, Marshall, and Richard (1990); Mailath and Zemsky (1991); Hendricks, Porter, and Tan (1999).

1.10 Multi-unit Auctions

1.10.1 Optimal Auctions
Maskin and Riley (*1989); Palfrey (*1983); Avery and Hendershott (2000); Armstrong (2000); Rothkopf, Pekeč, and Harstad (1998).

1.10.2 Simultaneous Auctions
Wilson (*1979); Back and Zender (*1993); Anton and Yao (*1992); Klemperer and Meyer (*1989); Hansen (*1988); Maxwell (1983); Bernheim and Whinston (1986); Anton and Yao (1989); Daripa (1996a); Daripa (1996b); Nyborg (1997); Engelbrecht-Wiggans and Kahn (1998a); Engelbrecht-Wiggans and Kahn (1998b); Wang and Zender (2002).

1.10.3 Sequential Auctions
(i) *Bidders who demand only a single unit each:* Milgrom and Weber (*2000); Bulow and Klemperer (*1994); McAfee and Vincent (*1993); Bernhardt and Scoones (1994); Engelbrecht-Wiggans (1994); von der Fehr (1994);

Gale and Hausch (1994); Robert, Laffont, and Loisel (1994); Beggs and Graddy (1997); McAfee and Vincent (1997).

(ii) *Bidders with multi-unit demand:* Weber (*1983); Ortega Reichert (*1968b); Hausch (1986); Pitchik and Schotter (1988); Black and de Meza (1992); Krishna (1993); Robert ($\approx$1995); Gale and Stegeman (2001); Pitchik (1995); Gale, Hausch, and Stegeman (2000); von der Fehr and Riis (1999).

1.10.4 Efficient Auctions
Ausubel (1998); Ausubel and Cramton (1998a,b); Dasgupta and Maskin (2000); Jehiel and Moldovanu (2001); Perry and Reny (1998); Bikhchandani (1999).

1.11 Royalties, Incentive Contracts, and Payments for Quality

Riley (*1988); Laffont and Tirole (*1987); Che (*1993); McAfee and McMillan (1986); McAfee and McMillan (1987d); Riordan and Sappington (1987); Branco (1997).

1.12 Double Auctions, etc.

1.12.1 Double Auctions
Chatterjee and Samuelson (*1983); Wilson (*1985); Rustichini, Satterthwaite, and Williams (*1994); McAfee (*1992); Leininger, Linhart, and Radner (1989); Satterthwaite and Williams (1989a); Satterthwaite and Williams (1989b).

1.12.2 Related Two-Sided Trading Mechanisms
Myerson and Satterthwaite (*1983); Cramton, Gibbons, and Klemperer (*1987).

1.13. Other Topics

1.13.1 Budget Constraints
Che and Gale (*1998); Pitchik and Schotter (1988); Pitchik (1995); Che and Gale (1996); Benoît and Krishna (2001).

1.13.2 Externalities between Bidders
Jehiel and Moldovanu (*1996); Jehiel, Moldovanu, and Stacchetti (1996); Caillaud and Jehiel (1998).

1.13.3 Jump Bidding
Avery (*1998); Fishman (*1988); Daniel and Hirshleifer (1995).

1.13.4 The War of Attrition
Bulow and Klemperer (*1999); Riley (1980); Bliss and Nalebuff (1984);
Fudenberg and Tirole (1986); Krishna and Morgan (1997).

1.13.5 Competing Auctioneers
McAfee (*1993); Peters and Severinov (1997); Burguet and Sákovics (1999).

1.14. Testing the Theory

1.14.1 Empirical
Laffont (*1997); Hendricks and Porter (1988); Hendricks and Paarsch (1995);
Laffont, Ossard, and Vuong (1995); Porter (1995); Laffont and Vuong (1996).

1.14.2 Experimental
Kagel (*1995).

1.15. More on Specific Auction Forms

1.15.1 More on First Price Auctions
Lebrun (1996); Maskin and Riley (2000a); Maskin and Riley (forthcoming);
Athey (2001); Lizzeri and Persico (2000).

1.15.2 More on Second Price Auctions
Rothkopf, Teisberg, and Kahn (1990); Bikhchandani and Riley (1991);
Bulow, Huang, and Klemperer (1995); Lopomo (1998); Wilson (1998);
Bulow and Klemperer (2002).

1.16 Miscellaneous

Cassady (1967); Shubik (1983); Ashenfelter (1989); McAfee and McMillan
(1994); McAfee and McMillan (1996); Riley and Li (1997); Ginsburgh
(1998); Bulow and Klemperer (1998, Appendix B); Milgrom (2004).

1.17 Surveys

Klemperer (*1999a); McAfee and McMillan (*1987a); Milgrom (1985);
Weber (1985); Milgrom (1987); Milgrom (1989); Riley (1989b); Maskin
(1992); Wilson (1992); Bikhchandani and Huang (1993); Harstad and Rothkopf (1994); Rothkopf (1994); Wolfstetter (1996).

1.18 Collection of Articles

Klemperer (2000a).

Afterword

Although auction theory has remained an extremely active area of research since this survey was written in 1999, an introductory survey written today in 2004 would not be very different. The important changes would be in three areas: multi-unit auctions, collusion, and entry, in which much work has been stimulated by the practical concerns and experience arising from the many newly created auction markets (especially the recent government auctions of mobile-phone licenses) that we will discuss in parts C and D.[1]

There has been particular interest in multi-unit auctions of heterogeneous goods, especially in auctions in which there are complementarities between the goods. This work has yielded few definite answers about what mechanisms might be optimal (either revenue maximizing, or socially most efficient), but much effort has focused on what might be practical auction designs.[2]

The most important new design is the Simultaneous Ascending Auction (SAA). This is a fairly natural extension of the basic ascending auction to multiple objects; the bidding remains open on all the objects until no one wants to make any more bids on any object. Some complexity arises from the fact that a bidder may be reluctant to place bids until he sees other players' bids, in order to learn others' valuations. In particular, a bidder may be concerned about the risk of being "stranded" winning an object that he had wanted to win only if he had won other objects which were in fact won by other bidders. So "activity" rules that specify what bids a bidder must make to remain eligible to win objects are necessary to ensure that the bidding proceeds at a reasonable pace.

Although the germ of the SAA idea can perhaps be traced back to Vickrey (1976), it was first developed for practical use by Milgrom, Wilson, and McAfee who proposed the rules that were necessary to make the SAA effective in the context of US radio spectrum auctions. A full description of one version of the SAA is given in section 6.5.2.[3] We also show in that section that

---

[1] The increased attention to collusion and entry may perhaps have been reinforced by my urgings, in Klemperer (1998, 1999b, 2000b).

[2] If there is no complementarity or substitutability between objects, that is, a bidder's valuation for a bundle of objects just equals the sum of his (private) valuations of the individual objects in the bundle, it is efficient to auction the objects separately, but it may nevertheless increase expected revenue to auction the objects in bundles, see section 1.10.1 of our survey. If no bidder is interested in more than one unit, and units are homogeneous, most standard auctions (whether simultaneous or sequential) are revenue equivalent, see section 1.10.3 of the survey.

[3] The description given there is for a context in which bidders are permitted to win just one object each, so the activity rules are particularly simple.

the SAA is, in theory, an efficient mechanism for the sale of heterogeneous objects when bidders have private values, but want (or are permitted) to win at most a single object each.[4] However, the design has also been used in many other circumstances than these, and we will describe some of its successes and failures in practice in parts C and D.

One reason the SAA was originally proposed for the US radio spectrum auctions was that it was thought it might work well when bidders have complementarities between objects, but this will not be true if the complementarities are sufficiently important. The reason is the one noted above that bidders are required (by the activity rules) to make firm bids on some objects before they know which other objects they will win.[5] Some bidders may therefore end up stuck with objects that are worth very little to them because they failed to win complementary objects (this is called the *exposure problem*), while other bidders may quit the bidding early because of fear of this. Thus inefficiencies are likely. So if complementarities are important, it is natural to use some form of "combinatorial auction" in which a buyer can place bids for one or more packages of items and/or make contingent bids.[6] (A package bid is a single price offered for a set of items; a contingent bid is one that applies only under specified circumstances such as the buyer winning a particular other object; these auctions are called "combinatorial" because the auctioneer must solve a combinatorial optimization problem).

The most famous combinatorial auction is the Vickrey auction, in the general version of which the auctioneer maximizes social surplus and sets prices so that each participant's net profits equal her contribution to social surplus, assuming participants bid truthfully (i.e., the participant pays a price for those items she wins equal to her declared value for those items *less* the total social surplus achieved by the allocation *plus* the social surplus that the auctioneer could have achieved if that participant had not been present). However, as noted in section 1.10.4, a Vickrey auction is usually totally impracticable even in those private-value contexts in which it is, in theory,

---

[4] Milgrom (2000) gives more detail.

[5] If there is no penalty for withdrawing bids, the bidding process may never end, and there may also be substantially enhanced possibilities of collusion.

[6] Although combinatorial auctions can often reduce inefficiency, they also sometimes have the opposite effect. Just as with ordinary monopolists who bundle products or use non-linear pricing and quantity discounts, a combinatorial auction that permits or requires bids for packages rather than individual objects can result in bundling items that would be more efficiently allocated to different bidders, but may nevertheless increase expected seller revenue. (Thus, for example, if one bidder values objects A and B at x and $2x$ respectively, while a second bidder values A and B at $2x$ and x respectively, and x is known to the bidders but not to the seller, selling the two objects in two separate auctions (either ascending or sealed bid) is efficient, but yields total revenues of just $x + x = 2x$, while selling the two objects as a bundle in a single "combinational" auction obtains revenues of $3x$ (which both bidders will bid) but inefficiently sells both objects to the same winner.)

efficient.[7] There has therefore been considerable renewed interest in alternative combinatorial auction forms. Examples include Bernheim and Whinston's (1986) first-price package auctions (in which bidders submit package bids, the seller selects the combination that maximizes her revenue, and each bidder pays the amount it bid for the package it receives), and ascending package auctions in which bidders raise their offers over a series of rounds, such as Ausubel and Milgrom's (2002) "ascending proxy auction", and Banks, Ledyard, and Porter's (1989) "adaptive user selection mechanism" or AUSM (pronounced "awesome", and developed—as can, of course, be inferred from its name—in California). Milgrom (2004) is an excellent introduction to the state of the art in combinatorial auctions, and to multi-unit auctions more generally.

The practical use of multi-unit auctions has also reinforced the importance of the *demand reduction* problem we noted in section 1.10.4 of our survey, above, that bidders in these auctions, like oligopsonists in other kinds of markets, can often lower the prices they pay by buying fewer units than they actually want (because offering to buy fewer units means the auction closes at lower prices).[8] This behavior can arise even if there is just one "large" bidder who wants more than one unit, and if all bidders bid independently. When there are several "large" bidders, multi-unit auctions also open up the possibility of these bidders coordinating their behavior to reduce their demand in concert. Such "collusion", whether tacit or otherwise, has been a serious problem in multi-unit auctions, especially in ascending designs such as the SAA, as we will emphasize in chapters 3 and 5.

Thus multi-unit auctions have focused renewed attention on the point made in section 1.9 of our survey, above, that "A crucial concern about auctions in practice is the ability of bidders to collude, but the theoretical work on this issue is rather limited." Although the importance of this issue is now generally recognized, and research on it is beginning to develop,[9] this literature remains in its infancy. In particular, as we will emphasize in chapter 4, it is not clear that it has yet taught us very much more than could be gleaned from an intelligent reading of the industrial organization literature.

---

[7] Policy makers usually find a Vickrey auction very hard to understand and operate; it often results in bidders with high values paying less for objects than bidders who win identical objects but have lower values for them (which seems strange and unfair to many people); it offers unusual opportunities for collusive behavior which are also hard to guard against; and it sometimes yields low revenues. Furthermore, it is not efficient (and may perform very badly) if bidders are risk-averse or have budget constraints or have common-value elements to their valuations.

[8] This problem has been emphasized by Ausubel and Cramton (1998a) and Ausubel (forthcoming).

[9] For example, Menezes (1996), Weber (1997), Engelbrecht-Wiggans and Kahn (1998c), Ausubel and Schwartz (1999), Cramton and Schwartz (2000, 2002), Brusco and Lopomo (2002a), and Grimm, Riedel, and Wolfstetter (2003) all discuss how vulnerable multi-unit ascending auctions are to collusive outcomes. See also Marshall and Meurer (2002).

Finally, and also prompted by practical experience, there is a much greater general understanding than previously that, as emphasized in section 1.8.1 of the survey above, "In practical auction design, persuading bidders to take the time and trouble to enter the contest is a major concern." Although no general principles have yet emerged beyond those in section 1.7 (about asymmetries between bidders) or section 1.8 (explicitly about entry) of the survey, this issue is now an area of active research.

We will give considerable attention to the problems of encouraging entry and discouraging collusion, often in the context of multi-unit auctions, in Parts C and D of this volume.[10]

---

[10] Klemperer et al. (forthcoming) is a case-study of a multi-unit auction of environmental goods that emphasizes entry issues.

Exercises

These are the Oxford University MPhil in Economics examination questions that I set in the period 1995–2003, for a short course roughly corresponding to the "graduate course outline" at the back of the book.

Questions 1, 9, and 11 are somewhat easier than the rest, though for introductory examples the reader is referred to Appendix 1.D. Solutions are at the end of the book.

REVENUE EQUIVALENCE THEOREM—THEORY

1. An auctioneer of a single object faces n risk-neutral bidders with private valuations for the object that are independently drawn from a distribution $F(\cdot)$ with density $f(\cdot)$.

(i) State, and sketch a proof of the revenue equivalence theorem for this situation.

(ii) Write down how players bid in a Japanese (i.e., English, or ascending, auction), and hence derive their expected payments conditional on winning, when their values are independently drawn from a uniform distribution on $[0, \bar{v}]$.

(iii) Consider an "all-pay" auction (i.e., a simultaneous sealed-bid auction in which the high bidder wins the object, but every bidder pays her bid). Use the revenue equivalence theorem, together with your solution to part (ii), to solve for the bidding functions for the "all-pay" auction when bidders' values are independently drawn from a uniform distribution on $[0, \bar{v}]$.

(iv) Write down the differential equation for a player's bid as a function of her value in the symmetric equilibrium of an "all-pay" auction when bidders' values are independently drawn from the distribution $F(\cdot)$. Solve the differential equation for the special case in which $F(\cdot)$ is uniform on $[0, \bar{v}]$. (Your solution should be consistent with (iii)!)

[Oxford, 1st Year Micro, 2000]

2. Consider an auctioneer with a single unit facing two risk-neutral buyers with independent private valuations. Each buyer is equally likely to be a "type H" who has value $v_H = 1$ or a "type L" with value $v_L = 0$.

(i) Consider the auction form in which the seller begins by offering a price $a \in (0, \frac{2}{3})$ and buyers simultaneously accept or reject. If one buyer accepts, she receives the unit at price a. If both buyers accept price a, then the unit is allocated by a fair lottery between both players at price a. If both buyers reject price *a* then the unit is allocated by a fair lottery between both players at price 0. Show that there is an equilibrium in which type *H*s always accept. What are the seller's equilibrium profits, and the expected surpluses of different types of buyers?

(ii) Why does the revenue equivalence theorem not apply when comparing auction forms of the type described in part (i) with different values of *a*?

(iii) Write down incentive compatibility constraints relating the amounts of surplus that types *H* and *L* can receive in any mechanism which always assigns the unit to one of the buyers, and always does so efficiently (and gives the two buyers the same probability of winning if they are of the same type). Hence deduce a mechanism that maximizes the seller's profits in this class of mechanisms.

(iv) Assume the seller need not assign the unit to either buyer. What mechanism maximizes her profits?

[Oxford, Economic Theory, 1999]

3. Each of six risk-neutral bidders has a privately known value independently drawn from a uniform distribution on $[0, \bar{v}]$ for a single unit. (No bidder desires more than 1 unit.) An auctioneer has two identical units available. Denote by v_i^j the *i*th highest remaining valuation when *j* bidders remain in the auction.

(i) State, and sketch a proof of a version of the revenue equivalence theorem that applies to this context.

(ii) Two successive first-price sealed-bid auctions are held for one unit each. (In each auction only the winning bid is revealed.) In equilibrium, what is the bid in the *second* auction of a bidder with value *v* who failed to win in the first auction?

(iii) What is the bid in the *first* auction of a bidder with value *v?*

(iv) Now assume *n* objects are sold by successive sealed-bid auctions to $(n + 4)$ bidders. Derive whether prices are generally higher or lower in later auctions than in earlier auctions.

(v) Briefly discuss how your answer to (iv) might be sensitive to the assumptions of the problem.

[Oxford, Economic Theory, 2000]

REVENUE EQUIVALENCE THEOREM—APPLICATIONS

4. In 1991 US Vice-President Quayle proposed that the loser in a lawsuit be required to transfer an amount equal to her own legal expenses to the winner. Quayle claimed this would reduce the amount spent on legal services. (Under current US rules each party pays its own costs.) We will model this by assuming each party $i = 1, 2$ has a privately known value v_i, independently drawn from $F(v)$(with $F(\underline{v}) = 0$) for winning a lawsuit, the two parties independently and simultaneously decide how much to spend on legal services, and the party that spends the most money wins.

(i) Obtain an expression for the amount each player spends under current US rules, by using revenue equivalence with an ascending auction for the prize of winning the lawsuit. What additional assumption(s), if any, did you have to make to use the revenue equivalence theorem?

(ii) Without doing any more calculations, use our model to evaluate Quayle's claim. What additional assumption(s), if any, have you made?

(iii) In European legal systems the loser usually pays a fraction of the winner's actual expenses. Without doing any more calculations do you think this rule will increase or reduce expected legal expenses?

(iv) Use the revenue equivalence theorem to obtain a differential equation for the amount $l(v)$ each party spends under Quayle's rules. Show that

$$l(v) = \frac{v^2}{3} \frac{3-v}{(2-v)^2}$$

satisfies your equation when $F(v) = v$.

(v) Very briefly, how satisfactory is the model?

[Oxford, Economic Theory, 1998]

5. It is sometimes said that firms dislike sealed-bid auctions because they can be very embarrassing for managers who find they have paid a lot more than runners-up.

(i) Consider n firms whose values, v_i, are independently drawn from the uniform distribution on $[0, 1]$. i's managers' utility from winning with bid b_i equals

$$u_i = v_i - b_i - k\left(b_i - \max_{j \neq i} b_j\right)$$

(in which the term proportional to k reflects the embarrassment of winning) and a non-winner's utility is zero. Write down the first-order condition that bidding must satisfy, and hence show that there is a linear equilibrium.

(ii) Compute the seller's expected profit, and the bidders' expected utilities from the auction.

(iii) How do the bidders' expected utilities depend on k? How can you explain this result? Hence explain how the seller's expected profit depends on k.

(iv) How do you expect your results would change if losers also suffered embarrassment costs based on the difference between their bids and the winner's bid? [You are not expected to solve such a model.]

(v) Using, but without limiting yourself to, the models discussed in (i) and (iv) briefly discuss why firms often lobby against government proposals to use sealed-bid auctions.

[Oxford, Economic Theory, 2002]

6. This problem explores the institution of "buy prices".

(i) Two bidders compete in a standard ascending auction for a single prize for which they have private values independently drawn from the uniform distribution on [0, 1]. What is the expected price, conditional on winning, that a bidder with value x will pay?

(ii) Now assume that prior to the auction the seller announces that at any point during the auction either bidder can immediately end the auction by announcing her willingness to pay the fixed "buy price" of $b \geq 0.5$, in which case that bidder wins the prize and pays the buy price b. Assume that there is an equilibrium in which a bidder with value $x \geq b$ bids the buy price when the bidding has reached $p(x)$, with $p'(x) < 0$. What is the expected price, conditional on winning, that a bidder with value x will pay, as a function of x and $p(x)$?

(iii) Assuming the bidders are risk-neutral, explain why the expected price that a bidder with value x pays conditional on winning is the same in parts (i) and (ii). Now use this to solve for $p(x)$.
[*Hint*: You should get a quadratic equation, one root of which is $p = x$. This root is not the solution, since by assumption $p'(x) < 0$.]

(iv) If the seller is risk-averse (and the bidders are risk-neutral) does she prefer the buy-price auction to (a) a pure ascending auction? and (b) a first-price sealed-bid auction? Why?

(v) If the bidders are risk-averse, do you conjecture expected revenue is higher or lower than in (a) a pure ascending auction? and (b) a first-price sealed-bid auction? Why?

[Oxford, Economic Theory, 2003]

MARGINAL REVENUES

7. (i) Consider a monopolist with a single unit facing two markets with demands $p = 1 - q$ and $p = 2 - q$, respectively, between which she can price discriminate. What are her optimal prices and sales in each market?

(ii) Consider an auctioneer with a single unit facing two risk-neutral buyers with independent valuations uniformly distributed on [0, 1] and [1, 2], respectively. Construct an optimal auction for him. What are the probabilities with which he sells to each buyer?

(iii) By reference to parts (i) and (ii) explain the similarities between, and the differences between, the theory of optimal auctions and the theory of price discrimination.

[Oxford, Economic Theory, 1996]

8. (i) Sketch why the expected revenue from an ascending auction equals the expected marginal revenue of the winning bidder. Under what assumptions does the result extend to any auction form?

(ii) Consider an auction with three risk-neutral bidders. Bidder A has a value of 10. Bidder B has a value that is drawn from a uniform distribution between 0 and 30. Bidder C has a value that is drawn from a uniform distribution between 0 and 50, independently of B's. The seller has a value of 0 and can pre-commit to any allocation mechanism she wishes. Construct the optimal auction.

(iii) Now consider an auction in which each of three risk-neutral bidders observes a private signal independently drawn from a uniform distribution on [0, 1], and the value to any of the bidders is equal to the maximum of the three signals.

> (a) What expected price does a standard ascending auction in which all three bidders participate yield?
> (b) If one bidder, chosen at random, had been excluded from the auction, what would the expected price have been?
> (c) If the auctioneer had been able to transact with only one of the bidders, chosen at random, what is the highest take-it-or-leave-it price she could have set while guaranteeing acceptance?
> (d) Comment on your findings in (a), (b), (c).

[Oxford, Economic Theory, 2001]

COMMON VALUES

9. Risk neutral bidders $i = 1, 2$ each receive a private signal z_i independently drawn from the uniform distribution on [0, 1]. Bidder i's value for an object is $v_i = 3z_i + z_j; i, j = 1, 2; i \neq j$.

(i) A single item is sold by English (i.e., Japanese, or ascending) auction. Compute equilibrium bidding strategies.

(ii) A single object is sold by Dutch (i.e., descending) auction.

> (a) Use your solution in (i) together with the revenue equivalence theorem to deduce equilibrium bidding strategies.
> (b) Solve for the equilibrium strategies directly, by writing out i's surplus when her signal is z_i and she bids as if her type was $\tilde{z}_i$ and then obtaining a differential equation from the first-order condition.

(iii) Would the seller prefer a Japanese or a Dutch auction

> (a) If the buyers are risk-averse (but the seller is risk-neutral)?
> (b) If the seller is risk-averse (but the buyers are risk-neutral as before)?

[Oxford, Economic Theory, 1997]

10. Three risk-neutral bidders $i = 1, 2, 3$ each receive a private signal t_i that is independently drawn from the uniform distribution on $[0, 1]$. Each of two objects has an actual value equal to the average of the three signals.

(i) State a version of the revenue equivalence theorem that applies to this context.

(ii) Describe bidders' strategies in the symmetric equilibrium of the English auction (i.e., an ascending auction in which the two remaining bidders win at the price at which the other quits).

(iii) Compute the expected surplus of a bidder with signal t in the above equilibrium.

(iv) Deduce equilibrium strategies in a sealed-bid discriminatory auction (i.e., each of the two highest bidders wins an object and pays her actual bid).

[Oxford, Economic Theory, 1995]

RISK AVERSION

11. Two players $i = 1, 2$ have private values v_i that are independently drawn from the uniform distribution on $[0, 1]$, for a single object.

(i) Assume players' utilities u_i are given by $u_i = v_i - t_i$ when the player receives the object for payment t_i and $u_i = 0$ otherwise.

  (a) How do players bid in an ascending auction? What are expected revenues?

  (b) Solve for the symmetric equilibrium bidding functions $b(v_i)$ in a first-price sealed-bid auction by obtaining the first-order condition that optimal bidding must satisfy and solving the resulting differential equation. What are expected revenues?

  (c) Comment on the comparison of the results of (a) and (b).

(ii) Now assume $u_i = \sqrt{v_i - t_i}$ when the player receives the object. Repeat (a), (b) and (c) above, and provide intuition.

[Oxford, 1st Year Micro, 2002]

ESSAY QUESTIONS

12. "As a mechanism for allocating resources, auctions are efficient and fair." Discuss.

[Oxford, 1st Year Micro, 1999]

13. Are first-price or second-price auctions better?

[Oxford, Economic Theory, 1997]

14. Sketch a proof of the revenue equivalence theorem. Explain why the theorem fails, and how the seller's revenue comparison between first- and second-price auctions is affected, if (i) bidders are risk-averse, and (ii) bidders' information is affiliated.

[Oxford, Economic Theory, 1996]

15. Does behavior in common-value auctions differ importantly from that in private-value auctions?

[Oxford, Economic Theory, 1999]

16. Is the commonly made assumption that bidders' private-information is independent an important one in auction theory? Why? Is it a good assumption?

[Oxford, Economic Theory, 2000]

17. How does the correlation of bidders' information signals affect the design of an auction?

[Oxford, Economic Theory, 2003]

18. When several similar objects are auctioned sequentially, should we expect later prices to be on average higher, or on average lower, than earlier prices?

[Oxford, Economic Theory, 2001]

19. Does it matter that most auction theory has been developed in a single-unit context?

[Oxford, Economic Theory, 2002]

20. What are the main strengths and limitations of existing auction theory for practical applications?

[Oxford, Economic Theory, 1998]

PART B
_____

Applications to *Other* Areas of Economics

CHAPTER TWO

Why Every Economist Should Learn Some Auction Theory*

We discuss the strong connections between auction theory and "standard" economic theory; we show that situations that do not at first sight look like auctions can be recast to use auction-theoretic techniques; and we argue that auction-theoretic tools and intuitions can provide useful arguments and insights in a broad range of mainstream economic settings. We also discuss some more obvious applications, especially to industrial organization.

Auction Theory **Heineken.**
Refreshes the parts other
economics **beers cannot reach**

Disclaimer: We do not contend that the following ideas are all as important as the one illustrated here, merely that those who have not imbibed auction theory are missing out on a potent brew!

* This was an Invited Lecture to the 8th World Congress of the Econometric Society, and was originally published under the title "Why Every Economist Should Learn Some Auction Theory", in Dewatripont, M., Hansen, L., and Turnovsky, S. (eds.) (2003) *Advances in Economics and Econometrics: Theory and Applications*. Cambridge University Press, vol. 1, pp. 25–55. Susan Athey was an excellent discussant of my lecture. I also received extremely helpful comments and advice from many other friends and colleagues, including Larry Ausubel, Mike Baye, Alan Beggs, Simon Board, Jeremy Bulow, Peter Cramton, Joe Farrell, Giulio Federico, Nils Hendrik von der Fehr, Dan Kovenock, David McAdams, Peter McAfee, Flavio Menezes, Meg Meyer, Jonathan

2.1 INTRODUCTION

Auction theory has attracted enormous attention in the last few years.[1] It has been increasingly applied in practice, and this has itself generated a new burst of theory. It has also been extensively used, both experimentally and empirically, as a testing ground for game theory.[2] Furthermore, by carefully analyzing very simple trading models, auction theory is developing the fundamental building blocks for our understanding of more complex environments. But some people still see auction theory as a rather specialized field, distinct from the main body of economic theory, and as an endeavor for management scientists and operations researchers rather than as a part of mainstream economics. This chapter aims to counter that view.

This view may have arisen in part because auction theory was substantially developed by operational researchers, or in operations research journals,[3] and using technical mathematical arguments rather than standard economic intuitions. But it need not have been this way. This chapter argues that the connections between auction theory and "standard" economic theory run deeper than many people realize; that auction-theoretic tools provide useful arguments in a broad range of contexts; and that a good understanding of auction theory is valuable in developing intuitions and insights that can inform the analysis of many mainstream economic questions. In short, auction theory is central to economics.

We pursue this agenda in the context of some of the main themes of auction theory: the revenue equivalence theorem, marginal revenues, and ascending vs. (first-price) sealed-bid auctions. To show how auction-theoretic tools can be applied elsewhere in economics, section 2.2 exploits the revenue equivalence theorem to analyze a wide range of applications that are not, at first sight, auctions, including litigation systems, financial crashes, queues, and wars of attrition. (Section 4.6 briefly discusses an application of the theory of affiliation.) To illustrate how looser analogies can usefully be made between auction theory and economics, section 2.3 applies some intuitions from the compar-

Mirrlees-Black, John Morgan, Marco Pagnozzi, Nicola Persico, Eric Rasmussen, David Salant, Margaret Stevens, Rebecca Stone, Lucy White, Mark Williams, Xavier Vives, Caspar de Vries, and Charles Zheng.

[1] See chapter 1 for a review of auction theory; many of the most important contributions are collected in Klemperer (2000a).

[2] Kagel (1995) and Laffont (1997) are excellent recent surveys of the experimental and empirical work, respectively. Section 2.6 and chapters 3–7 discuss practical applications.

[3] The earliest studies appear in the operations research literature, for example, Friedman (1956). Myerson's (1981) breakthrough article appeared in *Mathematics of Operations Research*, while Rothkopf's (1969) and Wilson's (1967, 1969) classic early papers appeared in *Management Science*. Ortega Reichert's (1968a) pathbreaking models of auctions, including a model of signaling that significantly predated Spence (1972), remain relatively little known by economists, perhaps because they formed an operations research PhD thesis.

ison of ascending and sealed-bid auctions to other economic settings such as rationing, and e-commerce. To demonstrate the deeper connections between auction theory and economics, section 2.4 discusses and applies the close parallel between the optimal auction problem and that of the discriminating monopolist; both are about maximizing marginal revenues.

Furthermore, auction-theoretic ways of thinking are also underutilized in more obvious areas of application, for instance, price-setting oligopolies which we discuss in section 2.5.[4] Few non-auction-theorists know, for example, that marginal-cost pricing is *not* always the only equilibrium when identical firms with constant marginal costs set prices, or know the interesting implications of this fact. Section 2.6 briefly discusses direct applications of auction theory to markets that are literally auction markets, including electricity markets, treasury auctions, spectrum auctions, and internet markets, and we conclude in section 2.7.

2.2 USING AUCTION-THEORETIC TOOLS IN ECONOMICS: THE REVENUE EQUIVALENCE THEOREM

Auction theory's most celebrated theorem, the revenue equivalence theorem (RET) states conditions under which different auction forms yield the same expected revenue, and also allows revenue rankings of auctions to be developed when these conditions are violated.[5] Our purpose here, however, is to apply it in contexts where the use of an auction model might not seem obvious.

Revenue Equivalence Theorem (RET). *Assume each of a given number of risk-neutral potential buyers has a privately known valuation independently drawn from a strictly increasing atomless distribution, and that no buyer wants more than one of the k identical indivisible prizes. Then any mechanism in which (i) the prizes always go to the k buyers with the highest valuations and (ii) any bidder with the lowest feasible valuation expects zero surplus, yields the same expected revenue (and results in each bidder making the same expected payment as a function of her valuation).[6]*

---

[4] Of course, standard auction models form the basic building blocks of models in many contexts. See, for example, Stevens' (1994, 2000) models of wage determination in oligopsonistic labor markets, Bernheim and Whinston (1986), Feddersen and Pesendorfer (1996, 1998), Persico (2000a), and many others' political economy models, and many models in finance (including, of course, takeover battles, to which we give an application in section 2.4).

Another major area we do not develop here is the application of auction-theorists' understanding of the winner's curse to adverse selection more generally.

[5] See chapter 1.

[6] See Appendix 1.A for more general statements and an elementary proof. The theorem was first derived in an elementary form by Vickrey (1961, 1962) and subsequently extended to greater generality by Myerson (1981), Riley and Samuelson (1981), and others.

More general statements are possible, but are not needed for the current purpose. Our first example is very close to a pure auction.

2.2.1 Comparing Litigation Systems

In 1991, US Vice President Dan Quayle suggested reforming the US legal system in the hope, in particular, of reducing legal expenditures. One of his proposals was to augment the current rule according to which parties pay their own legal expenses, by a rule requiring the losing party to pay the winner an amount equal to the loser's own expenses. Quayle's intuition was that if spending an extra $1 on a lawsuit might end up costing you $2, then less would be spent. Was he correct?[7]

A simple starting point is to assume each party has a privately known value of winning the lawsuit relative to losing, independently drawn from a common, strictly increasing, atomless distribution;[8] that the parties independently and simultaneously choose how much money to spend on legal expenses; and that the party who spends the most money wins the "prize" (the lawsuit).[9] It is not too hard to see that both the existing US system and the Quayle system satisfy the assumptions of the RET, so the two systems result in the same expected total payments on lawyers.[10] So Quayle was wrong (as usual); his argument is precisely offset by the fact that the value of winning the lawsuit is greater when you win your opponent's expenses.[11]

Ah, Quayle might say, but this calculation has taken as given the set of lawsuits that are contested. Introducing the Quayle scheme will change the

[7] This question was raised and analyzed (though not by invoking the RET) by Baye, Kovenock, and de Vries (1997). The ideas in this section, except for the method of analysis, are drawn from them. See also Baye, Kovenock, and de Vries (1998). (See chapter 1, exercise 4.)

[8] For example, a suit about which party has the right to a patent might fit this model. The results extend easily to common-value settings, for example, contexts in which the issue is the amount of damages that should be transferred from one party to another.

[9] American seminar audiences typically think this is a natural assumption, but non-Americans often regard it as unduly jaundiced. Of course, we use it as a benchmark only, to develop insight and intuition (just as the lowest price does not win the whole market in most real "Bertrand" markets, but making the extreme assumption is a common and useful starting point). Extensions are possible to cases in which with probability $(1 - \lambda)$ the "most deserving" party wins, but with probability $\lambda > 0$ the biggest spender wins.

[10] The fact that no single "auctioneer" collects the players' payments as revenues, but that they are instead dissipated in legal expenses in competing for the single available prize (victory in the lawsuit), is of course irrelevant to the result.

Formally, checking our claims requires confirming that there are equilibria of the games that satisfy the RET's assumptions. The assumption we made that the parties make a one-shot choice of legal expenses is not necessary but makes confirming this relatively easy. See Baye, Kovenock, and de Vries (1997) for explicit solutions.

[11] Some readers might argue they could have inferred the effectiveness of the proposal from the name of the proponent, without need of further analysis. In fact, however, this was one of Dan Quayle's policy interventions that was not subject to immediate popular derision.

"bidding functions", that is, change the amount any given party spends on litigation, so also change who decides to bring suits. Wrong again Dan! Although it is correct that the bidding functions change, the RET also tells us (in its parenthetical remark) that any given party's *expected* payoffs from the lawsuit are unchanged, so the incentives to bring lawsuits are unchanged.

What about other systems, such as the typical European system in which the loser pays a fraction of the winner's expenses? This is a trick question: it is no longer true that a party with the lowest possible valuation can spend nothing and lose nothing. Now this party always loses in equilibrium and must pay a fraction of the winner's expenses, so makes negative expected surplus. That is, condition (ii) of the RET now fails. Thinking through the logic of the proof of the RET makes clear that all the players are worse off than under the previous systems.[12] That is, legal bills are higher under the European rule. The reason is that the incentives to win are greater than in the US system, and there is no offsetting effect. Here of course the issue of who brings lawsuits is important since low-valuation parties would do better not to contest suits in this kind of system; consistent with our theory there is empirical evidence (e.g., Hughes and Snyder, 1995) that the American system leads to more trials than, for example, the British system.

This last extension demonstrates that even where the RET in its simplest form fails, it is often possible to see how the result is modified; Appendix 2.A shows how to use the RET to solve for the relative merits of a much broader class of systems of which those we have discussed are special cases. We also show there that a system that might be thought of as the exact opposite of Quayle's system is optimal in this model. Of course, many factors are ignored (e.g.,, asymmetries); the basic model should be regarded as no more than a starting point for analysis.

2.2.2 The War of Attrition

Consider a war of attrition in which N players compete for a prize. For example, N firms compete to be the unique survivor in a natural monopoly market, or N firms each hold out for the industry to adopt the standard they prefer.[13] Each player pays costs of 1 per unit time until she quits the game. When just one player remains, that player also stops paying costs and wins the prize. There is no discounting. The two-player case, where just one quit is

---

[12] As Appendix 2.A discusses, every type's surplus is determined by reference to the lowest-valuation type's surplus (see also Appendix 1.A), and the lowest type is worse off in the European system. Again, our argument depends on condition (i) of the RET applying. See Appendix 2.A and Baye, Kovenock, and de Vries (1997).

[13] Another related example analyzed by Bulow and Klemperer (1999) is that of N politicians each delaying in the hope of being able to avoid publicly supporting a necessary but unpopular policy that requires the support of $N - 1$ to be adopted.

needed to end the game, has been well analyzed.[14] Does the many-player case yield anything of additional interest?

Assume players' values of winning are independently drawn from a common, strictly increasing, atomless distribution, and the game has an equilibrium satisfying the other conditions of the RET. Then the RET tells us that in expectation the total resources spent by the players in the war of attrition equal those paid by the players in any other mechanism satisfying the RET's conditions—for example, a standard ascending auction in which the price rises continuously until just one player remains and (only) the winner pays the final price. This final price will equal the second-highest actual valuation, so the expected total resources dissipated in the war of attrition is the expectation of this quantity.

Now imagine the war of attrition has been under way long enough that just the two highest-valuation players remain. What are the expected resources that will be dissipated by the remaining two players, starting from this time on? The RET tells us that they equal the auctioneer's expected revenue if the war of attrition were halted at this point and the objects sold to the remaining players by an ascending auction, that is, the expected second-highest valuation of these two remaining players. This is the same quantity, on average, as before![15] So the expected resources dissipated, and hence the total time taken until just two players remain, must be zero; all but the two highest-valuation players must have quit at once.

Of course this conclusion is, strictly speaking, impossible; the lowest-valuation players cannot identify who they are in zero time. However, the conclusion is correct in spirit, in that it is the limit point of the unique symmetric equilibria of a sequence of games which approach this game arbitrarily closely (and there is no symmetric equilibrium of the limit game).[16]

---

[14] See, for example, Maynard Smith (1974) and Riley (1980) who discuss biological competition, Fudenberg and Tirole (1986) who discuss industrial competition, Abreu and Gul (2000), Kambe (1999), and others who analyze bargaining, and Bliss and Nalebuff (1984) who give a variety of amusing examples.

Bliss and Nalebuff note that extending to $K + 1$ players competing for K prizes does not change the analysis in any important way, since it remains true that just one quit is needed to end the game.

[15] Of course the expectation of the second-highest valuation of the last two players is computed when just these two players remain, rather than at the beginning of the war of attrition as before. But on average these two expectations must be the same.

[16] Bulow and Klemperer (1999) analyze games in which each player pays costs at rate 1 before quitting but must continue to pay costs even after quitting at rate c per unit time until the whole game ends. The limit $c \to 0$ corresponds to the war of attrition discussed here. (The case $c = 1$ corresponds, for example, to "standards battles" or political negotiations in which all players bear costs equally until *all* have agreed on the same standard or outcome; this game also has interesting properties—see Bulow and Klemperer.) Other series of games, for example, games in which being kth to last to quit earns a prize of ε^{k-1} times one's valuation, with $\varepsilon \to 0$, or games in which players can only quit at the discrete times $0, \varepsilon, 2\varepsilon, \ldots$, with $\varepsilon \to 0$, also yield the same outcome in the limit.

Here, therefore, the role of the RET is less to perform the ultimate analysis than it is to show that there is an interesting and simple result to be obtained.[17] Of course by developing intuition about what the result must be, the RET also makes proving it much easier. Furthermore the RET was also useful in the actual analysis of the more complex games that Bulow and Klemperer (1999) used to approximate this game. In addition, anyone armed with a knowledge of the RET can simplify the analysis of the basic two-player war of attrition.

2.2.3 Queuing and Other "All-Pay" Applications

The preceding applications have both been variants of "all-pay" auctions. As another elementary example of this kind consider different queuing systems, for example, for tickets to a sporting event. Under not unreasonable assumptions, a variety of different rules of queue management, for example, making the queue more or less comfortable, informing or not informing people whether the number queuing exceeds the number who will receive a ticket, etc., will make no difference to the social cost of the queuing mechanism. As in our litigation example (section 2.2.1), we think of these results as a starting point for analysis rather than as final conclusions.[18]

Many other issues such as lobbying battles, political campaigns,[19] tournaments in firms, contributions to public goods,[20] patent races, and some kinds of price-setting oligopoly (see section 2.5.2) can be modeled as all-pay auctions and may provide similar applications.

2.2.4 Solving for Equilibrium Behavior: Market Crashes and Trading "Frenzies"

The examples thus far have all proceeded by computing the expected total payments made by all players. But the RET also states that each individual's

---

[17] It was the RET that showed Bulow and Klemperer that there was an analysis worth doing. Many people, and some literature, had assumed the many-player case would look like the two-player case but with more-complicated expressions, although Fudenberg and Kreps (1987) and Haigh and Cannings (1989) observed a similar result to ours in games without any private information and in which all players' values are equal.

However, an alternative way to see the result in our war of attrition is to imagine the converse but that a player is within ε of her planned quit time when $n > 1$ other players remain. Then the player's cost of waiting as planned is of order ε, but her benefit is of order ε^n since only when all n other players are within ε of giving up will she ultimately win. So for small ε she will prefer to quit now rather than wait, but in this case she should of course have quit ε earlier, and so on. So only when $n = 1$ is delay possible.

[18] Holt and Sherman (1982) compute equilibrium behavior and hence obtain these results without using the RET.

[19] See, especially, Persico (2000a).

[20] Menezes, Monteiro, and Temimi (2000) uses the RET in this context.

expected payment must be equal across mechanisms satisfying the assumptions. This fact can be used to infer what players' equilibrium actions must be in games which would be too complex to solve by any direct method of computing optimal behavior.[21]

Consider the following model. The aim is to represent, for example, a financial or housing market and show that trading "frenzies" and price "crashes" are the inevitable outcome of rational strategic behavior in a market that clears through a sequence of sales rather than through a Walrasian auctioneer. There are N potential buyers, each of whom is interested in securing one of K available units. Without fully modeling the selling side of the market, we assume it generates a single asking price at each instant of time according to some given function of buyer behavior to date. Each potential buyer observes all prices and all past offers to trade, and can accept the current asking price at any instant, in which case, supply permitting, the buyer trades at that price.

So traders have to decide both whether *and when* to offer to buy, all the while conditioning their strategies on the information that has been revealed in the market to date. Regarding the function generating the asking prices, we specify only that (i) if there is no demand at a price, then the next asking price is lower, and (ii) if demand exceeds remaining supply at any instant, then no trade actually takes place at that time but the next asking price is higher and only those who attempted to trade are allowed to buy subsequently.[22] Note, however, that even if we did restrict attention to a specific price-setting process, the direct approach of computing buyers' optimal behavior using first-order conditions as a function of all prior behavior to solve a dynamic program would generally be completely intractable.

To use the RET we must first ensure that the appropriate assumptions are satisfied. We assume, of course, that buyers' valuations are independently drawn from a common, strictly increasing, atomless distribution, and that there is no discounting during the time the mechanism takes. And the objects do eventually go to the highest-valuation buyers, and the lowest-possible-valuation buyer makes zero surplus in equilibrium, because of our assumption that if demand ever exceeds remaining supply then no trade takes place and non-demanders are henceforth excluded. So

---

[21] The same approach is also an economical method of computing equilibrium bids in many standard auctions. For example, in an ascending auction for a single unit, the expected payment of a bidder equals her probability of winning times the expected second-highest valuation among all the bidders conditional on her value being higher. So the RET implies that her equilibrium bid in a standard all-pay auction equals this quantity. Similarly, the RET implies that her equilibrium bid in a first-price sealed-bid auction equals the expected second-highest valuation among all the bidders conditional on her value being higher. See Appendix 1.A for more details and discussion.

[22] Additional technical assumptions are required to ensure that all units are sold in finite time. See Bulow and Klemperer (1994) for full details.

the RET applies, and it also applies to any subgame of the whole game.[23]

Under our assumptions, then, starting from any point of the process, the remainder of the game is revenue equivalent to what would result if the game were halted at that point and the remaining k objects were sold to the remaining buyers using a standard ascending auction (which sells all k objects at the $(k + 1)$th highest valuation among the remaining buyers). So at any point of our game we know the expected payment of any buyer in the remainder of our game, and therefore also the buyer's expected payment conditional on winning.[24] But any potential buyer whose expected payment conditional on winning equals or exceeds the current asking price will attempt to buy at the current price.[25] This allows us to completely characterize buyer behavior, so fully characterizes the price path for any given rule generating the asking prices.

It is now straightforward to show (see Bulow and Klemperer, 1994) that potential buyers are extremely sensitive to the new information that the price process reveals. So almost any seller behavior—for example, starting at a very high price and slowly lowering the price continuously until all the units are sold or there is excess demand—will result in "frenzies" of trading activity in which many buyers bid simultaneously, even though there is zero probability that two buyers have the same valuation.[26] Furthermore these frenzies will

[23] If, instead, excess demand resulted in random rationing, the highest-valuation buyers might not win, violating the requirements of the RET, so even if we thought this was more natural it would make sense to begin with our assumption to be able to analyze and understand the process using the RET. The effects of the alternative assumption could then be analyzed with the benefit of the intuitions developed using the RET. Bulow and Klemperer (1994) proceed in exactly this way.

[24] Specifically, if k objects remain, the buyer's expected payment conditional on winning will be the expected $(k + 1)$th highest valuation remaining conditional on the buyer having a valuation among the k highest remaining, and conditional on all the information revealed to date. This is exactly the buyer's expected payment conditional on winning an object in the ascending auction, since in both cases only winners pay and the probability of a bidder winning is the same.

[25] The marginal potential buyer, who is just indifferent about bidding now, will either win now or will never win an object. (If bidding now results in excess demand, this bidder will lose to inframarginal current bidders, since there is probability zero that two bidders have the same valuation.) So conditional on winning, this bidder's actual payment is the current price. Inframarginal bidders, whose expected payment conditional on winning exceeds the current price, may eventually end up winning an object at above the current price.

[26] To see why a frenzy must arise if the price is lowered continuously, note that for it to be rational for any potential buyer to jump in and bid first, there must be positive probability that there will be a frenzy large enough to create excess demand immediately following the first bid. Otherwise the strategy of waiting to bid until another player has bid first would guarantee a lower price.

For more general seller behavior, the point is that while buyers' valuations may be very dispersed, higher-valuation buyers are all almost certainly inframarginal in terms of whether to buy and are therefore all solving virtually identical optimization problems of when to buy. So a small change in asking price, or a small change in market conditions (such as the information revealed by a single trade) at a given price, can make a large number of buyers change from being unwilling to trade to wanting to trade.

The only selling process that can surely avoid a frenzy is a repeated Dutch auction.

sometimes lead to "crashes" in which it becomes common knowledge that the market price must fall a substantial distance before any further trade will take place.[27] Bulow and Klemperer also show that natural extensions to the model (e.g., "common values", the possibility of resale, or an elastic supply of units) tend to accentuate frenzies and crashes. Frenzies and crashes arise precisely because buyers are rational and strategic; by contrast buyer irrationality might lead to "smoother" market behavior.

Of course our main point here is not the details of the process, but rather that the RET permits the solution and analysis of the dynamic price path of a market that would otherwise seem completely intractable to solve for.

2.3 TRANSLATING LOOSER ANALOGIES FROM AUCTIONS INTO ECONOMICS: ASCENDING VS. (FIRST-PRICE) SEALED-BID AUCTIONS

A major focus of auction theory has been contrasting the revenue and efficiency properties of "ascending" and "sealed-bid" auctions.[28] Ideas and intuitions developed in these comparisons have wide applicability.

2.3.1 Internet Sales Versus Dealer Sales

There is massive interest in the implications of e-commerce and internet sales. For example, the advent of internet sales in the automobile industry as a partial replacement for traditional methods of selling through dealers has been widely welcomed in Europe;[29] the organization of the European automobile market is currently a major policy concern both in official circles and the popular press, and the internet sales are seen as increasing "transparency". But is transparency a good thing?

Auction theory shows that internet sales need *not* be good for consumers. Clearly transparent prices benefit consumers if they reduce consumers' search costs so that in effect there are more competitors for every consumer.[30] And of course internet sales may also lower prices by cutting out the fixed costs of dealerships, albeit by also cutting out the additional services that dealers

---

[27] The price process is also extremely sensitive to buyer valuations; an arbitrarily small change in one buyer's value can discontinuously and substantially change all subsequent trading prices.

[28] By "sealed-bid" we mean standard first-price sealed-bid auctions. "Ascending" auctions have similar properties to second-price sealed-bid auctions. See sections 1.1.2–1.1.4 for an introduction to the different types of auctions.

[29] See, for example, "May the net be with you", *Financial Times*, 21 October 1999, p. 22. In the United Kingdom, Vauxhall began selling a limited number of special models over the internet late in 1999, while Ford began a pilot project in Finland.

[30] There may be both a direct effect (that consumers can observe more firms), and an indirect effect (that new entry is facilitated). See Baye and Morgan (2001) and Kühn and Vives (1995) for more discussion.

provide. But transparency also makes internet sales more like ascending auctions, by contrast with dealer sales that are more like (first-price) sealed-bid auctions, and we will show this is probably *bad* for consumers.

Transparent internet prices are readily observable by a firm's competitors so result, in effect, in an "ascending" auction; a firm knows if and when its offers are being beaten and can rapidly respond to its competitors' offers if it wishes. So, viewing each car sale as a separate auction, the price any consumer faces falls until all but one firm quits bidding to sell to him. (The price is, of course, descending because firms are competing to sell, but the process corresponds exactly to the standard ascending auction among bidders competing to buy an object, and we therefore maintain the standard "ascending" terminology.)

On the other hand, shopping to buy a car from one of competing dealers is very like procuring in a (first-price) "sealed-bid" auction. It is typically impossible to credibly communicate one dealer's offer to another. (Car dealers often deliberately make this hard by refusing to put an offer in writing.) So from the buyer's perspective it is as if sellers were independently making sealed-bid offers in ignorance of the competition.

Of course, the analogies are imperfect,[31] but they serve as a starting point for analysis. So what does auction theory suggest?

Since, under the conditions of the revenue equivalence theorem, there is no difference between the auction forms for either consumer or producer welfare, we consider the implications of the most important violations of the conditions.

First, market demand is downward sloping, not inelastic.[32] Hansen (1988) showed that this means consumers always prefer the sealed-bid setting, and firms may prefer it also; the sum of producer and consumer surpluses is always higher in a sealed-bid auction.[33] The intuition is that in an "ascending" auction the sales price equals the runner-up's cost, so is less reflective of the winner's cost than is the sealed-bid price. So the sealed-bid auction is more productively efficient (the quantity traded better reflects the winner's cost) and provides greater incentive for aggressive bidding (a more aggressive sealed bid not only increases the probability of winning, but also increases the quantity traded contingent on winning).

---

[31] The analogies are less good for many other products. For lower-value products than cars, internet sales are less like an "ascending" auction since search costs will allow price dispersion, while traditional sales through posted prices in high-street stores are more like "ascending" auctions than are dealer sales of cars.

  Note also that the outcomes of the two auction types differ most when competitors have private information about their costs, which is more likely when competitors are original manufacturers than when competitors are retailers selling goods bought at identical prices from the same wholesaler.

[32] For an individual consumer, demand might be inelastic for a single car up to a reservation price. From the point of view of the sellers who do not know the consumer's reservation price, the expected market demand is downward sloping.

[33] Of course, Hansen is maintaining the other important assumptions of the revenue equivalence theorem.

Second, we need to consider the possibilities for collusion, implicit or explicit. The general conclusion is that ascending auctions are more susceptible to collusion, and this is particularly the case when, as in our example, many auctions of different car models and different consumers are taking place simultaneously.[34] As has been observed in the US and German auctions of radio spectrum, for example, bidders may be able to tacitly coordinate on dividing up the spoils in a simultaneous ascending auction. Bidders can use the early rounds when prices are still low[35] to signal their views about who should win which objects, and then, when consensus has been reached, tacitly agree to stop pushing prices up.[36] The same coordination cannot readily be achieved in simultaneous sealed-bid auctions, where there is neither the opportunity to signal, nor the ability to retaliate against a bidder who fails to cooperate.[37] The conclusion is less stark when there are many repetitions over time, but it probably remains true that coordination is easier in ascending auctions. Furthermore, as is already well understood in the industrial-organization literature,[38] this conclusion is strengthened by the different observabilities of internet and dealer sale prices which make mutual understanding of firms' strategies, including defections from "agreements", far greater in the internet case. So selling over the internet probably makes it easier for firms to collude.

A third important issue is that bidders may be asymmetric. Then "ascending" auctions are generally more efficient (because the lowest-cost bidders win[39]), but

[34] See Robinson (1985) and Milgrom (1987) for discussion of the single-unit case, Menezes (1996), Weber (1997), Engelbrecht-Wiggans and Kahn (1998c), Ausubel and Schwartz (1999), Brusco and Lopomo (2002a), and Cramton and Schwartz (2000) for the multi-unit case. Sections 3.2 and 4.3.2 review these arguments and gives many examples.

[35] Bidders are competing to buy rather than sell spectrum, so prices are ascending rather than descending.

[36] For example, in a 1999 German spectrum auction Mannesman bid a low price for half the licenses and a slightly lower price for the other half. One of T-Mobil's managers said. "There were no agreements with Mannesman. But [T-Mobil] interpreted Mannesman's first bid as an offer." T-Mobil understood that it could raise the bid on the other half of the licenses slightly, and that the two companies would then "live and let live" with neither company challenging the other on "their" half. Just that happened. The auction closed after just two rounds with each of the bidders having half the licenses for the same low price (Jehiel and Moldovanu, 2000; Grimm, Riedel, and Wolfstetter, 2002).

In US FCC auctions, bidders have used the final three digits of multi-million dollar bids to signal the market ID codes of the areas they coveted, and a 1997 auction that was expected to raise $1,800 million raised less than $14 million. See Cramton and Schwartz (2001), and "Learning to Play the Game", The Economist, 17 May 1997, p. 120.

Sections 3.2 and 4.3.2 and chapter 5 give many more examples.

[37] The low prices in the ascending auction are supported by the threat that if a bidder overbids a competitor anywhere, then the competitor will retaliate by overbidding the first bidder on markets where the first bidder has the high bids.

[38] At least since Stigler (1964).

[39] To the extent that the auctions for individual consumers are independent single-unit auctions, an ascending auction is efficient under a broad class of assumptions if bidders' private signals are single-dimensional, even with asymmetries among bidders and common-value components to valuations. See Maskin (1992).

sealed-bid auctions typically yield lower consumer prices.[40] In this case economists generally favor ascending auctions, but competition-policy practitioners should usually prefer sealed-bid auctions because most competition regimes concentrate on consumer welfare.

Furthermore, this analysis ignores the impact of auction type on new entry in the presence of asymmetries. Because an "ascending" auction is generally efficient, a potential competitor with even a slightly higher cost (or lower quality) than an incumbent will see no point in entering the auction. However, the same competitor might enter a sealed-bid auction which gives a weaker bidder a shot at winning. The extra competition may lower prices very substantially. Of course the entry of the weaker competitor may also slightly reduce efficiency, but if competition is desirable per se, or if competition itself improves efficiency, or if the objective is consumer welfare rather than efficiency, then the case for sealed-bid auctions is very strong (see sections 2.3.2, 3.3, 3.5.2, and 4.3.1).

Although there are other dimensions in which our setting fails the revenue equivalence assumptions, they seem less important.[41] So the transparency induced between firms that makes internet sales more like ascending auctions than sealed-bid auctions is probably bad for consumers. While gains from lower consumer search costs and dealer costs could certainly reverse this conclusion, auction-theoretic considerations mount a strong case against "transparent" internet sales.[42]

In another application of auction-theoretic insights to e-commerce, Bulow and Klemperer (forthcoming) apply Milgrom and Weber's (1982a) celebrated *linkage principle* to show when the price discrimination that internet markets make possible *helps* consumers.

---

[40] A price-minimizing auction allocates the object to the bidder with the lowest "virtual cost", rather than to the one with the lowest actual cost. (See section 2.4; virtual cost is the analogous concept to marginal revenue for an auction to buy an object.) Compared to an ascending auction, a sealed-bid auction discriminates in favor of selling to "weaker" bidders, whose costs are drawn from higher distributions, because they bid more aggressively (closer to their actual costs) than stronger ones. But, for a given cost, a weaker bidder has a lower virtual cost than a stronger one. So in the sealed-bid auction often, but not always, yields lower prices. See section 1.7.1.

[41] Other violations of the revenue equivalence assumptions may include buyer and seller risk aversion which both favor sealed-bid auctions, and affiliation of costs which favors ascending auctions.

[42] Empirical evidence is limited. Lee (1998) and Lee, Westland, and Hong (1999) find electronic markets yield higher prices than conventional markets for cars. Scott Morton, Zettelmeyer, and Silva Risso (2001) find that California customers get lower prices if they use automobile internet sites, but this is unsurprising since these sites merely refer customers to dealers for price quotes, so behave more like traditional dealers than like the "transparent" sites that we have described and that are being promised in Europe.

88CHAPTER TWO

2.3.2 Anglo-Dutch Auctions, a Theory of Rationing, and Patent Races

The last disadvantage of ascending auctions discussed above—the dampening effect on entry—has been very important in practical auction contexts (see parts C and D). For example, in the main (1995) auction of US mobile-phone licenses some large potential bidders such as MCI, the United States's third-largest phone company, failed to enter at all, and many other bidders were deterred from competing seriously for particular licenses such as the Los Angeles and New York licenses which therefore sold at very low prices.[43] Entry was therefore a prominent concern when the United Kingdom planned an auction of four UMTS "third generation" mobile-phone licenses in 1998 for a market in which four companies operated mobile telephone services and therefore had clear advantages over any new entrant.[44]

In this case the design chosen was an "Anglo-Dutch" auction as first proposed in Klemperer (1998):[45] in an Anglo-Dutch auction for four licenses the price rises continuously until five bidders remain (the "English" stage), after which the five survivors make sealed-bids (required to be no lower than the current price level) and the four winners pay the fourth-highest bid (the "Dutch" stage). Weak bidders have an incentive to enter such an auction because they know they have a chance of winning at the sealed-bid stage if they can survive to be among the five finalists. The design accepts some risk of an ex-post inefficient allocation in order to increase the chance of attracting the additional bidders that are necessary for a successful auction and reasonable revenues.[46,47]

[43] See Klemperer and Pagnozzi (forthcoming) for econometric evidence of these kinds of problems in US spectrum auctions, Klemperer (1998) and Bulow and Klemperer (2002) for extensive discussion, and Bulow, Huang, and Klemperer (1999) for related modeling.

[44] Bidders could not be allowed to win more than one license each.

[45] See Klemperer (1998), Radiocommunications Agency (1998a,b) and sections 3.5.3 and 6.5.1 for more details and for variants on the basic design. (The Agency was advised by Binmore, Klemperer and others.)

[46] The additional bidders might yield a higher price even after the English stage, let alone after the final stage, than in a pure ascending auction.

[47] The design performed very successfully in laboratory testing, but the auction was delayed until 2000 and technological advances made it possible to offer five licenses, albeit of different sizes. The additional license resolved the problem of attracting new entrants, and since collusion was not a serious problem in this case (bidders were not allowed to win more than one license each), it was decided to switch to a simultaneous ascending design.

The actual UK auction was very successful, but the wisdom of the UK decision not to run an ascending auction when the number of strong bidders equaled the number of licenses was confirmed when the Netherlands did just this three months later, and raised little more than one-quarter of the per capita revenue raised by the United Kingdom. In large part the Netherlands' problem was that their ascending auction deterred entry.

Denmark also had the same number of strong bidders as licenses, and (successfully) used a sealed-bid auction for similar reasons that the United Kingdom would have run an Anglo-Dutch auction in this context. (In Denmark it was clear that there were too few potential bidders to make an Anglo stage worthwhile.)

See parts C and D for more detail.

Translating this idea into a more traditional economics context suggests a theory of why firms might ration their output at prices at which there is excess demand as, for example, microprocessor manufacturers routinely do after the introduction of a new chip. Raising the price to clear the market would correspond to running an ascending auction. It would be ex-post efficient and ex-post profit maximizing, but would give poor incentives for weaker potential customers who fear being priced out of the market to make the investments necessary to enter the market (such as the product design necessary to use the new chip). Committing to rationing at a fixed price at which demand exceeds supply is ex-post inefficient,[48] but may encourage more entry into the market and so improve ex-ante profits. Details and more examples are in Gilbert and Klemperer (2000).

A similar point is that a weaker firm may not be willing to enter a patent race in which all parties can observe others' progress. Such a race is akin to an ascending auction in which a stronger rival can always observe and overtake a weaker firm which therefore has no chance of winning.[49] A race in which rivals' progress cannot be monitored is more akin to a sealed-bid auction and may attract more entry.

These analogies illustrate how an insight that is routine in auction theory may help develop ideas in economics more broadly.

2.4 EXPLOITING DEEPER CONNECTIONS BETWEEN AUCTIONS AND ECONOMICS: MARGINAL REVENUES

The previous sections showed how a variety of economic problems can be thought of in auction-theoretic terms, allowing us to use tools such as the revenue equivalence theorem and intuitions such as those from the comparison of ascending and sealed-bid auctions. This section explains that the connections between auction theory and standard economic theory run much deeper.

Much of the analysis of optimal auctions can be phrased, like the analysis of monopoly, in terms of "marginal revenues". Imagine a firm whose demand curve is constructed from an arbitrarily large number of bidders whose values are independently drawn from a bidder's value distribution. When bidders have independent private values, a bidder's "marginal revenue" is defined as the marginal revenue of this firm at the price that equals the bidder's actual value (see figure 2.1).[50]

---

[48] We assume any resale is inefficient. But see Cramton, Gibbons, and Klemperer (1987).

[49] Of course, this point is closely related to the idea of "ε-preemption" in R&D races with observability that has already been well discussed in the standard industrial organization literature (Fudenberg, Gilbert, Stiglitz, and Tirole, 1983).

[50] The point of this construction is particularly clear when a seller faces a single bidder whose private value is distributed according to $F(v)$. Then setting a take-it-or-leave-it price of v yields expected sales, or "demand", $1 - F(v)$, expected revenue of $v(1 - F(v))$ and expected marginal revenue $d(qv)/dq = v - [1 - F(v)]/f(v)$. See Appendix 1.B.

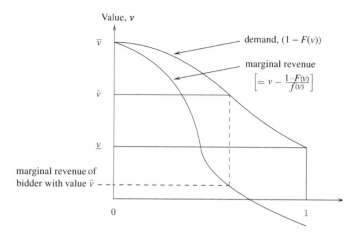

Figure 2.1 Construction of marginal revenue of bidder with value $\tilde{v}$ drawn from distribution $F(v)$ on $[\underline{v}, \overline{v}]$.

Although it had been hinted at before,[51] the key point was first explicitly drawn out by Bulow and Roberts (1989) who showed that under the assumptions of the revenue equivalence theorem *the expected revenue from an auction equals the expected marginal revenue of the winning bidder(s)*. The new results in the article were few—the paper largely mimicked Myerson (1981) while renaming Myerson's concept of "virtual utility" as "marginal revenue"[52,53]—but their contribution was nevertheless important. Once the connection had been made it was possible to take ways of thinking that are second nature to economists from the standard theory of monopoly pricing and apply them to auction theory.

For example, once the basic result above (that an auction's expected revenue equals the winning bidder's expected marginal revenue) was seen,

---

[51] For example, Mussa and Rosen's (1978) analysis of monopoly and product quality contained expressions for 'marginal revenue' that look like Myerson's (1981) analysis of optimal auctions.

[52] Myerson's results initially seemed unfamiliar to economists in part because his basic analysis (although not all his expressions) expressed virtual utilities as a function of bidders' values, which correspond to *prices*, and so computed revenues by integrating along the vertical axis, whereas we usually solve monopoly problems by expressing marginal revenues as functions of *quantities* and integrating along the horizontal axis of the standard (for monopoly) picture.

[53] Bulow and Roberts emphasize the close parallel between a monopolist third-degree price-discriminating across markets with different demand curves, and an auctioneer selling to bidders whose valuations are drawn from different distributions. For the $\left\{{monopolist \atop auctioneer}\right\}$, $\left\{{revenue \atop expected\ revenue}\right\}$ is maximized by selling to the $\left\{{consumers \atop bidder}\right\}$ with the highest marginal revenue(s), *not* necessarily the highest value(s), subject to never selling to a $\left\{{consumer \atop bidder}\right\}$ with marginal revenue less than the $\left\{{monopolist's\ marginal\ cost \atop auctioneer's\ own\ valuation}\right\}$, assuming (i) resale can be prohibited, (ii) credible commitment can be made to $\left\{{no\ future\ sales \atop sticking\ to\ any\ reserve\ price}\right\}$, and (iii) $\left\{{marginal\ revenue\ curves\ are\ all\ downward\ sloping \atop higher\ "types"\ of\ any\ bidder\ have\ higher\ marginal\ revenues\ than\ lower\ "types"\ of\ the\ same\ bidder}\right\}$, etc.

Bulow and Klemperer (1996) were able to use a simple monopoly diagram to derive it more simply and under a broader class of assumptions than had previously been done by Myerson or Bulow and Roberts.[54] Bulow and Klemperer also used standard monopoly intuition to derive additional results in auction theory.

The main benefits from the marginal-revenue connection come from translating ideas from monopoly analysis into auction analysis, since most economists' intuition for and understanding of monopoly is much more highly developed than for auctions. But it is possible to go in the other direction too, from auction theory to monopoly theory.

Consider, for example, the main result of Bulow and Klemperer (1996).

Proposition (Auction-Theoretic Version).   *An optimal auction of K units to Q bidders earns less profit than a simple ascending auction (without a reserve price) of K units to Q + K bidders, assuming (a) bidders are symmetric, (b) bidders are serious (i.e., their lowest-possible valuations exceed the seller's supply cost), and (c) bidders with higher valuations have higher marginal revenues.*[55]

Proof.   See Bulow and Klemperer (1996).

Application.   One application is to selling a firm (so $K = 1$). Since the seller can always resort to an ascending auction, attracting a single additional bidder is worth more than any amount of negotiating skill or bargaining power against an existing bidder or bidders, under reasonable assumptions. So there is little justification for, for example, accepting a "lock-up" bid for a company without fully exploring the interest of alternative possible purchasers.

The optimal auction translates, for large Q and K, to the monopolist's optimum. An ascending auction translates to the competitive outcome, in which price-taking firms make positive profits only because of the fixed supply of units. (An ascending auction yields the $(K + 1)$th highest value among the bidders; in a perfectly competitive market an inelastic supply of K units is in equilibrium with demand at any price between the Kth and $(K + 1)$th highest value, but the distinction is unimportant for large K.) So one way of expressing the result in the market context is:

---

[54] See Appendix 1.B for an exposition.

[55] See Bulow and Klemperer (1996) for a precise statement. We do not require bidders' valuations to be private, but do place some restrictions on the class of possible mechanisms from which the "optimal" one is selected, if bidders are not risk-neutral or their signals are not independent. We assume bidders demand a single unit each.

Proposition (Monopoly-Theoretic Version). *A perfectly competitive industry with (fixed) capacity K and Q consumers would gain less by fully cartelizing the industry (and charging the monopoly price) than it would gain by attracting K new potential customers into the industry with no change in the intensity of competition, assuming (a') the K new potential consumers have the same distribution of valuations as the existing consumers, (b') all consumers' valuations for the product exceed sellers' supply costs (up to sellers' capacity), and (c') the marginal–revenue curve constructed from the market–demand curve is downward sloping.*[56]

Proof. No proof is required—the proposition is implied by the auction-theoretic version—but once we know the result we are looking for and the necessary assumptions, it is very simple to prove it directly using introductory undergraduate economics and we do this in a brief Appendix 2.B.

Application. One application is that this provides conditions under which a joint-marketing agency does better to focus on actually marketing rather than (as some of the industrial organization literature suggests) on facilitating collusive practices.[57]

2.5 APPLYING AUCTION THEORY TO PRICE-SETTING OLIGOPOLIES

We have stressed the applications of auction theory to contexts that might not be thought of as auctions, but even though price-setting oligopolies are obviously auctions, the insights that can be obtained by thinking of them in this way are often passed by.

2.5.1 Marginal-Cost Pricing is NOT the Unique Bertrand Equilibrium

One of the most famous results in economics is the "Bertrand paradox" that with just two firms with constant and equal marginal costs in a homogeneous-products industry the unique equilibrium is for both firms to set price equal to marginal cost and firms earn zero profit. This "theorem" is widely quoted in standard texts. But it is *false*. There are other equilibria with large profits, for some standard demand curves, a fact that seems until recently to have been known only to a few auction theorists.[58]

---

[56] We are measuring capacity in units such that each consumer demands a single unit of output. Appendix 2.B makes it clear how the result generalizes.

[57] Of course the agency may wish to pursue both strategies in practice.

[58] We assume firms can choose any prices. It is well known that if prices can only be quoted in whole pennies, there is an equilibrium with positive (but small) profits in which each firm charges one penny above cost. (With perfectly inelastic demand, there is also an equilibrium in which each firm charges two pennies above cost.)

Auction theorists are familiar with the fact that a boundary condition is necessary to solve a sealed-bid auction. Usually this is imposed by assuming no bidder can bid less than any bidder's lowest-possible valuation, but there are generally a continuum of equilibria if arbitrarily negative bids are permitted.[59] Exactly conversely, with perfectly inelastic demand for one unit and, for example, two risk-neutral sellers with zero costs, it is a mixed-strategy equilibrium for each firm to bid above any price p with probability k/p, for any fixed k. (Each firm therefore faces expected residual demand of constant elasticity -1, and is therefore indifferent about mixing in this way; profits are k per firm.)

It is not hard to see that a similar construction is possible with downward-sloping demand, for example, standard constant-elasticity demand, provided that monopoly profits are unbounded. (See especially, Baye and Morgan (1999a) and Kaplan and Wettstein (2000)). One point of view is that the non-uniqueness of the "Bertrand paradox" equilibrium is a merely technical point since it requires "unreasonable" (even though often assumed[60]) demand. However, the construction immediately suggests another more important result: quite generally (including for demand which becomes zero at some finite choke price) there are very profitable mixed-strategy ε-equilibria to the Bertrand game, even though there are no pure-strategy ε-equilibria. That is, there are mixed strategies that are very different from marginal-cost pricing in which no player can gain more than a very small amount, ε, by deviating from the strategies.[61] (There are also "quantal response" equilibria with a similar flavor.) Experimental evidence suggests that these strategies may be empirically relevant (see Baye and Morgan, 1999b).[62]

2.5.2 The Value of New Consumers

The Revenue Equivalence Theorem (RET) can of course be applied to price-setting oligopolies.[63]

[59] For example, if each of two risk-neutral bidders' private values is independently drawn from a uniform distribution on the open interval $(0, 1)$ then for any non-negative k there is an equilibrium in which a player with value v bids $(v/2) - (k/v)$. If it is common knowledge that both bidders have value zero, there is an equilibrium in which each player bids below any price $-p$ with probability k/p, for any fixed non-negative k.

[60] This demand can, for example, yield unique and finite-profit Cournot equilibrium.

[61] Of course, the concept of mixed-strategy ε equilibrium used here is even more contentious than either mixed-strategy (Nash) equilibria or (pure-strategy) ε equilibrium. The best defense for it may be its practical usefulness.

[62] Spulber (1995) uses the analogy with a sealed-bid auction to analyze a price-setting oligopoly in which, by contrast with our discussion, firms do not know their rivals' costs. For a related application of auction theory to price-setting oligopoly, see Athey, Bagwell, and Sanchirico (forthcoming).

[63] See section 2.2 for discussion of the RET. As another example of its application to price-setting oligopolies, Vives (2002) uses the revenue equivalence theorem to compare oligopoly equilibria with incomplete and complete (or shared) information about firms' constant marginal costs, and so shows information sharing is socially undesirable in this context.

For example: what is the value of new consumers in a market with strong brand loyalty? If firms can price discriminate between new uncommitted consumers and old "locked-in" consumers, Bertrand competition for the former will mean their value is low, but what if price discrimination is impossible?

In particular, it is often argued that new youth smokers are very valuable to the tobacco industry because brand loyalty (as well as loyalty to the product) is very high (only about 10 percent of smokers switch brands in any year), so price-cost margins on all consumers are very high. Is there any truth to this view?

The answer, of course, under appropriate assumptions, is that the RET implies that the ability to price discriminate is irrelevant to the value of the new consumers: With price discrimination, we can model the oligopolists as acting as monopolists against their old customers, and as being in an "ascending"[64] price auction for the uncommitted consumers with the firm which is prepared to price the lowest selling to all these consumers at the cost of the runner-up firm. Alternatively, we can model the oligopolists as making sealed bids for the uncommitted consumers with the lowest bidder selling to these consumers at its asking price. The expected profits are the same under the RET assumptions. Absent price discrimination, a natural model is the latter one, but in addition each oligopolist must discount its price to its own locked-in customers down to the price it bids for the uncommitted consumers. The RET tells us that the total cost to the industry of these "discounts" to old consumers will on average precisely compensate the higher sale price achieved on new consumers.[65] That is, the net value to the industry of the new consumers is exactly as if there was Bertrand competition for them, even when the inability to price discriminate prevents this.

So Bulow and Klemperer (1998) argue that the economic importance to the tobacco companies of the youth market is actually very tiny, even

---

[64] The price is descending because the oligopolists are competing to sell rather than buy, but it corresponds to an ascending auction in which firms are competing to buy, and we stick with this terminology as in section 2.3.1.

[65] Specifically let n "old" consumers be attached to each firm i, and firms' costs c_i be independently drawn from a common, strictly increasing, atomless distribution. There are m "new" consumers who will buy from the cheapest firm. All consumers have reservation price r.

Think of firms competing for the prize of selling to the new consumers, worth $m(r - c_i)$ to firm i. Firms set prices $p_i = r - d_i$ to "new" consumers; equivalently they set "discounts" d_i to consumers' reservation prices. If price discrimination is feasible, the winner pays md_i for the prize and all firms sell to their old consumers at r. Absent price discrimination, the prices p_i apply to all firms' sales, so relative to selling just to old consumers at price r, the winner pays $(m + n)d_i$ for the prize and the losers pay nd_i each.

For the usual reasons, the two sets of payment rules are revenue equivalent. For more discussion of this result, including its robustness to multi-period contexts, see Bulow and Klemperer (1998); if the total demand of new consumers is more elastic, their economic value will be somewhat less than our model suggests; for a fuller discussion of the effects of "brand loyalty" or "switching costs" in oligopoly see, especially, Klemperer (1987a,b, 1995) and Beggs and Klemperer (1992).

though from an accounting perspective new consumers appear as valuable as any others.[66]

Similarly, applying the same logic to an international trade question, the value of a free-trading market to firms each of which has a protected home market is independent (under appropriate assumptions) of whether the firms can price discriminate between markets.[67]

Section 2.3.1's discussion of oligopolistic e-competition develops this kind of analysis further by considering implications of failures of the RET.

2.5.3 Information Aggregation in Perfect Competition

Although the examples above, and in section 2.3,[68] suggest auction theory has been underused in analyzing oligopolistic competition, it has been very important in influencing economists' ideas about the limit as the number of firms becomes large.

An important strand of the auction literature has focused on the properties of pure-common-value auctions as the number of bidders becomes large, and asked: does the sale price converge to the true value, thus fully aggregating all of the economy's information even though each bidder has only partial information? Wilson (1977) and Milgrom (1979) showed assumptions under which the answer is "yes" for a first-price sealed-bid auction, and Milgrom (1981) obtained similar results for a second-price auction (or for a $(k + 1)$th price auction for k objects).[69] So these models justify some of our ideas about perfect competition.

2.6 Applying Auction Theory (and Economics) to Auction Markets

Finally, although it has not always been grasped by practitioners, some markets are literally auctions. The increasing recognition that many real markets are best understood through the lens of auction theory has stimulated a burst of new theorizing,[70] and created the new subject of market design that stands in similar relation to auction theory as engineering does to physics.

---

[66] If industry executives seem to value the youth segment, it is probably due more to concern for their own future jobs than concern for their shareholders.

[67] See also Rosenthal (1980).

[68] Bulow and Klemperer (forthcoming) provides an additional example.

[69] Matthews (1984), on the other hand, showed that the (first-price) sale price does not in general converge to the true value when each bidder can acquire information at a cost.

Pesendorfer and Swinkels (1997) recently breathed new life into this literature, by showing convergence under weaker assumptions than previously if the number of objects for sale, as well as the number of bidders, becomes large. See also Pesendorfer and Swinkels (2000), Swinkels (2001), and Kremer (2002).

[70] Especially on multi-unit auctions in which bidders are not restricted to winning a single unit each, since most markets are of this kind.

2.6.1 Important Auction Markets

It was not initially well understood that deregulated *electricity markets,* such as in the United Kingdom, are best described and analyzed as auctions of infinitely divisible quantities of homogeneous units.[71] Although much of the early analysis of the UK market was based on Klemperer and Meyer (1989), which explicitly followed Wilson's (1979) seminal contribution to multi-unit auctions, the Klemperer and Meyer model was not thought of as an "auctions" paper and only recently received much attention among auction theorists.[72] Indeed von der Fehr and Harbord (1993) were seen as rather novel in pointing out that the new electricity markets could be viewed as auctions. Now, however, it is uncontroversial that these markets are best understood through auction theory, and electricity market design has become the province of leading auction theorists, such as Wilson, who have been very influential.

Treasury bill auctions, like electricity markets, trade a divisible homogeneous good, but although treasury auctions have always been clearly understood to be "auctions", and the existing auction theory is probably even more relevant to treasury markets than to electricity markets,[73] auction theorists have never been as influential as they now are in energy markets. In part this is because the treasury auctions predated any relevant theory,[74] and the auctions seemed not to have serious problems. In part it may be because no clear view has emerged about the best form of auction to use; indeed one possibility is that the differences between the main types of auction may not be too important in this context (see section 3.4.6).[75]

---

[71] von der Fehr and Harbord (1998) provide a useful overview of electricity markets.

[72] Klemperer and Meyer (1989) was couched as a traditional industrial organization study of whether competition is more like Bertrand or Cournot, following Klemperer and Meyer (1986).

[73] Non auction-theoretic issues which limit the direct application of auction theory to electricity markets include the very high frequency of repetition among market participants who have stable and predictable requirements which makes the theory of collusion in repeated games also very relevant; the nature of the game the major electricity suppliers are playing with the industry regulator who may step in and attempt to change the rules (again) if the companies are perceived to be making excessive profits; the conditions for new entry; and the effects of vertical integration of industry participants.

On the other hand, the interaction of a treasury auction with the financial markets for trading the bills both before and after the auction complicates the analysis of that auction.

[74] By contrast, the current UK government sales of gold are a new development, and government agencies have now consulted auction theorists (including myself) about the sale method.

[75] In a further interesting contrast the UK electricity market—the first major market in the world to be deregulated and run as an auction—was set up as a uniform price auction, but its perceived poor performance has led to a planned switch to an exchange market followed by a discriminatory auction (see sections 3.2 and 3.5.2; Office of Gas and Electricity Markets, 1999; Newbery, 1998; Wolfram, 1998, 1999). Meanwhile the vast majority of the world's treasury bill markets have until recently been run as discriminatory auctions (see Bartolini and Cottarelli, 1997), but the United States switched to uniform price auctions in late 1998 and several other countries have been experimenting with these. In fact, it seems unlikely that either form of auction is best either for all electricity markets or for all treasury markets (see, e.g., Klemperer, 1999b; Federico and Rahman, 2000; McAdams, 1998; Nyborg and Sundaresan, 1996).

Academics were involved at all stages of the *radio spectrum auctions* from suggesting the original designs to advising bidders on their strategies. The original US proponents of an auction format saw it as a complex environment that needed academic input, and a pattern of using academic consultants was set in the United States and spread to other countries (see part D).[76]

Many other new auction markets are currently being created using the *Internet*, such as the online consumer auctions run by eBay, Amazon, and others which have over 10 million customers, and the business-to-business autoparts auctions being planned by General Motors, Ford, and Daimler-Chrysler which are expected to handle $250 million in transactions a year. Here too auction theorists have been in heavy demand, and there is considerable ongoing experimentation with different auction forms.[77] Furthermore, we have already argued that internet markets that are not usually thought of as auctions can be illuminated by auction theory (see section 2.3.1 and Bulow and Klemperer, forthcoming).

2.6.2 Applying Economics to Auction Design

While many economic markets are now fruitfully analyzed as auctions, the most significant problems in auction markets and auction design are probably those with which industry regulators and competition authorities have traditionally been concerned—discouraging collusive, predatory and entry-deterring behavior, and analyzing the merits of mergers or other changes to market structure.

[76] Evan Kwerel was especially important in promoting the use of auctions. The dominant design has been the simultaneous ascending auction sketched by Vickrey (1976), and proposed and developed by McAfee, Milgrom, and Wilson for the US auctions (see McMillan, 1994; McAfee and McMillan, 1996; and especially Milgrom, 2004). Although some problems have emerged, primarily its susceptibility to collusion and its inhospitability to entry (see section 2.3.2), it has generally been considered a success in most of its applications (see, e.g., Board, 1999; Cramton, 1997; Plott, 1997; Salant, 1997; Weber, 1997; Zheng, 2001).

A large part of the motivation for the US design was the possibility of complementarities between licenses (see Ausubel, Cramton, McAfee, and McMillan, 1997), although it is unproven either that the design was especially helpful in allowing bidders to aggregate efficient packages, or that it would work well if complementarities had been very significant. Ironically, the simultaneous ascending auction is most attractive when each of an exogenously fixed number of bidders has a privately known value for each of a collection of heterogenous objects, but (contrary to the US case) is restricted to buying at most a single license. In this case entry is not an issue, collusion is very unlikely, and the outcome is efficient. For this reason a version of the simultaneous ascending auction was designed by Binmore and Klemperer for the UK 3G auction (in which each bidder was restricted to a single license) after concerns about entry had been laid to rest.

A sealed-bid design was recently used very successfully in Denmark where attracting entry was a serious concern (see section 2.3.2). (See part D for discussion of the recent European spectrum auctions.)

[77] See, for example, Hall (2001). The UK government recently used the internet to run the world's first auction for greenhouse gas emissions reductions. (Peter Cramton, Eric Maskin and I advised on the design, and Larry Ausubel and Jeremy Bulow also helped with the implementation.)

This contrasts with most of the auction literature which focuses on Nash equilibria in one-shot games with a fixed number of bidders, and emphasizes issues such as the effects of risk aversion, correlation of information, budget constraints, complementarities, asymmetries, etc. While these are also important topics—and auction theorists have made important progress on them which other economic theory can learn from—they are probably not the main issues.

Although the relative thinness of the auction-theoretic literature on collusion and entry deterrence may be defensible to the extent general economic principles apply, there is a real danger that auction theorists will underemphasize these problems in applications. In particular, ascending, second-price, and uniform-price auction forms, while attractive in many auction theorists' models, are more vulnerable to collusive and predatory behavior than (first-price) sealed-bid and hybrid forms such as the Anglo-Dutch auction described in sections 2.3.2, 3.5.3, and 6.5.1. Part C provides an extensive discussion of these issues.

While auction theorists are justly proud of how much they can teach economics, they must not forget that the classical lessons of economics continue to apply.

2.7 CONCLUSION

Auction theory is a central part of economics, and should be a part of every economist's armory; auction theorists' ways of thinking shed light on a whole range of economic topics.

We have shown that many economic questions that do not at first sight seem related to auctions can be recast to be solvable using auction-theoretic techniques such as the revenue equivalence theorem. The close parallels between auction theory and standard price theory—such as those between the theories of optimal auctions and of price discrimination—mean ideas can be arbitraged from auction theory to standard economics, and vice versa. And the insights and intuitions that auction theorists have developed in comparing different auction forms can find fertile application in many other contexts.

Furthermore, while standard auction theory models already provide the basis of much work in labor economics, political economy, finance, and industrial organization, we have used the example of price-setting oligopoly to show that a much greater application of auction-theoretic thinking may be possible in these more obvious fields.

"Heineken refreshes the parts other beers cannot reach" was recently voted one of the top advertising campaigns of all time, worldwide. The moral of this chapter is that "Auction theory refreshes the parts other economics cannot reach." Like Heineken, auction theory is a potent brew that we should all imbibe.

APPENDIX 2.A: COMPARING LITIGATION SYSTEMS

Assume that after transfers between the parties, the loser ends up paying fraction $\alpha \geq 0$ of his own expenses and fraction $\beta \leq 1$ of his opponent's. (The winner pays the remainder.)[78] So the American system is $\alpha = 1$, $\beta = 0$, the British system is $\alpha = \beta = 1$, the Netherlands system is roughly, $\alpha = 1$, $0 < \beta < 1$, and Quayle's is $\alpha = 2$, $\beta = 0$. It is also interesting to consider a "reverse-Quayle" rule $\alpha = 1$, $\beta < 0$ in which both parties pay their own expenses but the winner transfers an amount proportional to her own expenses to the loser. Let L be the average legal expenses spent per player.

The following slight generalization of the RET is the key: assuming the conditions of the RET all hold except for assumption (ii) (that is, the expected surplus of a bidder with the lowest-feasible valuation, say $\underline{S}$, may not be zero), it remains true that the expected surplus of any other types of bidder is a fixed amount above $\underline{S}$ (see, e.g., Appendix 1.A); the fixed amount depends on the distribution of the parties' valuations, but unlike $\underline{S}$ and L does not depend on the mechanism $\{\alpha, \beta\}$.

It follows that the average bidder surplus is $\underline{S}$ plus a constant. But the average bidder surplus equals the average lawsuit winnings (expectation of {probability of winning} × {valuation}) minus L, equals a constant minus L by assumption (i) of the RET. So $\underline{S} = K - L$ in which K is a constant independent of α and β. But since the lowest-valuation type always loses in equilibrium (by assumption (i) of the RET) she bids zero so $\underline{S} = -\beta L$ because in a one-shot game her opponent, on average, incurs expenses of L. Solving, $L = K/(1 - \beta)$ and the expected surplus of any given party is a constant minus $\beta K/(1 - \beta)$.

It follows that both expected total expenses and any party's expected payoff are invariant to α, hence the remarks in the text about the Quayle proposal. But legal expenses are increasing in β, indeed become unbounded in the limit corresponding to the British system. So the mechanism that minimizes legal expenses taking the set of lawsuits as given is the reverse-Quayle. The intuition is that it both increases the marginal cost of spending on a lawsuit and reduces the value of winning the suit. On the other hand, of course, bringing lawsuits becomes more attractive as β falls.

---

[78] As in the main text, we assume a symmetric equilibrium with strictly increasing bidding functions. For extreme values of α and β this may not exist (and we cannot then use the RET directly). See Baye, Kovenock, and de Vries (1997) for explicit solutions for the equilibria for different α and β.

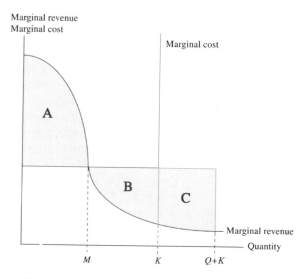

Figure 2.2 Marginal revenue if demand is expanded.

APPENDIX 2.B: DIRECT PROOF OF MONOPOLY-THEORETIC VERSION OF
PROPOSITION IN SECTION 2.4

The proof rests precisely on the assumptions (a'), (b'), and (c'). Without loss of generality let firms' marginal costs be flat up to capacity,[79] and consider what would be the marginal revenue curve for the market if the K new consumers were attracted into it (see figure 2.2).

A monopolist on this (expanded) market would earn area A in profits, that is, the area between the marginal revenue and marginal cost curves up to the monopoly point, M. The perfectly competitive industry in the same (expanded) market would earn $\Pi^c = A - B$, that is, the integral of marginal revenue less marginal cost up to industry capacity, K. By assumption (a'), a monopolist (or fully cartelized industry) in the original market would earn $\Pi^m = [Q/(Q + K)]A$. Now the average marginal revenue up to quantity $Q + K$ equals the price at demand $Q + K$ (because total marginal revenue = price × quantity), which exceeds marginal cost by assumption (b'), so $B + C \le A$. Furthermore, by assumption (c'), and elementary geometry, $B \le [(K - M)/((Q + K) - M)](B + C)$. So $B \le [(K - M)/(Q + K - M)]A$, and therefore $\Pi^c = A - B \ge Q/(Q + K - M)A \ge \Pi^m$, as required.

---

[79] If the industry cost curve is not flat up to the capacity, then use the argument in the text to prove the result for a cost curve that is flat and everywhere weakly above the actual cost curve. A fortiori, this proves the result for the actual curve, since a monopoly saves less from a lower cost curve than a competitive industry saves from the lower cost curve.

Practical Auction Design

CHAPTER THREE

What Really Matters in Auction Design*

The most important issues in auction design are the traditional concerns of competition policy—preventing collusive, predatory, and entry-deterring behavior. Ascending and uniform-price auctions are particularly vulnerable to these problems. The Anglo-Dutch auction—a hybrid of the sealed-bid and ascending auctions—may perform better. Effective antitrust is also critical. Notable fiascoes in auctioning, mobile-phone licenses, TV franchises, companies, electricity, etc., and especially the European "third-generation" (UMTS) spectrum auctions, show that everything depends on the details of the context. Auction design is not "one size fits all".

3.1 INTRODUCTION

Auctions have became enormously popular in recent years. Governments are now especially keen, using auctions to sell mobile-phone licenses, to operate decentralized electricity markets, and to privatize companies, etc. And the growth of e-commerce has led to many business-to-business auctions for goods whose trade was previously negotiated bilaterally.

Economists are proud of their role in pushing for auctions; for example, Coase (1959) was among the first to advocate auctioning radio spectrum. But many auctions—including some designed with the help of leading academic economists—have worked very badly.

For example, six European countries auctioned off spectrum licenses for "third-generation" mobile phones in 2000. In Germany and the United Kingdom, the spectrum sold for over 600 euros per person ($80 billion in all, or over 2 percent of GDP). But in Austria, the Netherlands, Italy, and Switzerland the revenues were just 100, 170, 240 and 20 euros per person, respectively. (See chapter 5.) To be sure, investors became more skeptical about the underlying value of the spectrum during 2000 (and they are even more skeptical today). But this is just a fraction of the story. The Netherlands auction was sandwiched between the UK and German auctions, and analysts and government officials predicted revenues in excess of 400 euros per person from the Italian and Swiss auctions just a few days before they began (Michelson, 2000;

* This chapter was originally published under its current title in the *Journal of Economic Perspectives* 2002, 16, 169–189. I am very grateful to many colleagues including Sushil Bikhchandani, Nils-Henrik von der Fehr, Tim Harford, Emiel Maasland, Margaret Meyer, Mike Rothkopf, David Salant, Rebecca Stone, Tim Taylor, Chuck Thomas, Tommaso Valletti, Michael Waldman, Mark Williams, and especially my co-authors Jeremy Bulow and Marco Pagnozzi, for helpful advice on this chapter.

Roberts, 2000; Total Telecom, 2000; and chapter 5). These other auctions were fiascoes primarily because they were poorly designed.

So what makes a successful auction?

What really matters in auction design are the same issues that any industry regulator would recognize as key concerns: discouraging collusive, entry-deterring and predatory behavior. In short, good auction design is mostly good elementary economics.

By contrast, most of the extensive auction literature (summarized in, e.g., chapter 1 and Klemperer, 2000a) is of second-order importance for *practical* auction design. The literature largely focuses on a fixed number of bidders who bid non-cooperatively, and it emphasizes issues such as the effects of risk aversion, correlation of information, budget constraints, complementarities, etc. Auction theorists have made important progress on these topics which other economic theory has benefited from, and auction theory has also been fruitfully applied in political economy, finance, law and economics, labor economics, industrial organization, etc. often in contexts not usually thought of as auctions (see chapter 2). But most of this literature is of much less use for actually designing auctions.

This chapter lists and gives examples of some critical pitfalls in auction design, and discusses what to do about them. We show that ascending and uniform-price auctions are both very vulnerable to collusion, and very likely to deter entry into an auction. We consider including a final sealed-bid stage into an otherwise ascending auction to create an "Anglo-Dutch" auction, and emphasize the need for stronger antitrust policy in auction markets.

3.2 COLLUSION

A first major set of concerns for practical auction design involves the risk that participants may explicitly or tacitly collude to avoid bidding up prices. Consider a multi-unit (simultaneous) *ascending* auction. (This is just like the standard auction used, for example, to sell a painting in Sotheby's or Christies—the price starts low and competing bidders raise the price until no one is prepared to bid any higher, and the final bidder then wins the prize at the final price he bid—except that several objects are sold at the same time, with the price rising on each of them independently, and none of the objects is finally sold until no one wishes to bid again on any of the objects.) In such an auction, bidders can use the early stages when prices are still low to signal who should win which objects, and then tacitly agree to stop pushing prices up.

For example, in 1999 Germany sold ten blocks of spectrum by a simultaneous ascending auction with the rule that any new bid on a block had to exceed the previous high bid by at least 10 percent. Mannesman's first bids were 18.18 million deutschmarks (DM) per megahertz on blocks 1–5 and 20 million DM per MHz on blocks 6–10; the only other credible bidder—T-Mobil—bid even less in the first round. One of T-Mobil's managers then said. "There were no agreements with Mannesman. But [T-Mobil] interpreted Mannesman's first bid as an offer" (Stuewe, 1999, p. 13). The point is that 18.18 plus a 10 percent raise equals approximately 20. It seems T-Mobil understood that if it bid 20 million DM per MHz on blocks 1–5, but did not bid again on blocks 6–10, the two companies would then live and let live with neither company challenging the other on the other's half. Exactly that happened. So the auction closed after just two rounds with each of the bidders acquiring half the blocks for the same low price (Jehiel and Moldovanu, 2001b; Grimm, Riedel, and Wolfstetter, 2003).

Ascending auctions can also facilitate collusion by offering a mechanism for punishing rivals. The threat of punishment may be implicit; for example, it was clear to T-Mobil that Mannesman would retaliate with high bids on blocks 1–5 if T-Mobil continued bidding on blocks 6–10. But an ascending auction can also allow more explicit options for punishment.

In a multi-license US spectrum auction in 1996–97, U.S. West was competing vigorously with McLeod for lot number 378—a license in Rochester, Minnesota. Although most bids in the auction had been in exact thousands of dollars, U.S. West bid $313,378 and $62,378 for two licenses in Iowa in which it had earlier shown no interest, overbidding McLeod who had seemed to be the uncontested high bidder for these licenses. McLeod got the point that it was being punished for competing in Rochester, and dropped out of that market. Since McLeod made subsequent higher bids on the Iowa licenses, the "punishment" bids cost U.S. West nothing (Cramton and Schwartz, 2002).

A related phenomenon can arise in one special kind of sealed-bid auction, namely a *uniform-price* auction in which each bidder submits a sealed bid stating what price it would pay for different quantities of a homogenous good, for example, electricity (i.e., it submits a demand function), and then the good is sold at the single price determined by the lowest winning bid. In this format, bidders can submit bids that ensure that any deviation from a (tacit or explicit) collusive agreement is severely punished: each bidder bids very high prices for smaller quantities than its collusively agreed share. Then if any bidder attempts to obtain more than its agreed share (leaving other firms with less than their agreed shares), all bidders will have to pay these very high prices. However, if everyone sticks to their agreed shares then these very high prices will never need to be paid. So deviation from the collusive agreement is unprofitable.[1]

---

[1] Since, with many units, the lowest winning bid in a uniform-price auction is typically not importantly different from the highest losing bid, this auction is analogous to an ascending auction (in which every winner pays the runner-up's willingness-to-pay). The "threats" that support collusion in a uniform-price auction are likewise analogous to the implicit threats supporting collusion in an ascending auction. Collusion in a uniform-price auction is harder if supply is uncertain since this reduces the number of points on the bid schedule that are inframarginal and can be used as threats (Klemperer and Meyer, 1989; Back and Zender, 1993, 2001).

The electricity regulator in the United Kingdom believes the market in which distribution companies purchase electricity from generating companies has fallen prey to exactly this kind of "implicit collusion" (Office of Gas and Electricity Markets, 1999, pp. 173–174). "Far from being the success story trumpeted around the world, the story of the UK generation market and the development of competition has been something of a disaster" (*Power U.K.*, issue 66, 31 August 1999, p. 14; see also von der Fehr and Harbord, 1998; Newbery, 1998; Wolfram, 1998, 1999). In addition, a frequently repeated auction market such as that for electricity is particularly vulnerable to collusion, because the repeated interaction among bidders expands the set of signaling and punishment strategies available to them, and allows them to learn to cooperate.

Much of the kind of behavior discussed so far is hard to challenge legally. Indeed, trying to outlaw it all would require cumbersome rules that restrict bidders' flexibility and might generate inefficiencies, without being fully effective. It would be much better to solve these problems with better auction designs.

3.3 ENTRY DETERRENCE AND PREDATION

The second major area of concern of practical auction design is to attract bidders, since an auction with too few bidders risks being unprofitable for the auctioneer (Bulow and Klemperer, 1996) and potentially inefficient. Ascending auctions are often particularly poor in this respect, since they can allow some bidders to deter the entry, or depress the bidding, of rivals.

In an ascending auction, there is a strong presumption that the firm which values winning the most will be the eventual winner, because even if it is outbid at an early stage, it can eventually top any opposition. As a result, other firms have little incentive to enter the bidding, and may not do so if they have even modest costs of bidding.

Consider, for example, Glaxo's 1995 takeover of the Wellcome drugs company. After Glaxo's first bid of 9 billion pounds, Zeneca expressed willingness to offer about 10 billion pounds if it could be sure of winning, while Roche considered an offer of 11 billion pounds. But certain synergies made Wellcome worth a little more to Glaxo than to the other firms, and the costs of bidding were tens of millions of pounds. Eventually, neither Roche nor Zeneca actually entered the bidding, and Wellcome was sold at the original bid of 9 billion pounds, literally a billion or two less than its shareholders might have received. Wellcome's own chief executive admitted "…there was money left on the table" (Wighton, 1995a,b).

While ascending auctions are particularly vulnerable to lack of entry, other auction forms can result in similar problems if the costs of entry and the asymmetries between bidders are too large.

The 1991 UK sale of TV franchises by a sealed-bid auction is a dramatic example. While the regions in the South and South East, South West, East, Wales, and West, North East, and Yorkshire all sold in the range 9.36 to 15.88 pounds per head of population, the only—and therefore winning—bid for the Midlands region was made by the incumbent firm and was just one-twentieth of one penny (!) per head of population. Much the same happened in Scotland, where the only bidder for the Central region generously bid one-seventh of one penny per capita. What had happened was that bidders were required to provide very detailed region-specific programming plans. In each of these two regions, the only bidder had figured out that no one else had developed such a plan.[2]

Another issue that can depress bidding in some ascending auctions is the "winner's curse". This applies when bidders have the same, or close to the same, actual value for a prize, but they have different information about that actual value (what auction theorists call the "common values" case). The winner's curse reflects the danger that the winner of an auction is likely to be the party who has most greatly overestimated the value of the prize. Knowing about the winner's curse will cause everyone to bid cautiously. But weaker firms must be especially cautious, since they must recognize that they are only likely to win when they have overestimated the value by even more than usual. Therefore, an advantaged firm can be less cautious, since beating very cautious opponents need not imply one has overestimated the prize's value. Because the winner's curse affects weak firms much more than strong ones, and because the effect is self-reinforcing, the advantaged bidder wins most of the time. And because its rivals bid extremely cautiously, it also generally pays a low price when it does win (Klemperer, 1998).

The bidding on the Los Angeles license in the 1995 US auction for mobile-phone broadband licenses illustrates this problem. While the license's value was hard to estimate, it was probably worth similar amounts to several bidders. But Pacific Telephone, which already operated the local fixed-line telephone business in California, had distinct advantages from its database on potential local customers, its well-known brand name, and its familiarity with doing business in California. The auction was an ascending auction. And the result was that the bidding stopped at a very low price. In the end, the Los Angeles license yielded only $26 per capita. In Chicago, by contrast, the main local fixed-line provider was ineligible to compete and it was not obvious who would win, so the auction yielded $31 per capita even though Chicago was thought less valuable than Los Angeles because of its lower household incomes, lower expected population growth, and more dispersed population (Klemperer, 1998; Bulow and Klemperer, 2002). For broader, formal econometric evidence for the FCC auctions, see Klemperer and Pagnozzi (forthcoming).

[2] While I have advised the UK government on several auctions, I have never had anything to do with TV licenses!

Of course, the "winner's curse" problem exacerbates the problem that weaker bidders may not bother to participate in an ascending auction. GTE and Bell Atlantic made deals that made them ineligible to bid for the Los Angeles license, and MCI failed to enter this auction at all. Similarly, takeover battles are essentially ascending auctions, and there is empirical evidence that a firm that makes a takeover bid has a lower risk of facing a rival bidder if the firm has a larger shareholding or "toehold" in the target company (Betton and Eckbo, 1995).

Because outcomes in an ascending auction can be dramatically influenced by a seemingly modest advantage, developing such an advantage can be an effective way to predate on rivals. An apparent example was the 1999 attempt by BSkyB (Rupert Murdoch's satellite television company) to acquire Manchester United (England's most successful soccer club). The problem was the advantage this would give BSkyB in the auction of football TV rights. Since Manchester United receives 7 percent of the Premier League's TV revenues, BSkyB would have received 7 percent of the price of the league's broadcasting rights, whoever won them. So BSkyB would have had an incentive to bid more aggressively in an ascending auction to push up the price of the rights, and knowing this, other potential bidders would have faced a worse "winner's curse" and backed off. BSkyB might have ended up with a lock over the TV rights with damaging effects on the TV market more generally. Largely for this reason the UK Government blocked the acquisition.[3]

A strong bidder also has an incentive to create a reputation for aggressiveness that reinforces its advantage. For example, when Glaxo was bidding for Wellcome, it made it clear that it "would almost certainly top a rival bid" (Wighton, 1995b). Similarly, before bidding for the California phone license, Pacific Telephone announced in the *Wall Street Journal* that "if somebody takes California away from us, they'll never make any money" (Cauley and Carnevale, 1994, p. A4). Pacific Telephone also hired one of the world's most prominent auction theorists to give seminars to the rest of the industry to explain the winner's curse argument that justifies this statement, and reinforced the point in full page ads that it ran in the newspapers of the cities where their major competitors were headquartered (Koselka, 1995, p. 63). It also made organizational changes that demonstrated its commitment to winning the Los Angeles license.

Predation may be particularly easy in repeated ascending auctions, such as, for example, in a series of spectrum auctions. A bidder who buys assets that are complementary to assets for sale in a future auction, or simply bids very aggressively in early auctions, can develop a reputation for aggressiveness (Bikhchandani, 1988). Potential rivals in future auctions will both be less

---

[3] Although the term "toehold effect" coined by Bulow, Huang and Klemperer (1999), and Klemperer (1998) in the related context of takeover battles (see above) entered the popular press, and these papers were cited by the UK Monopolies and Mergers Commission (1999) report which effectively decided the issue, neither I nor my co-authors had any involvement in this case.

willing to participate, and bid less aggressively if they do participate. Even in the absence of predation, weaker bidders learn that they are weaker and became reluctant to enter future ascending auctions (see section 5.7.2).

Finally, because an ascending auction often effectively blocks the entry of "weaker" bidders, it encourages "stronger" bidders to bid jointly or to collude; after all, they know that no one else can enter the auction to steal the collusive rents they create. In the disastrous November 2000 Swiss sale of four third-generation mobile-phone licenses, there was considerable initial interest from potential bidders. But weaker bidders were put off by the auction form—at least one company hired bidding consultants and then gave up after learning that the ascending-bidding rules would give the company very little chance against stronger rivals. Moreover, the government permitted last-minute joint-bidding agreements—essentially officially sanctioned collusion. In the week before the auction, the field shrank from nine bidders to just four bidders for the four licenses! Since no bidder was allowed to take more than one license, the sale price was determined by the reserve price which was just one-thirtieth of the UK and German per capita revenues, and one-fiftieth of what the Swiss had once hoped for!

3.4 OTHER PITFALLS

3.4.1 Reserve Prices

Many of the disasters above were greatly aggravated by failure to set a proper reserve price (the minimum amount the winner is required to pay). Take the last example. It was ridiculous for the Swiss government to set its reserve at just one-thirtieth of the per capita revenue raised by the German and UK governments for similar properties. Since the government's own spokesman predicted just five days prior to the auction that twenty times the reserve price would be raised, what was the government playing at?

Inadequate reserves also increase the incentives for predation and may encourage collusion that would not otherwise have been in all bidders' interests. A stronger bidder in an ascending auction has a choice between either tacitly colluding to end the auction quickly at a low price, or forcing the price up to drive out weaker bidders. The lower the reserve price at which the auction can be concluded, the more attractive is the first option—this factor may have been an important contributor to several of the fiascoes we have discussed.

3.4.2 Political Problems

Serious reserve prices are often opposed not only by industry groups, but also by government officials for whom the worst outcome is that the reserve price is not met so the object is not sold and the auction is seen as a "failure".

Similarly, standard (first-price) sealed-bid auctions—in which the bidders simultaneously make "best and final" offers, and the winner pays the price he bid—can sometimes be very embarrassing for bidders, as BSCH (Spain's biggest bank) found out when Brazil privatized the Sao Paulo state bank Banespa. When the bids were opened, BSCH's managers were horrified to learn that their bid of over 7 million Reals ($3.6 billion) was more than three times the runner-up's bid, and that they were therefore paying 5 billion Reals ($2.5 billion) more than was needed to win. In other auctions, meanwhile, losers who have just narrowly underbid the winners have found it equally hard to explain themselves to their bosses and shareholders. So firms, or at least their managers, can oppose first-price auctions.

On the other hand, a *second-price* sealed-bid auction—in which the winner pays the runner-up's bid—can be embarrassing for the auctioneer if the winner's actual bid is revealed to be far more than the runner-up's, even if the auction was ex-ante both efficient and revenue maximizing. McMillan (1994) reports a second-price New Zealand auction in which the winner bid NZ $7 million but paid the runner-up's bid of NZ $5,000. Of course, New Zealand should have set a minimum reserve price that the winner had to pay, but even if that had been politically possible, the winner would probably have bid more than it had to pay, so this might have been an economically but not politically sensible auction.

3.4.3 Loopholes

In some cases, the auction rules may leave gaping loopholes for behavior to game the auction. In 2000, Turkey auctioned two telecom licenses sequentially, with an additional twist that set the reserve price for the second license equal to the selling price of the first. One firm then bid far more for the first license than it could possibly be worth if the firm had to compete in the telecom market with a rival holding the second license. But the firm had rightly figured that no rival would be willing to bid that high for the second license, which therefore remained unsold, leaving the firm without a rival operating the second license!

As another example, McMillan (1994) reports an Australian auction for satellite-television licenses in which two bidders each made large numbers of different sealed bids on the same objects and then, after considerable delays, defaulted on those bids they did not like after the fact—since the government had neglected to impose any penalties for default. More recently, the US spectrum auctions have been plagued by bidders "winning" licenses and subsequently defaulting on their commitments, often after long delays. (India also recently fell into the same trap.) If default costs are small, then bidders are bidding for *options* on prizes rather than the prizes themselves. Furthermore, if smaller, underfinanced firms can avoid commitments through bankruptcy, then an auction actually favors these bidders over better-financed competitors who cannot default.

3.4.4 Credibility of the Rules

It may not be credible for the auctioneer to punish a bidder violating the auction rules when just one bidder needs to be eliminated to end an auction, because excluding the offending bidder would end the auction immediately, and it might be hard to impose fines large enough to have a serious deterrent effect. Fines of hundreds of millions or even billions of dollars might have been required to deter improper behavior in some of the European third-generation mobile-phone license auctions. In the Netherlands sale, for example, six bidders competed for five licenses in an ascending auction in which bidders were permitted to win just one license each. One bidder, Telfort, sent a letter to another, Versatel, threatening legal action for damages if Versatel continued to bid! Telfort claimed that Versatel "believes that its bids will always be surpassed by [others' … so it] must be that Versatel is attempting to either raise its competitors' costs or to get access to their … networks", but many observers felt Telfort's threats against Versatel were outrageous. However, the government took no action—not even an investigation. As a result, Versatel quit the auction and the sale raised less than 30 percent of what the Dutch government had forecast based on the results of the United Kingdom's similar auction just three months earlier.

Ascending auctions are particularly vulnerable to rule breaking by the bidders since they necessarily pass through a stage where there is just one (or a few) excess bidders, and the ascending structure allows a cheat time to assess the success of its strategy. Sealed-bid auctions, by contrast, may be more vulnerable to rule changing by the auctioneer. For example, excuses for not accepting a winning bid can often be found if losing bidders are willing to bid higher. The famous RJR-Nabisco sale went through several supposedly final sealed-bid auctions (Burrough and Helyar, 1990). But if, after a sealed-bid auction, the auctioneer can re-open the auction to higher offers, the auction is really an ascending-bid auction and needs to be recognized as such. In fact, genuine sealed-bid auctions may be difficult to run in takeover battles, especially since a director who turns down a higher bid for his company after running a "sealed-bid auction" may be vulnerable to shareholder lawsuits.

Sealed-bid auctions can also be especially hard to commit to if the auctioneer has any association with a bidder as, for example, would have been the case in the UK football TV-rights auction discussed earlier if BSkyB (a bidder) had taken over Manchester United (an influential member of the football league which was the auctioneer).

Committing to future behavior may be a particular problem for governments. For example, it may be difficult to auction a license if the regulatory regime may change, but binding future governments (or even the current government) to a particular regulatory regime may prove difficult.

The credibility of reserve prices is of special importance. If a reserve price is not a genuine commitment to not sell an object if it does not reach its reserve, then it has no meaning and bidders will treat it as such. For example, returning to the Turkish tale of woe, the government is now considering new arrangements to sell the second license, but at what cost to the credibility of its future auctions?[4]

3.4.5 Market Structure

In some auctions, for example of mobile-phone licenses, the structure of the industry that will be created cannot be ignored by the auction designer. It is tempting to simply "let the market decide" the industry structure by auction-ing many small packages of spectrum, which individual firms can aggregate into larger licenses. But the auction's outcome is driven by bidders' profits, not by the welfare of consumers or society as a whole.

The most obvious possible distortion is that since firms' joint profits in the telecom market are generally greater the fewer competitors there are in the market, it is worth more to any group of firms to prevent entry of an additional firm than the additional firm is willing to pay to enter. So too few firms may win spectrum, and these winners may each win too much, exactly as a "hands-off" policy to merger control will tend to create an overly concentrated industry. The Turkish fiasco discussed earlier was a spectacular example of how an auction can be biased towards generating monopoly.[5]

But this outcome is not the only socially suboptimal possibility. A firm with a large demand may prefer to reduce its demand to end the auction at a low price, rather than raise the price to drive out its rivals, even when the latter course would be socially more efficient (Ausubel and Cramton, 1998a). There can also be too many winners if firms collude to divide the spoils at a low price. In the Austrian third-generation mobile spectrum sale, for example, six firms competed for twelve identical lots in an ascending auction and not surprisingly seemed to agree to divide the market so each firm won two lots each at not much more than the very low reserve price. Perhaps six winners was the efficient outcome. But we certainly cannot tell from the behavior in the auction. (It was rumored that the bidding lasted only long enough to create some public perception of genuine competition and reduce the risk of the government changing the rules.)

---

[4] Re-auctioning with a lower reserve price after a delay may sometimes be sensible, to allow further entry if there are high costs of entering the auction (Burguet and Sákovics, 1996; McAfee and McMillan, 1988), but in this case the auctioneer should make clear in advance what he would do if the reserve is not met.

[5] Similarly, the Greek second-generation spectrum auction in July 2001 led to a more concentrated telecom market than seems likely to be socially efficient.

So it may sometimes be wiser to predetermine the number of winners by auctioning off fewer, larger, licenses, but limiting bidders to one license apiece, rather than to auction many licenses and to allow bidders to buy as many as they wish.

3.4.6 When Is Auction Design Less Important?

The fact that collusion and entry deterrence and, more generally, buyer market power is the key to auction problems suggests that auction design may not matter very much when there is a large number of potential bidders for whom entry to the auction is easy. For example, though much ink has been spilt on the subject of government security sales, auction design may not matter much for either price or efficiency in this case. Indeed the US Treasury's recent experiments with different kinds of auctions yielded inconclusive results (Simon, 1994; Malvey, Archibald and Flynn, 1996; Nyborg and Sundaresan 1996; Reinhart and Belzar, 1996; Ausubel and Cramton 1998a), and the broader empirical literature is also inconclusive. Of course, even small differences in auction performance can be significant when such large amounts of money are involved, and collusion has been an issue in some government-security sales, so further research is still warranted.[6]

3.5 SOLUTIONS

3.5.1 Making the Ascending Auction More Robust

Much of our discussion has emphasized the vulnerability of ascending auctions to collusion and predatory behavior. However, ascending auctions have several virtues, as well. An ascending auction is particularly likely to allocate the prizes to the bidders who value them the most, since a bidder with a higher value always has the opportunity to rebid to top a lower-value bidder who may initially have bid more aggressively.[7] Moreover, if there are complementarities between the objects for sale, a multi-unit ascending auction makes it more likely that bidders will win efficient bundles than in a pure sealed-bid

---

[6] These views are personal; I have advised UK government agencies on the related issue of the sale of gold.

[7] This applies in many "common values" and "private values" settings (Maskin, 1992), but is not necessarily the same as maximizing efficiency; when bidders are firms, it ignores consumer welfare (which is likely to favor a more widely dispersed ownership than firms would choose) and, of course, it ignores government revenue. We assume governments (as well as other auctioneers) care about revenue because of the substantial deadweight losses (perhaps 33 cents per dollar raised) of raising government funds through alternative methods (Ballard, Shoven, and Whalley, 1985). Resale is not a perfect substitute for an efficient initial allocation, because even costless resale cannot usually ensure an efficient outcome in the presence of incomplete information (Myerson and Satterthwaite, 1983; Cramton, Gibbons and Klemperer, 1987).

auction in which they can learn nothing about their opponents' intentions. Allowing bidders to learn about cthers' valuations during the auction can also make the bidders more comfortable with their own assessments and less cautious, and often raises the auctioneer's revenues if information is "affiliated" in the sense of Milgrom and Weber (1982a).

A number of methods to make the ascending auction more robust are clear enough. For example, bidders can be forced to bid "round" numbers, the exact increments can be prespecified, and bids can be made anonymous. These steps make it harder to use bids to signal other buyers. Lots can be aggregated into larger packages to make it harder for bidders to divide the spoils, and keeping secret the number of bidders remaining in the auction also makes collusion harder (Cramton and Schwartz, 2000; Salant, 2000). Ausubel's (1998) suggested modification of the ascending auction mitigates the incentive of bidders to reduce their demands in order to end the auction quickly at a low price. Sometimes it is possible to pay bidders to enter an auction; for example, "white knights" can be offered options to enter a takeover battle against an advantaged bidder.

But while these measures can be useful, they do not eliminate the risks of collusion or of too few bidders. An alternative is to choose a different type of auction.

3.5.2 Using Sealed-bid Auctions

In a standard sealed-bid auction (or "first-price" sealed-bid auction), each bidder simultaneously makes a single "best and final" offer. As a result, firms are unable to retaliate against bidders who fail to cooperate with them, so collusion is much harder than in an ascending auction. Tacit collusion is particularly difficult since firms are unable to use the bidding to signal. True, both signaling and retaliation are possible in a series of sealed-bid auctions, but collusion is still usually harder than in a series of ascending auctions.

From the perspective of encouraging more entry, the merit of a sealed-bid auction is that the outcome is much less certain than in an ascending auction. An advantaged bidder will probably win a sealed-bid auction, but it must make its single final offer in the face of uncertainty about its rivals' bids, and because it wants to get a bargain its sealed-bid will not be the maximum it could be pushed to in an ascending auction. So "weaker" bidders have at least some chance of victory, even when they would surely lose an ascending auction (Vickrey, 1961, Appendix III). It follows that potential entrants are likely to be more willing to enter a sealed-bid auction than an ascending auction.

A sealed-bid auction might even encourage bidders who enter only in order to resell, further increasing the competitiveness of the auction. Such bidders seem less likely to enter an ascending auction, since it is generally more difficult to profit from reselling to firms one has beaten in an ascending auction.

Because sealed-bid auctions are more attractive to entrants, they may also discourage consortia from forming. If the strong firms form a consortium, they may simply attract other firms into the bidding in the hope of beating the consortium. So strong firms are more likely to bid independently in a sealed-bid auction, making this a much more competitive auction.

Consistent with all this, there is some evidence from timber sales that sealed-bid auctions attract more bidders than ascending auctions do, and that this makes sealed-bid auctions considerably more profitable for the seller, and this seems to be believed in this industry (Mead and Schneipp, 1989; Rothkopf and Engelbrecht-Wiggans, 1993), even though *conditional* on the number of bidders, sealed-bid auctions seem only slightly more profitable than ascending auctions (Hansen, 1986).

Furthermore, in the "common values" case in which bidders have similar actual values for a prize, the "winner's curse" problem for a weaker bidder is far less severe in a sealed-bid auction. Winning an ascending auction means the weaker bidder is paying a price his rival is unwilling to match— which should make the weaker bidder very nervous. But the weaker player has a chance of winning a sealed-bid auction at a price the stronger rival *would* be willing to match, but did not. Since beating the stronger player is not necessarily bad news in a sealed-bid auction, the weaker player can bid more aggressively. So auction prices will be higher, even for a given number of bidders (Klemperer, 1998; Bulow, Huang and Klemperer, 1999).[8]

But while sealed-bid auctions have many advantages, they are not without flaws. Mainly, by giving some chance of victory to weaker bidders, sealed-bid auctions are less likely than ascending auctions to lead to efficient outcomes. Moreover, in standard sealed-bid auctions in which winners pay their own bids, bidders need to have good information about the distribution of their rivals' values to bid intelligently (Persico, 2000b). By contrast, in an ascending or uniform-price auction the best strategy of a bidder who knows his own value is just to bid up to that value, and winners' payments are determined by non-winners' bids. So "pay-your-bid" sealed-bid auctions may discourage potential bidders who have only small amounts to trade and for whom the costs of obtaining market information might not be worth paying. For example, in March 2001 the UK electricity regulator replaced the problematic uniform-price auction we described earlier by an exchange market followed by a "pay-your-bid" sealed-bid auction, which makes collusion harder because bids can no longer be used as costless threats. But a major concern is that the new

---

[8] In Milgrom and Weber's (1982a) model, sealed-bid auctions are less profitable than ascending auctions if signals are "affiliated". But they assume symmetric bidders, and the effect does not seem large in practice (Riley and Li, 1997). Sealed-bid auctions are generally more profitable if bidders are risk-averse or budget-constrained (see sections 1.5 and 1.13.1).

trading arrangements may deter potential entrants from investing the sunk costs necessary to enter the electricity market.[9]

However, the entry problem in many-unit auctions is much less serious if small bidders can buy from larger intermediaries who can aggregate smaller bidders' demands and bid in their place as, for example, occurs in auctions of treasury bills. And the entry problem is also alleviated if smaller bidders are permitted to make "non-competitive bids", that is, to state demands for fixed quantities for which they pay the average winning price, as is also the case in some treasury bill auctions.

3.5.3 The Anglo-Dutch Auction

A solution to the dilemma of choosing between the ascending (often called "English") and sealed-bid (or "Dutch") forms is to combine the two in a hybrid, the "Anglo-Dutch", which often captures the best features of both, and was first described and proposed in Klemperer (1998). (See also sections 2.3.2 and 6.5.1.)

For simplicity, assume a single object is to be auctioned. In an Anglo-Dutch auction the auctioneer begins by running an ascending auction in which price is raised continuously until all but two bidders have dropped out. The two remaining bidders are then each required to make a final sealed-bid offer that is not lower than the current asking price, and the winner pays his bid. The process is much like the way houses are often sold, although unlike in many house sales the procedure the auctioneer will follow in an Anglo-Dutch auction is clearly specified in advance.

Another auction with similar features—and probably similar motivations to the Anglo-Dutch—is W. R. Hambrecht's *OpenBook* auction for corporate bonds. The early bidding is public and ascending in style but bidders can make final sealed-bids in the last hour. Although all bidders are permitted to make final bids, higher bidders in the first stages are given an advantage that is evidently large enough to induce serious bidding early on (Hall, 2001, p. 71).

The process also has some similarity to auctions on eBay (by far the world's most successful e-commerce auctioneer) which are ascending price, but with a fixed ending time so that many bidders often bid only in the last few seconds in essentially sealed-bid style. eBay attracts far more bidders than its rival, Yahoo, which runs a standard ascending auction with a traditional "going, going, gone" procedure that does not close the auction until there have been no bids for 10 minutes.

The main value of the Anglo-Dutch procedure arises when one bidder (e.g., the incumbent operator of a license that is to be re-auctioned) is thought to be stronger than potential rivals. Potential rivals might be unwilling to enter a

---

[9] Also, the new arrangements may not fully resolve the collusion problem anyway since the market is so frequently repeated (Klemperer, 1999b).

pure ascending-bid auction against the strong bidder, who would be perceived to be a sure winner. But the sealed bid at the final stage induces some uncertainty about which of the two finalists will win, and entrants are attracted by the knowledge that they have a chance to make it to this final stage. So the price may easily be higher even by the end of the first, ascending, stage of the Anglo-Dutch auction, than if a pure ascending auction were used.

The Anglo-Dutch auction should capture the other advantages of the sealed-bid auction discussed in the previous section. Collusion will be discouraged because the final sealed-bid round allows firms to renege on any deals without fear of retaliation, and because the Anglo-Dutch auction eliminates the stage of the ascending auction when just one excess bidder remains, at which point rules against collusion and predation may not be credible.

Consortium formation will also be discouraged. Imagine there are two strong bidders for an item. In an ascending auction they are unlikely to be challenged if they form a consortium so they have an incentive to do so. But in an Anglo-Dutch auction, forming the consortium would open up an opportunity for new entrants who would now have a chance to make it to the final sealed-bid stage. So the strong firms are much less likely to bid jointly.

But the Anglo-Dutch should also capture much of the benefit of an ascending auction. It will be more likely to sell to the highest valuer than a pure sealed-bid auction, both because it directly reduces the numbers allowed into the sealed-bid stage and also because the two finalists can learn something about each other's and the remaining bidders' perceptions of the object's value from behavior during the ascending stage.

When the Anglo-Dutch auction is extended to contexts in which individual bidders are permitted to win multiple units and there are complementarities between the objects, the ascending stage makes it more likely that bidders will win efficient bundles than in a pure sealed-bid auction.

Finally, I conjecture that the ascending stages of the Anglo-Dutch auction may extract most of the information that would be revealed by a pure ascending auction, raising revenues if bidders' information is "affiliated", while the sealed-bid stage may do almost as well as a pure sealed-bid auction in capturing extra revenue due to the effects of bidders' risk aversion, budget constraints, and asymmetries. This suggests the Anglo-Dutch auction may outperform ascending and sealed-bid auctions even if it attracts no additional bidders.

In short, the Anglo-Dutch auction often combines the best of both the ascending and the sealed-bid worlds.

3.5.4 Antitrust

Effective antitrust is critical to fighting collusion and predation in auctions. But antitrust enforcement seems much lighter than in "ordinary" economic markets.

    The US Department of Justice has pursued some signaling cases, but the legal
status of many of the kinds of behavior discussed in this chapter remains ambiguous, and collusion in takeover battles for companies is legal in the United States.

    European antitrust has been even weaker, as evidenced by T-Mobil's will-
ingness to explicitly confirm the signaling behavior described earlier. True,
when apparently similar behavior was observed in the more recent German
third-generation spectrum auction, firms refused to confirm officially that they
were signaling to rivals to end the auction. Even so, the *Financial Times*
reported: "One operator has privately admitted to altering the last digit of
its bid in a semi-serious attempt to signal to other participants that it was
willing to accept [fewer lots to end the auction]" (Roberts and Ward, 2000,
p. 21). This kind of signaling behavior could perhaps be challenged as an
abuse of "joint dominance" under EU and UK law. But European regulators
have showed no interest in pursuing such matters.

    Firms are also permitted to make explicit statements about auctions that
would surely be unacceptable if made about a "normal" economic market.
For example, before the Austrian third-generation spectrum auction Telekom
Austria, the largest incumbent and presumably the strongest among the six
bidders, said it "would be satisfied with just 2 of the 12 blocks of frequency on
offer" and "if the [5 other bidders] behaved similarly it should be possible to
get the frequencies on sensible terms", but "it would bid for a 3rd block if one
of its rivals did" (*Reuters*, 31 October 2000). It seems inconceivable that a
dominant firm in a "normal" market would be allowed to make the equivalent
offer and threat that it "would be satisfied with a market share of just 1/6" and
"if the other five firms also stick to 1/6 of the market each, it should be
possible to sell at high prices", but "it would compete aggressively for a
larger share, if any of its rivals aimed for more than 1/6".[10]

    Just as damaging has been the European authorities' acceptance of joint-
bidding agreements that are, in effect, open collusion. Combinations that are
arranged very close to the auction date (as in the example of Switzerland
discussed earlier) should be particularly discouraged since they give no
time for entrants to emerge to threaten the new coalition. One view is that
auction participants should generally be restricted to entities that exist when
the auction is first announced, although exceptions would clearly be necessary.

    The antitrust agencies' response to predation in auction markets has also been
feeble. Dominant bidders such as Glaxo and Pactel in the examples above are
apparently allowed to make open threats that they will punish new entrants. For
example, Glaxo's letting it be known that it "would almost certainly top a rival

---

[10] Similarly, during the German third-generation spectrum auction, MobilCom told a newspaper
that "should [Debitel] fail to secure a license [it could] become a 'virtual network operator' using
MobilCom's network while saving on the cost of the license" (Benoit, 2000, p. 28). This translates
roughly to a firm in a "normal" market saying it "would supply a rival should it choose to exit the
market", but MobilCom's remarks went unpunished.

bid", would roughly translate to an incumbent firm in a "normal" economic market saying it "would almost certainly undercut any new entrant's price".[11]

Regulators should take such threats seriously, and treat auction markets more like "ordinary" economic markets.

3.6 TAILORING AUCTION DESIGN TO THE CONTEXT

Good auction design is *not* "one size fits all" and must be sensitive to the details of the context. A good example of this—and of our other principles—is afforded by the year 2000 European third-generation (UMTS) mobile phone license auctions.

The United Kingdom, which ran the first of these auctions, originally planned to sell just *four* licenses.[12] In this case the presence of exactly four incumbent operators who had the advantages of existing brand names and networks suggested that an ascending auction might deter new firms from bidding strongly in the auction, or even from entering at all. So the government planned an Anglo-Dutch auction. An ascending stage would have continued until just five bidders remained, after which the five survivors would have made sealed-bids (required to be no lower than the current price level) for the four licenses.[13] The design performed extremely well in laboratory experiments in both efficiency and revenue generation.

But, when it became possible to sell *five* licenses, an ascending auction made more sense. Because no bidder was permitted to win more than one license, at least one license had to be sold to a new entrant. This would be a sufficient carrot to attract several new entrants in the UK context in which it was very unclear which new entrant(s) might be successful.[14] Because licenses

---

[11] Similarly, Pacific Telephone's remark that "if somebody takes California away from us, they'll never make any money" seems to correspond to threatening that "if anyone tries to compete with us, we'll cut the price until they lose money". And Pacific Telephone's hiring of an auction theorist to explain the winner's curse to competitors might correspond to hiring an industrial economist to explain the theory of the difficulties of entering new markets to potential entrants.

[12] I was the principal auction theorist advising the UK government's Radiocommunications Agency, which designed and ran the recent UK mobile-phone license auction. Ken Binmore led the team and supervised experiments testing the proposed designs. Other academic advisors included Tilman Börgers, Jeremy Bulow, Philippe Jehiel, and Joe Swierzbinski.

[13] It was proposed that all four winners would pay the fourth-highest sealed bid. Since the licenses were not quite identical, a final simultaneous ascending stage would have followed to allocate them more efficiently among the winners. The sealed-bid stage could be run using an ascending mechanism that would hide the actual bids even from the auctioneer, if this would reduce political problems. See Klemperer (1998), Radiocommunications Agency (1998a,b), and section 6.5.1, for more details.

[14] In large part this was because the United Kingdom ran the first third-generation auction. Going to market first was a deliberate strategy of the auction team, and the sustained marketing campaign was also important. The UK auction attracted 13 bidders who then learnt about others' strengths, and none of the eight subsequent auctions had more than seven bidders.

could not be divided, bidders could not collude to divide the market without resort to side payments. So the problems of collusion and entry deterrence were minimal, and a version of an ascending auction was therefore used for efficiency reasons. The auction was widely judged a success; nine new entrants bid strongly against the incumbents, creating intense competition and record-breaking revenues of £22.5 billion ($34 billion).

The Netherlands' sale came next. Their key blunder was to follow the actual British design when they had an equal number (five) of incumbents and licenses. It was not hard to predict (indeed prior to the auction, an early draft of this paper, Klemperer, 2000b, quoted in the Dutch press and Maasland, 2000, *did* predict) that very few entrants would show up. Netherlands antitrust policy was as dysfunctional as the auction design, allowing the strongest potential entrants to make deals with incumbent operators. In the end just one weak new entrant (Versatel) competed with the incumbents. As we have already discussed, with just one excess bidder in an ascending auction it was unsurprising when the weak bidder quit early amid allegations of predation, at less than 30 percent of the per capita UK prices. Six months later, the Dutch parliament began an investigation into the auction process.

A version of the Anglo-Dutch design would probably have worked better in the Netherlands context. There are reasons to believe Versatel would have bid higher in the sealed-bid stage than the price at which it quit the ascending auction. And the fear of this would have made the incumbents bid higher. Furthermore, the "hope and dream" that a sealed-bid stage gives weaker bidders might have attracted more bidders and discouraged the formation of the joint-bidding consortia.

The Italian government thought it had learned from the Netherlands fiasco. It also chose roughly the UK design, but stipulated that if there were no more "serious" bidders (as defined by prequalification conditions) than licenses, then the number of licenses could, and probably would be reduced. At first glance this seemed a clever way to avoid an uncompetitive auction but (as I and others argued) the approach was fundamentally flawed. First, it is "putting the cart before the horse" to create an unnecessarily concentrated mobile-phone market in order to make an auction look good. Second, our earlier discussion demonstrates that a rule that allows the possibility that there will be just one more bidder than license does *not* guarantee a competitive ascending auction! And it was clear that the number of likely entrants into an ascending auction was much smaller than it had been for the United Kingdom, in large part because weaker potential entrants had figured out from the earlier auctions that they were weaker, and that they therefore had little chance of winning such an auction. In the event, just six bidders competed for five licenses and the auction ended amid allegations of collusion after less than two days of bidding with per capita revenues below 40 percent of the UK level, about half the amount the government was expecting. Again, an Anglo-Dutch or pure sealed-bid design would probably have performed better.

Part D discusses all nine 2000–2001 western European spectrum auctions in much more detail.

3.7 CONCLUSION

Much of what we have said about auction design is no more than an application of standard antitrust theory. The key issues in both fields are collusion and entry. The signaling and punishment strategies that support collusion in auctions are familiar from "ordinary" industrial markets, as are firms' verbal encouragements to collude and the predatory threats they make. Our point that even modest bidding costs may be a serious deterrent to potential bidders is analogous to the industrial-organization point that the contestability of a market is non-robust to even small sunk costs of entry. We also argued that because an ascending auction is more likely than a sealed-bid auction to be won by the strongest firm, the ascending auction may therefore be less attractive to bidders and so be less profitable than a sealed-bid auction; this is just an example of the standard industrial-organization argument that a market that is in principle more competitive (e.g., "Bertrand" rather than "Cournot") is less attractive to enter, so may in fact be less competitive. A particular feature of auction markets is that "winner's curse" effects may mean that sealed-bid and Anglo-Dutch auctions not only attract more firms than ascending auctions, but may also lead to better outcomes for the auctioneer for a given number of firms. But there is no justification for the current feebleness of antitrust policy in auction markets: regulators should treat them much more like "ordinary" economic markets.

However, none of our examples of auction failures should be taken as an argument against auctions in general. Most auctions work extremely well. Occasionally—for example, when there are too few potential bidders, or large costs of supplying necessary information to bidders—a form of structured negotiations may be better, but an auction is usually more attractive to potential buyers who are crucial to a sale's success (Bulow and Klemperer, 1996). And even relatively unsuccessful auctions, such as the Netherlands and Italian spectrum auctions we discussed, were probably more successful than the "beauty contest" administrative hearings used to allocate third-generation spectrum in several other European countries. For example, the Spanish beauty contest yielded just 13 euros per head of population, but generated considerable political and legal controversy and a widespread perception that the outcome was both unfair and inefficient, all problems that are typical of such procedures (see section 6.2), while the difficulties with the French beauty contest mean that France has not only missed its government's originally planned date for allocation of the spectrum (already by a year at the time of writing) but also missed EU deadlines.

In conclusion, the most important features of an auction are its robustness against collusion and its attractiveness to potential bidders. Failure to attend to these issues can lead to disaster. And anyone setting up an auction would be foolish to blindly follow past successful designs; auction design is *not* "one size fits all". While the sealed-bid auction performs well in some contexts, and the Anglo-Dutch auction is ideal in other contexts, the ascending auction has also frequently been used very successfully. In the practical design of auctions, local circumstances matter and the devil is in the details.

Using and Abusing Auction Theory*

Economic theory is often abused in practical policy-making. There is frequently excessive focus on sophisticated theory at the expense of elementary theory; too much economic knowledge can sometimes be a dangerous thing. Too little attention is paid to the wider economic context, and to the dangers posed by political pressures. Superficially trivial distinctions between policy proposals may be economically significant, while economically irrelevant distinctions may be politically important. I illustrate with some disastrous government auctions, but also show the value of economic theory.

4.1 INTRODUCTION

For half a century or more after the publication of his *Principles* (1890), it was routinely asserted of economic ideas that "they're all in Marshall". Of course, that is no longer true of the theory itself. But Marshall was also very concerned with applying economics, and when we think about how to use the theory, the example that Marshall set still remains a valuable guide. In this chapter, therefore, I want to use some of Marshall's views, and my own experience in auction design, to discuss the use (and abuse) of economic theory.[1]

* This chapter was originally published under the title "Using and Abusing Economic Theory", in the *Journal of the European Economic Association*, 2003, 1, 272–300. (It is also reprinted in *Advances in Economics and Econometrics: Theory and Applications*, S. Hurn (ed.), forthcoming.) It was improved by an enormous number of helpful comments from Tony Atkinson, Sushil Bikhchandani, Erik Eyster, Nils-Henrik von der Fehr, Tim Harford, Michael Landsberger, Kristen Mertz, Meg Meyer, Paul Milgrom, David Myatt, Marco Pagnozzi, Rob Porter, Kevin Roberts, Mike Rothschild, Peter Temin, Chris Wallace, Mike Waterson, and many others.

[1] This is the text of the 2002 Alfred Marshall Lecture of the European Economic Association, given at its Annual Congress, in Venice.

I gave a similar lecture at the 2002 Colin Clark Lecture of the Econometric Society, presented to its Annual Australasian Meeting. Like Marshall, Clark was very involved in practical economic policy making. He stressed the importance of quantification of empirical facts which, I argue below, is often underemphasized by modern economic theorists.

Similar material also formed the core of the biennial 2002 Lim Tay Boh Lecture in Singapore. Lim was another very distinguished economist (and Vice-Chancellor of the National University of Singapore), who also made significant contributions to policy, as an advisor to the Singapore Government.

Finally, some of these ideas were presented in the Keynote Address to the 2002 Portuguese Economic Association's 2002 meetings.

I am very grateful to all those audiences for helpful comments.

Although the most elegant mathematical theory is often the most influential, it may not be the most useful for practical problems. Marshall (1906) famously stated that "a good mathematical theorem dealing with economic hypotheses [is] very unlikely to be good economics", and continued by asserting the rules "(1) Translate [mathematics] into English; (2) then illustrate by examples that are important in real life; (3) burn the mathematics; (4) if you can't succeed in 2, burn 1"! Certainly this view now seems extreme, but it is salutary to be reminded that good mathematics need not necessarily be good economics. To slightly update Marshall's rules, if we cannot (1) offer credible intuition and (2) supply empirical (or perhaps case-study or experimental) evidence, we should (4) be cautious about applying the theory in practice.[2]

Furthermore, when economics is applied to policy, proposals need to be robust to the political context in which they are intended to operate. Too many economists excuse their practical failure by saying "the politicians (or bureaucrats) didn't do exactly what I recommended". Just as medical practitioners must allow for the fact that their patients may not take all the pills they prescribe, or follow all the advice they are given, so economics practitioners need to foresee political and administrative pressures and make their plans robust to changes that politicians, bureaucrats, and lobbyists are likely to impose. And in framing proposals, economists must recognize that policies that seem identical, or almost identical, to them may seem very different to politicians, and vice versa.

Some academics also need to widen the scope of their analyses beyond the confines of their models which, while elegant, are often short on real-world detail. Marshall always emphasized the importance of a deep "historical knowledge of any area being investigated and referred again and again to the complexity of economic problems and the naivety of simple hypotheses."[3] Employing "know it all" consultants with narrowly focused theories instead of experienced people with a good knowledge of the wider context can sometimes lead to disaster.

One might think these lessons scarcely needed stating—and Marshall certainly understood them very well—but the sorry history of "expert" advice in some recent auctions shows that they bear repetition. So although the lessons are general ones, I will illustrate them using auctions and auction theory: Auction theory is often held up as a triumph of the application of economic theory to economic practice, but it has not, in truth, been an unalloyed success. For example, while the European and Asian 3G spectrum auctions famously raised over 100 billion euros in

---

[2] I mean cautious about the theory. Not dismissive of it. And (3) seems a self-evident mistake, if only because of the need for efficient communication among, and education of, economists, let alone the possibilities for further useful development of the mathematics.

[3] Sills (1968, p. 28). An attractively written appreciation of Marshall and his work is in Keynes (1933).

total revenues, Hong Kong's, Austria's, the Netherlands', and Switzerland's auctions, among others, were catastrophically badly run yielding only a quarter or less of the per capita revenues earned elsewhere—and economic theorists deserve some of the blame.[4,5] Hong Kong's auction, for example, was superficially well designed, but not robust to relatively slight political interference that should perhaps have been anticipated. Several countries' academic advisors failed to recognize the importance of the interaction between different countries' auction processes, and bidders advised by experts in auction theory who ignored (or were ignorant of) their clients' histories pursued strategies that cost them billions of euros. Many of these failures could have been avoided if the lessons had been learnt to: pay more attention to elementary theory, to the wider context of the auctions, and to political pressures—and pay less attention to sophisticated mathematical theory.[6]

Of course, mathematical theory, even when it has no direct practical application, is not merely beautiful. It can clarify the central features of a problem, provide useful benchmarks and starting points for analysis and—especially—show the deep relationships between problems that are superficially unconnected. Thus, for example, the sophisticated tools of auction theory that have sometimes been abused in practical contexts turn out to have valuable applications to problems that, at first blush, do not look like auctions.

Section 4.2 briefly discusses what is often taken to be the "standard auction theory", before discussing its real relevance. Sections 4.3–4.5 illustrate its abuse using examples from the Asian and European 3G auctions, and discuss the broader lessons that can be drawn from these misapplications. Section 4.3 is in large part based on Klemperer (2000b) and chapters

---

[4] We take the governments' desire for high revenue as given, and ask how well the auctions met this objective. While an efficient allocation of licenses was most governments' first priority, there is no clear evidence of any differences between the efficiencies of different countries' allocations, so revenues were seen as the measure of success. Section 6.2 argues that governments were correct to make revenue a priority because of the substantial deadweight losses of raising government funds by alternative means, and because the revenues were one-time sunk costs for firms so should be expected to have only limited effects on firms' subsequent investment and pricing behavior.)

[5] The six European auctions in year 2000 yielded 100 (Austria), 615 (Germany), 240 (Italy), 170 (Netherlands), 20 (Switzerland), and 650 (United Kingdom) euros per capita for very similar properties. True, valuations fell during the year as the stockmarkets also fell, but chapter 5 details a variety of evidence that valuations ranged from 300 to 700 euros per capita in all of these auctions. Chapter 5 gives a full description of all nine west European 3G auctions.

[6] Another topical example of overemphasis on sophisticated theory at the expense of elementary theory is European merger policy's heavy focus on the "coordinated" effects that may be facilitated by a merger (and about which we have learnt from repeated game theory) and, at the time of writing, relative lack of concern about the more straightforward "unilateral" effects of mergers (which can be understood using much simpler static game theory). (As a UK Competition Commissioner, I stress that this criticism does not apply to UK policy!)

3 and 5 where additional details can be found (and this section may be skipped by readers familiar with all that material) but the other sections make different points using additional examples. Section 4.6 illustrates how the same concepts that are abused can have surprisingly valuable uses in different contexts. Section 4.7 concludes.

4.2 THE RECEIVED AUCTION THEORY

The core result that everyone who studies auction theory learns is the remarkable *Revenue Equivalence Theorem* (RET).[7] This tells us, subject to some reasonable-sounding conditions, that all the standard (and many non-standard) auction mechanisms are equally profitable for the seller, and that buyers are also indifferent between all these mechanisms.

If that were all there was to it, auction design would be of no interest. But of course the RET rests on a number of assumptions. Probably the most influential piece of auction theory apart from those associated with the RET is Milgrom and Weber's (1982a) remarkable paper—it is surely no coincidence that this is also perhaps the most elegant piece of auction theory apart from the RET. Milgrom and Weber's seminal analysis relaxes the assumption that bidders have independent private information about the value of the object for sale, and instead assumes bidders' private information is *affiliated*. This is similar to assuming positive correlation,[8] and under this assumption they show that ordinary ascending auctions are more profitable than standard (first-price) sealed-bid auctions, in expectation.

Milgrom and Weber's beautiful work is undoubtedly an important piece of economic theory and it has been enormously influential.[9] As a result, many economists leave graduate school "knowing" two things about auctions. First, that if bidders' information is independent then all auctions are equally good, and second, that if information is affiliated (which is

---

[7] The RET is due in an early form to Vickrey (1961), and in its full glory to Myerson (1981), Riley and Samuelson (1981), and others. A typical statement is "Assume each of a given number of risk-neutral potential buyers has a privately known signal about the value of an object, independently drawn from a common, strictly increasing, atomless distribution. Then any auction mechanism in which (i) the object always goes to the buyer with the highest signal, and (ii) any bidder with the lowest feasible signal expects zero surplus, yields the same expected revenue (and results in each bidder making the same expected payment as a function of her signal)."

See chapter 1 for further discussion of the RET.

[8] Affiliation is actually a stronger assumption, but it is probably typically approximately satisfied.

[9] Not only is the concept of affiliation important in applications well beyond auction theory (see section 4.6) but this paper was also critical to the development of auction theory, in that it introduced and analyzed a general model including both private and common value components.

generally the plausible case) then the ascending auction maximizes the seller's revenue.[10] But is this correct?

4.2.1 Relevance of the Received Theory

Marshall's (updated) tests are a good place to start. The value of empirical evidence needs no defense, while examining the plausibility of an intuition helps check whether an economic model provides a useful caricature of the real world, or misleads us by absurdly exaggerating particular features of it.[11]

The intuition behind the exact RET result cannot, to my knowledge, be explained in words that are both accurate and comprehensible to lay people. Anyone with the technical skill to understand any verbal explanation would probably do so by translating the words back into the mathematical argument. But it is easier to defend the weaker claim that it is ambiguous which of the two most common auction forms is superior: it *is* easy to explain that participants in a sealed-bid auction shade their bids below their values (unlike in an ascending auction), but that the winner determines the price (unlike in an ascending auction), so it is not hard to be convincing that there is no clear reason why either auction should be more profitable than the other. This is not quite the same as arguing that the standard auction forms are approximately similarly profitable, but the approximate validity of the RET (under its key assumptions) in fact seems consistent with the available evidence. (Some would say that the mere fact that both the ascending auction and the sealed-bid auction are commonly observed in practice is evidence that neither is always superior.) So the "approximate RET" seems a reasonable claim in practice, and it then follows that issues assumed away by the RET's assumptions should be looked at to choose between the standard auction forms. These issues should include not just those made explicitly in the statement of the theorem, for example, bidders are symmetric and risk-neutral; but also those that are implicit, for example, bidders share common priors and play non-cooperative Nash equilibrium; or semi-implicit, for example, the number and types of bidders are independent of the auction form.

However, as already noted, much attention has focused on just one of the RET's assumptions, namely independence of the bidders' information, and the theoretical result that if information is non-independent (affiliated) then ascending auctions are more profitable than first-price sealed-bid auctions. There is no very compelling intuition for this result. The verbal explanations that are given

---

[10] Or, to take just one very typical example from a current academic article "The one useful thing that our single unit auction theory can tell us is that when bidders' [signals] are affiliated ... the English [i.e., ascending] auction should be expected to raise the most revenue."

[11] Whether the intuition need be non-mathematical, or even comprehensible to lay people, depends on the context, but we can surely have greater confidence in predicting agents' actions when the agents concerned understand the logic behind them, especially when there are few opportunities for learning.

are unconvincing and/or misleading, or worse. The most commonly given "explanation" is that ascending auctions allow bidders to be more aggressive, because their "winner's curses" are reduced,[12] but this argument is plain wrong: the winner's curse is only a feature of common-value auctions, but common values are neither necessary nor sufficient for the result.[13]

A better explanation of the theoretical result is that bidders' profits derive from their private information, and the auctioneer can profit by reducing that private information.[14] An ascending auction reveals the information of bidders who drop out early, so partially reveals the winner's information (if bidders' information is correlated), and uses that information to set the price (through the runner-up's bid), whereas the price paid in a sealed-bid auction cannot use that information. Since the ascending and sealed-bid auctions are revenue-equivalent absent any correlation (i.e., with independent signals), and provided the runner-up's bid responds to the additional information that an ascending auction reveals in the appropriate way (which it does when information is affiliated), this effect makes the ascending auction the more profitable. Of course, this argument is obviously still incomplete,[15,16] and even if it

---

[12] The "winner's curse" reflects the fact that winning an auction suggests one's opponents have pessimistic views about the value of the prize, and bidders must take this into account by bidding more conservatively than otherwise.

[13] The result applies with affiliated private values, in which bidders' values are unaffected by others' information, so there is no winner's curse, and the result does not apply to independent-signal common-value auctions which do suffer from the winner's curse. (Where there is a winner's curse, the "theory" behind the argument is that bidders' private information can be inferred from the points at which they drop out of an ascending auction, so less "bad news" is discovered at the moment of winning than is discovered in winning a sealed-bid auction, so bidders can bid more aggressively in an ascending auction. But this assumes that bidders' more aggressive bidding more than compensates for the reduced winner's curse in an ascending auction—in independent-signal common-value auctions it exactly compensates, which is why there is no net effect, as the RET proves.)

In fact, many experimental and empirical studies suggest bidders fail to fully account for winner's curse effects, so these effects may in practice make sealed-bid auctions more profitable than ascending auctions!

[14] Absent private information, the auctioneer would sell to the bidder with the highest expected valuation at that expected valuation, and bidders would earn no rents. The more general result that, on average, the selling price is increased by having it depend on as much information as possible about the value of the good, is Milgrom and Weber's (1982a, 2000) Linkage Principle. However, in more recent work, Perry and Reny (1999) show that the Principle applies less generally (even in theory) than was thought.

[15] Revealing more information clearly need not necessarily reduce bidders' profits (if bidders' information is negatively correlated, the contrary is typically true), the conditions that make the ascending price respond correctly to the additional information revealed are quite subtle, and nor does the argument say anything about how affiliation affects sealed bids. Indeed there are simple and not unnatural examples with the "wrong kind" of positive correlation in which the ranking of auctions' revenues is reversed (see Bulow and Klemperer, forthcoming), and Perry and Reny (1999) also show the trickiness of the argument by demonstrating that the result only holds for single-unit auctions. A more complete verbal argument for the theoretical result is given in Appendix 1.C, but it is very hard (certainly for the layman).

were fully convincing, it would depend on the *exact* RET applying—which seems a very strong claim.

Furthermore, before relying on any theory mattering in practice, we need to ask: what is the likely order of magnitude of the effect? In fact, numerical analysis suggests the effects of affiliation are often tiny, even when bidders who exactly fit the assumptions of the theory compute their bids exactly using the theory. Riley and Li (1997) analyze equilibrium in a natural class of examples and show that the revenue difference between ascending and first-price auctions is very small unless the information is very strongly affiliated: when bidders' values are jointly normally distributed, bidders' expected rents are about 10 percent (20 percent) higher in a sealed-bid auction than in an ascending auction even for correlation coefficients as high as 0.3 (0.5). So these results suggest affiliation could explain why a 3G spectrum auction earned, for example, 640 rather than 650 euros per capita when bidders' valuations were 700 euros per capita. But the actual range was from just 20 (*twenty*) to 650 euros per capita! Riley and Li also find that even with very strong affiliation, other effects, such as those of asymmetry, are more important and often reverse the effects of affiliation, even taking the numbers of bidders, non-cooperative behavior, common priors, etc., as given.[17] This kind of quantitative analysis surely deserves more attention than economists often give it.

---

[16] Another loose intuition is that in an ascending auction each bidder acts as if he is competing against an opponent with the same valuation. But in a sealed-bid auction a bidder must outbid those with lower valuations. With independent valuations, the RET applies. But if valuations are affiliated, a lower valuation bidder has a more conservative estimate of his opponent's valuation and therefore bids more conservatively. So a bidder in a sealed-bid auction attempting to outbid lower-valuation bidders will bid more conservatively as well. But this argument also rests on the RET applying exactly, and even so several steps are either far from compelling (e.g., the optimal bid against a more conservative opponent is not always to be more conservative), or very non-transparent.

[17] An easier numerical example than Riley and Li's assumes bidder i's value is $v_i = \theta + t_i$, in which θ and the t_i's are independent and uniform on $[0, 1]$, and i knows only v_i. With two bidders, expected revenue is 14/18 in a first-price sealed-bid auction and 15/18 in an ascending auction, so bidder rents are 7/18 and 6/18 respectively (though with n bidders of whom $n/2$ each win a single object, as $n \to \infty$ bidder rents are 42 percent higher in the sealed-bid auction).

With very extreme affiliation, an auctioneer's profits may be more sensitive to the auction form. Modifying the previous example so that there are two bidders who have completely diffuse priors for θ, bidder rents are 50 percent higher in a first-price sealed-bid auction than in an ascending auction (see Appendix 1.D), and Riley and Li's example yields a similar result for correlation coefficients around 0.9 (when bidder rents are anyway small). These examples assume private values. Auctioneers' profits may also be more sensitive to auction form with common values and, in the previous extreme-affiliation model with diffuse priors on θ, if bidders' signals are v_i and the true common value is θ, bidders' rents are twice as high in the sealed-bid auction as in the ascending auction. But, with common values, small asymmetries between bidders are very much more important than affiliation (see Klemperer, 1998; Bulow and Klemperer, 2002). Moreover, we will see that other effects also seem to have been quantitatively much more important in practice than affiliation is even in any of these theoretical examples.

Finally, all the previous discussion is in the context of single-unit auctions. Perry and Reny (1999) show that the result about affiliation does not hold—even in theory—in multi-unit auctions.[18]

Given all this, it is unsurprising that there is no empirical evidence (that I am aware of) that argues the affiliation effect is important.[19,20]

So there seems no strong argument to expect affiliation to matter much in most practical applications; independence is not the assumption of the RET that most needs relaxing.

The theory that really matters most for auction design is just the very elementary undergraduate economics of relaxing the implicit and semi-implicit assumptions of the RET about (fixed) entry and (lack of) collusion.[21] The intuitions are (as Marshall says they should be) easy to explain—we will see that it is clear that bidders are likely to understand and therefore to follow the undergraduate theory. By contrast the intuition for affiliation gives no sense of how bidders should compute their bids, and the calculations required to do so optimally require considerable mathematical sophistication and are sensitive to the precise assumptions bidders make about the "prior" distributions from which their and others' private information is drawn. Of course, this does not mean agents cannot intuitively make approximately optimal decisions (Machlup, 1946; Friedman, 1953), and individual agents need not understand the intuitions behind equilibrium group outcomes. But we can be more confident in predicting that agents will make decisions whose logic is very clear, especially in one-off events such as many auctions are.

Not surprisingly, practical examples of the undergraduate theory are easy to give (as Marshall also insists). But there is no elegant theory applying to the specific context of auctions; such theory is unnecessary since the basic point is that the main concerns in auctions are just the same as in other economic markets, so much of the same theory applies (see below). Furthermore, some

[18] The RET, also, only generalizes to a limited extent to multi-unit auctions.

[19] For example, empirical evidence about timber sales suggests rough revenue equivalence, or even that the sealed-bid auction raises more revenue given the number of bidders (Hansen, 1986; Mead and Schneipp, 1989; Paarsch, 1991; Rothkopf and Engelbrecht-Wiggans, 1993; Haile, 1996) though information is probably affiliated. The experimental evidence (see Kagel and Roth, 1995; Levin, Kagel, and Richard, 1996) is also inconclusive about whether affiliation causes any difference between the revenues from ascending and sealed-bid auctions.

[20] Like Marshall, Colin Clark (1939) emphasized the importance of quantification and real-world facts (see note 1), writing "I have … left my former colleagues in the English Universities … with dismay at their continued preference for the theoretical … approach to economic problems. Not one in a hundred … seems to understand [the need for] the testing of conclusions against … observed facts…" "…The result is a vast output of literature of which, it is safe to say, scarcely a syllable will be read in fifty years' time." I think he would be pleased that an academic from an English University is quoting his syllables well over 50 years after he wrote them.

[21] See chapter 3 and section 4.3. Risk-aversion and asymmetries (even absent entry issues) also arguably matter more than affiliation (and usually have the opposite effect). It is striking that Maskin and Riley's (1984, 2000b) important papers on these topics (see also Matthews, 1983, etc.) failed to have the same broad impact as Milgrom and Weber's work on affiliation.

of the key concerns are especially prominent when the assumption of symmetry is dropped, and models with asymmetries are often inelegant.

So graduate students are taught the elegant mathematics of affiliation and whenever, and wherever, I give a seminar about auctions in practice,[22] I am asked a question along the lines of "Haven't Milgrom and Weber shown that ascending auctions raise most revenue, so why consider other alternatives?". This is true of seminars to academics. It is even more true of seminars to policy makers. Thus, although a little knowledge of economic theory is a good thing, too much knowledge can sometimes be a dangerous thing. Moreover, the extraordinary influence of the concept of affiliation is only the most important example of this. I give a further illustration, involving over-attention to some of my own work, in the next subsection. In short, a little graduate education in auction theory can often distract attention from the straightforward "undergraduate" issues that really matter.[23]

4.3 THE ELEMENTARY ECONOMIC THEORY THAT MATTERS

What really matters in practical auction design is robustness against collusion and attractiveness to entry—just as in ordinary industrial markets.[24] Since I have repeatedly argued this, much of this section is drawn from Klemperer (2000b) and chapters 3 and 5 (any reader familiar with all this material may wish to skip to section 4.4).

4.3.1 Entry

The received theory described above takes the number of bidders as given. But the profitability of an auction depends crucially on the number of bidders who participate, and different auctions vary enormously in their

---

[22] I have done this in over twenty countries in five continents.

[23] True, the generally accepted notion of the "received auction theory" is changing and so is the auction theory that is emphasized in graduate programs. And recent auctions research has been heavily influenced by practical problems. But it will probably remain true that the elegance of a theory will remain an important determinant of its practical influence.

[24] Of course, auction theorists have not altogether ignored these issues—but the emphasis on them has been far less. The literature on collusion includes Robinson (1985), Cramton, Gibbons, and Klemperer (1987), Graham and Marshall (1987), Milgrom (1987), Hendricks and Porter (1989), Graham, Marshall, and Richard (1990), Mailath and Zemsky (1991), McAfee and McMillan (1992), Menezes (1996), Weber (1997), Engelbrecht-Wiggans and Kahn (1998c), Ausubel and Schwartz (1999), Brusco and Lopomo (2002a), Hendricks, Porter, and Tan (1999) and Cramton and Schwartz (2000). That on entry includes Matthews (1984), Engelbrecht-Wiggans (1987), McAfee and McMillan (1987c, 1988), Harstad (1990), Engelbrecht-Wiggans (1993), Levin and Smith (1994), Bulow and Klemperer (1996), Menezes and Monteiro (2000), Persico (2000b), Klemperer (1998) and Gilbert and Klemperer (2000). See also sections 1.8, 1.9 and the Afterword to chapter 1.

attractiveness to entry; participating in an auction can be a costly exercise that bidders will only undertake if they feel they have realistic chances of winning. In an ascending auction a stronger bidder can always top any bid that a weaker bidder makes, and knowing this the weaker bidder may not enter the auction in the first place—which may then allow the stronger bidder to win at a very low price. In a first-price sealed-bid auction, by contrast, a weaker bidder may win at a price that the stronger bidder could have beaten, but did not because the stronger bidder may risk trying to win at a lower price and cannot change his bid later. So more bidders may enter a first-price sealed-bid auction.[25]

The intuition is very clear, and there is little need for sophisticated theory. Perhaps because of this, or because the argument depends on asymmetries between bidders so any theory is likely to be inelegant, theory has largely ignored the point. Vickrey's (1961) classic paper contains an example (relegated to an appendix, and often overlooked) which illustrates the basic point that the player who actually has the lower value may win a first-price sealed-bid auction in Nash equilibrium, but that this cannot happen in an ascending auction (with private values). But little has been said since.

In fact, some of what has been written about the issue of attracting entry provides a further illustration of the potentially perverse impact of sophisticated theory. Although the point that weaker bidders are unlikely to win ascending auctions, and may therefore not enter them, is very general, some work—including Klemperer (1998)[26]—has emphasized that the argument is especially compelling for "almost-common-value" auctions, and this work may have had the unintended side-effect of linking the entry concern to common values in some people's minds;[27] I have heard economists who know the latter work all too well say that because an auction does not involve common values, therefore there is no entry problem![28] To the extent that the almost-common values theory (which is both of more limited application, and also assumes quite sophisticated reasoning by bidders) has distracted attention from the more general point, this is another example of excessive focus on sophisticated theory at the expense of more elementary, but more crucial, theory.

[25] The point is similar to the industrial-organization point that because a Bertrand market is more competitive than a Cournot market for any given number of firms, the Bertrand market may attract less entry, so the Cournot market may be more competitive if the number of firms is endogenous.

[26] See also Bikhchandani (1988), Bulow, Huang, and Klemperer (1999), Bulow and Klemperer (2002), and Klemperer and Pagnozzi (forthcoming).

[27] In spite of the fact that I have made the point that the argument applies more broadly in, for example, Klemperer (1999b, 2000b). See also sections 2.3.1, 3.3, and Gilbert and Klemperer (2000).

[28] Similarly others have asserted that the reason the United Kingdom planned to include a sealed-bid component in its 3G design if only four licenses were available for sale (see below), was because the auction designers (who included me) thought the auction was almost-common values—but publicly available government documents show that we did not think this was likely.

There is an additional important reason why a first-price sealed-bid auction may be more attractive to entrants: bidders in a sealed-bid auction may be much less certain about opponents' strategies, and the advantage of stronger players may therefore be less pronounced, than standard equilibrium theory predicts. The reason is that in practice, players are not likely to share common priors about distributions of valuations and, even if they do, they may not play Nash equilibrium strategies (i.e., a sealed-bid auction induces "strategic uncertainty"). So even if players were in fact ex-ante symmetric (i.e., their private information is drawn from identical distributions) the lower-value player might win a first-price sealed-bid auction, but would never win an ascending auction (in which bidders' strategies are very straightforward and predictable). When players are not symmetric, Nash equilibrium theory predicts that a weaker player will sometimes beat a stronger player in a sealed-bid auction, but I conjecture strategic uncertainty and the absence of common priors make this outcome even more likely than Nash equilibrium predicts. Since this point is very hard for standard economic theory to capture, it has largely been passed over. But it reinforces the point that a sealed-bid auction is in many circumstances more likely than an ascending auction to attract entry, and this will often have a substantial effect on the relative profit-abilities of the auctions.

The 3G auctions provide good examples of over-sensitivity to the significance of information revelation and affiliation at the expense of insensitivity to the more important issue of entry. For example, the Netherlands sold five 3G licenses in a context in which there were also exactly five incumbent mobile-phone operators who were the natural winners, leaving no room for any entrant. (For competition-policy reasons, bidders were permitted to win no more than one license each). The problem of attracting enough entry to have a competitive auction should therefore have been uppermost in planners' minds. But the planners seem instead to have been seduced by the fact that ascending auctions raise (a little) extra revenue because of affiliation and also increase the likelihood of an efficient allocation to those with the highest valuations.[29] The planners were probably also influenced by the fact that previous spectrum auctions in the United States and United Kingdom had used ascending designs,[30] even though they had usually done so in contexts in which entry was less

[29] It seems unlikely that the efficiency of the Netherlands auction was much improved by the ascending design.

[30] We discuss the UK design below. The design of the US auctions, according to McMillan (1994, p. 151–2) who was a consultant to the US government, was largely determined by faith in the linkage principle and hence the revenue advantages of an ascending auction in the presence of affiliation; the economic theorists advising the government judged other potential problems with the ascending design "to be outweighed by the bidders' ability to learn from other bids in the auction" (McMillan, 1994) (see also Perry and Reny, 1999). Efficiency was also a concern in the design of the US auctions.

of a concern, and even though some US auctions did suffer from entry problems. The result of the Netherlands auction was both predictable, and predicted (see, e.g. Maasland (2000) and Klemperer (2000b) quoted in the Dutch press prior to the auction). There was no serious entrant.[31] Revenue was less than a third of what had been predicted and barely a quarter of the per capita amounts raised in the immediately preceding and immediately subsequent 3G auctions (in the United Kingdom and Germany respectively). The resulting furor in the press led to a Parliamentary Inquiry.

By contrast, when Denmark faced a very similar situation in its 3G auctions in late 2001—four licenses for sale and four incumbents—its primary concern was to encourage entry.[32] (The designers had both observed the Netherlands fiasco, and also read Klemperer (2000b).) It chose a sealed-bid design (a "fourth-price" auction) and had a resounding success. A serious entrant bid, and revenue far exceeded expectations and was more than twice the levels achieved by any of the other three European 3G auctions (Switzerland, Belgium and Greece) that took place since late 2000.

The academics who designed the UK sale (which was held prior to the Netherlands and Danish auctions) also thought much harder about entry into their 3G auction.[33] The United Kingdom had four incumbent operators, and when design work began it was unclear how many licenses it would be possible to offer given the technological constraints. We realized that if there were just four licenses available it would be hard to persuade a non-incumbent to enter, so we planned in that case to use a design including a sealed-bid component (an "Anglo-Dutch" design) to encourage entry. In the event, five licenses were available so, given the UK context, we switched to an ascending auction, since there was considerable uncertainty about who the fifth strongest bidder would be (we ran the

---

[31] There was one entrant who probably did not seriously expect to win a license in an ascending auction—indeed it argued strongly prior to the auction that an ascending auction gave it very little chance and, more generally, reduced the likelihood of entry into the auction. Perhaps it competed in the hope of being bought off by an incumbent by, for example, gaining access rights to an incumbent's network, in return for its quitting the auction early. The Netherlands government should be very grateful that this entrant competed for as long as it did! See section 5.3.2 and van Damme (2002) for more details.

[32] Attracting entry was an even more severe problem in late 2001 than in early summer 2000 when the Netherlands auction was held. The dotcom boom was over, European telecoms stock prices at the time of the Danish auction were just one-third the levels they were at in the Dutch auction, and the prospects for 3G were much dimmer than they had seemed previously.

[33] I was the principal auction theorist advising the Radiocommunications Agency which designed and ran the UK auction. Ken Binmore led the team and supervised experiments testing the proposed designs. Other academic advisors included Tilman Börgers, Jeremy Bulow, Philippe Jehiel and Joe Swierzbinksi. Ken Binmore subsequently advised the Danish government on its very successful auction. The views expressed in this chapter are mine alone.

world's first 3G auction in part to ensure this; see section 4.5).[34] Thirteen bidders entered, ensuring a highly competitive auction which resulted in the highest per capita revenue among all the European and Asian 3G auctions.

4.3.2 Collusion

The received auction theory also assumes bidders play non-cooperatively in Nash equilibrium. We have already discussed how Nash equilibrium may be a poor prediction because of "strategic uncertainty" and the failure of the common priors assumption, but a more fundamental problem is that players may behave collusively rather than non-cooperatively. In particular, a standard ascending auction—especially a multi-unit ascending auction— often satisfies *all* the conditions that elementary economic theory tells us are important for facilitating collusion, even without any possibility of interaction or discussion among bidders beyond the information communicated in their bids.

For example, Waterson's (1984) standard industrial organization textbook lists five questions that must be answered affirmatively for firms to be able to support collusion in an ordinary industrial market: (1) can firms easily identify efficient divisions of the market? (2) Can firms easily agree on a division? (3) Can firms easily detect defection from any agreement? (4) Can firms credibly punish any observed defection? (5) Can firms deter non-participants in the agreement from entering the industry? In a multi-unit ascending auction: (1) the objects for sale are well defined, so firms can see how to share the collusive "pie" among them (by contrast with the problem of sharing an industrial market whose definition may not be obvious); (2) bids can be used to signal proposals about how the division should be made and to signal agreement; 3) firms' pricing (i.e., bidding) is immediately and perfectly observable, so defection from any collusive agreement is immediately detected; (4) the threat of punishment for defection from the agreement is highly credible, since punishment is quick and easy and often costless to the punisher in a multi-object auction in which a player has the ability to raise the price only on objects that the defector

---

[34] With five licenses, the licenses would be of unequal size, which argued for an ascending design. Note that in some contexts an ascending design may promote entry. For example, when Peter Cramton, Eric Maskin, and I advised the UK government on the design of its March 2002 auction of reductions in greenhouse gas emissions, we recommended an ascending design to encourage the entry of small bidders for whom working out how to bid sensibly in a discriminatory sealed-bid auction might have been prohibitively costly. (Strictly speaking the auction was a descending one since the auction was a reverse auction in which firms were bidding to sell emissions reductions to the government. But this is equivalent to an ascending design for a standard auction to sell permits.) (Larry Ausubel and Jeremy Bulow were also involved in the implementation of this design.) See Klemperer et al. (forthcoming).

will win;[35] and (5) we have already argued that entry in an ascending auction may be hard.

So collusion in an ascending auction seems much easier to sustain than in an "ordinary" industrial market, and it should therefore be no surprise that ascending auctions provide some particularly clear examples of collusion, as we illustrate below.

By contrast, a first-price sealed-bid auction is usually much more robust to collusion: bidders cannot "exchange views" through their bids, or observe opponents' bids until after the auction is over, or punish defection from any agreement during the course of the auction, or easily deter entry. But, perhaps because auction theorists have little that is new or exciting to say about collusion, too little attention has been given to this elementary issue in practical applications.

In the Austrian 3G auction, for example, twelve identical blocks of spectrum were sold to six bidders in a simultaneous ascending auction (bidders were allowed to win multiple blocks each). No one was in the least surprised when the bidding stopped just above the low reserve price with each bidder winning two blocks, at perhaps one-third the price that bidders valued them at.[36] Clearly the effect of "collusion" (whether explicit and illegal, or tacit and possibly legal) on revenues is first-order.

Another elegant example of bidders' ability to "collude" is provided by the 1999 German DCS-1800 auction in which ten blocks of spectrum were sold by ascending auction, with the rule that any new bid on a block had to exceed the previous high bid by at least 10 percent.[37] There were just two credible bidders, the two largest German mobile-phone companies T-Mobil and Mannesman, and Mannesman's first bids were 18.18 million deutschmarks per megahertz on blocks 1–5 and 20 million deutschmarks per MHz on blocks 6–10. T-Mobil—who bid even less in the first round—later said "There were no agreements with Mannesman. But [we] interpreted

---

[35] For example, in a multi-license US spectrum auction in 1996–97, U.S. West was competing vigorously with McLeod for lot number 378, a license in Rochester, Minnesota. Although most bids in the auction had been in exact thousands of dollars, U.S. West bid $313,378 and $62,378 for two licenses in Iowa in which it had earlier shown no interest, overbidding McLeod, who had seemed to be the uncontested high-bidder for these licenses. McLeod got the point that it was being punished for competing in Rochester, and dropped out of that market. Since McLeod made subsequent higher bids on the Iowa licenses, the "punishment" bids cost U.S. West nothing (Cramton and Schwartz, 2000).

[36] Although it did not require rocket science to determine the obvious way to divide twelve among six, the largest incumbent, Telekom Austria probably assisted the coordination when it announced in advance of the auction that it "would be satisfied with just two of the 12 blocks of frequency on offer" and "if the [five other bidders] behaved similarly it should be possible to get the frequencies on sensible terms", but "it would bid for a third frequency block if one of its rivals did" (Crossland, 2000).

[37] Unlike my other examples in this chapter this was not a 3G auction; however, it is highly relevant to the German 3G auction which we will discuss.

Mannesman's first bid as an offer." (Stuewe, 1999, p. 13). The point is that 18.18 plus a 10 percent raise equals 20.00. It seems T-Mobil understood that if it bid 20 million deutschmarks per MHz on blocks 1–5, but did not bid again on blocks 6–10, the two companies would then live and let live with neither company challenging the other on the other's half. Exactly that happened. So the auction closed after just two rounds with each of the bidders acquiring half the blocks for the same low price, which was a small fraction of the valuations that the bidders actually placed on the blocks.[38]

This example makes another important point. The elementary theory that tells us that "collusion" is easy in this context is important. The reader may think it obvious that bidders can "collude" in the setting described, but that is because the reader has been exposed to elementary undergraduate economic theory. This point was beautifully illustrated by the behavior of the subjects in an experiment that was specifically designed to advise one of the bidders in this auction by mimicking its setting and rules: the experimental subjects completely failed to achieve the low-price "collusive" outcome that was achieved in practice. Instead "… in [all] the [experimental] sessions the bidding was very competitive. Subjects went for all ten units in the beginning, and typically reduced their bidding rights only when the budget limit forced them to do so" (Abbink, Irlenbusch, Rockenbach, Sadrieh, and Selten, 2002). So the elementary economic theory of collusion which makes it plain, by contrast, that the "collusive" outcome that actually arose was to be expected from more sophisticated players does matter—and I feel confident that the very distinguished economists who ran the experiments advised their bidder more on the basis of the elementary theory than on the basis of the experiments.[39]

Both the United Kingdom's and Denmark's academic advisors gave considerable thought to preventing collusion. Denmark, for example, not only ran a sealed-bid auction, but also allowed bidders to submit multiple bids at multiple locations with the rule that only the highest bid made by any bidder would count, and also arranged for phony bids to be submitted—the idea was that bidders could not (illegally) agree to observe each other's bids without fear that their partners in collusion would double-

---

[38] See Jehiel and Moldovanu (2001b) and Grimm, Riedel, and Wolfstetter (2003). Grimm et al. argue that this outcome was a non-cooperative Nash equilibrium of the fully specified game. This is similar to the familiar industrial organization point that oligopolistic outcomes that we call "collusive" may be Nash equilibria of repeated oligopoly games. But our focus is on whether outcomes look like competitive, non-cooperative, behavior in the simple analyses that are often made, not on whether or not they can be justified as Nash equilibria in more sophisticated models.

[39] Abbink, Irlenbusch, Rockenbach, Sadrieh, and Selten (2002) write "The lessons learnt from the experiments are complemented by theoretical strategic considerations". Indeed, auctions policy advice should always, if possible, be informed by both theory and experiments.

cross them, and nor could bidders observe who had made bids, or how many had been made.[40]

4.4 Robustness to Political Pressures

To be effective, economic advice must also be sensitive to the organizational and political context; it is important to be realistic about how advice will be acted on. Economic advisors commonly explain a policy failure with the excuse that "it would have been okay if they had followed our advice". But medical practitioners are expected to take account of the fact that patients will not follow their every instruction.[41] Why should economic practitioners be different? Maybe it should be regarded as economic malpractice to give advice that will actually make matters worse if it is not followed exactly.

For example, the economic theorists advising the Swiss government on its 3G auction favored a multi-unit ascending auction, apparently arguing along the standard received- auction-theory lines that this was best for both efficiency and revenue. But they recognized the dangers of such an auction encouraging "collusive" behavior and deterring entry, and the advisors therefore also proposed setting a high reserve price. This would not only directly limit the potential revenue losses from collusion and/or inadequate entry but, importantly, also reduce the likelihood of collusion. (With a high reserve price, bidders are relatively more likely to prefer to raise the price to attempt to drive their rivals out altogether, than to collude with them at the reserve price; see section 3.4.1; Brusco and Lopomo, 2002b.)

But serious reserve prices are often unpopular with politicians and bureaucrats who—even if they have the information to set them sensibly—are often reluctant to run even a tiny risk of not selling the objects, which outcome they fear would be seen as "a failure".

---

[40] In the United Kingdom's ascending auction, the fact that bidders were each restricted to winning at most a single object, out of just five objects, ruled out tacit collusion to divide the spoils (provided that there were more than five bidders). More important, the large number of bidders expected (because the United Kingdom ran Europe's first 3G auction; see section 4.5) also made explicit (illegal) collusion much less likely (see chapter 5) and the fact that the United Kingdom retained the right to cancel the auction in some circumstances also reduced bidders' incentive to collude.

[41] Doctors are trained to recognize that some types of patients may not take all prescribed medicines or return for follow-up treatment. Pharmaceutical companies have developed one-dose regimens that are often more expensive or less effective than multiple-dose treatments, but that overcome these specific problems. For example, the treatment of chlamydial infection by a single dose of azithromycin is much more expensive and no more effective than a 7 day course of doxycycline; there is a short (2 month) course of preventive therapy for tuberculosis that is both more expensive, and seems to have more problems with side effects, than the longer 6 month course; and the abridged regimen for HIV+ women who are pregnant (to prevent perinatal transmission) is less effective than the longer, more extensive treatment.

The upshot was that no serious reserve was set. Through exit, joint-venture, and possibly—it was rumored—collusion,[42] the number of bidders shrank to equal the number of licenses available, so the remaining bidders had to pay only the trivial reserve price that had been fixed. (Firms were allowed to win just a single license each.) The outcome was met with jubilation by the bidders and their shareholders; per capita revenues were easily the lowest of any of the nine western European 3G auctions, and less than one-thirtieth of what the government had been hoping for.[43] Perhaps an ascending auction together with a carefully chosen reserve price was a reasonable choice. But an ascending auction with only a trivial reserve price was a disaster, and the economic-theorist advisors should have been more realistic that this was a likely outcome of their advice.[44]

4.4.1 Economic Similarity ≠ Political Similarity

Hong Kong's auction was another case where designers should perhaps have anticipated the political response to their advice. The Hong Kong auction's designers, like Denmark's, had observed the Netherlands fiasco (and had also read Klemperer, 2000b). So they were keen to use a sealed-bid design, given Hong Kong's situation.[45] Specifically, they favored a "fourth-price" sealed-

---

[42] Two bidders merged the day before the auction was to begin, and a total of five bidders quit in the last four days before the auction. At least one bidder had quit earlier after hearing from its bidding consultants that because it was a weaker bidder it had very little chance of winning an ascending auction. Furthermore, the regulator investigated rumors that Deutsche Telekom agreed not to participate in the auction in return for subsequently being able to buy into one of the winners.

[43] In fact, when the denouement of the auction had become clear, the Swiss government tried to cancel it and re-run it with different rules. But in contrast to the UK auction (see note 40), the designers had omitted to allow themselves that possibility.

The final revenues were 20 euros per capita, compared to analysts' estimates of 400–600 euros per capita in the week before the auction was due to begin. Meeks (2001) shows the jumps in Swisscom's share price around the auction are highly statistically significant and, controlling for general market movements, correspond to the market believing that bidders paid several hundred euros per capita less in the auction than was earlier anticipated.

[44] I am not arguing that an ascending auction plus reserve price is always bad advice, or even that it was necessarily poor advice here. But advisors must make it very clear if success depends on a whole package being adopted, and should think carefully about the likely implementation of their proposals.

Greece and Belgium did set reserve prices that seem to have been carefully thought out, but they were perhaps encouraged to do so by the example of the Swiss auction, and of the Italian and Austrian auctions which also had reserve prices that were clearly too low, even if not as low as Switzerland's.

[45] In Hong Kong, unlike in the Netherlands and Denmark, there were actually more incumbents than licenses. But not all Hong Kong's incumbents were thought strong. Furthermore, it is much more attractive for strong firms to form joint ventures or collude with their closest rivals prior to a standard ascending auction (when the strengthened combined bidder discourages entry) than prior to a standard sealed-bid auction (when reducing two strong bidders to one may attract entry). So even though the difference in strength between the likely winners and the also-rans seemed less dramatic in Hong Kong than in the Netherlands and Denmark, a standard ascending auction still seemed problematic. So there was a very serious concern—well-justified as it turned out—that a standard ascending auction would yield no more bidders than licenses.

bid design so that all four winners (there were four licenses and firms could win at most one license each) would pay the same fourth-highest bid—charging winners different amounts for identical properties might both be awkward and lead to cautious bidding by managements who did not want to risk the embarrassment of paying more than their rivals.[46]

However, the designers were also afraid that if the public could observe the top three bids after the auction, then if these were very different from the price that the firms actually paid (the fourth highest bid), the government would be criticized for selling the licenses for less than the firms had shown themselves willing to pay. Of course, such criticism would be ill-informed, but it could still be damaging, because even well-intentioned commentators find it hard to explain to the general public that requiring firms to pay their own bids would result in firms bidding differently. Thus far, nothing was different from the situation in Denmark. However, whereas the Danish government simply followed the advice it was given to keep all the bids secret and reveal only the price paid, the Hong Kong government felt it could not do this.

Openness and transparency of government was a big political issue in the wake of Hong Kong's return to Chinese rule, and it was feared that secrecy would be impossible to maintain. The advisors therefore proposed to run an auction that was *strategically equivalent* (i.e., has an identical game-theoretic structure and therefore should induce identical behavior) to a fourth-price auction, but that did not reveal the three high bids to *anyone*.[47] To achieve this, an ascending auction would be run for the four identical licenses, but dropouts would be kept secret and the price would continue to rise until the point at which the number of players remaining dropped from four to *three*. At this point the last four (including the firm that had just "dropped out") would pay the last price at which four players remained in the bidding. Since nothing was revealed to any player until the auction was over, no player had any decision to make except to choose a single dropout price, in the knowledge that if its price was among the top four then it would pay the fourth-highest dropout price; that is, the situation was identical from the firm's viewpoint to choosing a single bid in a fourth-price sealed-bid auction. But, unlike in Denmark, no one would ever see the "bids" planned by the top three winners

[46] In a simple model, if a winning bidder suffers "embarrassment costs" which are an increasing function of the difference between his payment and the lowest winning payment, then bidders are no worse off in expectation than in an auction which induces no embarrassment costs, but the auctioneer suffers. This is a consequence of the revenue equivalence theorem: under its assumptions, mechanisms that induce embarrassment costs cannot affect bidders' utilities (it is irrelevant to the bidders whether the "embarrassment costs" are received by the auctioneer or are social waste), so in equilibrium winning bidders' expected payments are lower by the expected embarrassment costs they suffer. (See chapter 1, exercise 5.)

[47] I had no direct involvement with this auction but, embarrassingly, I am told this "solution" was found in a footnote to Klemperer (2000b) that pointed out this method of running a strategically equivalent auction to the uniform fourth-price auction, and that it might (sometimes) be more politically acceptable. See also note 37 to chapter 6.

(and since these bids would never even have been placed, very little credibility would have attached to reports of them).

However, although the proposed auction was mathematically (i.e., strategically) equivalent to a sealed-bid auction, its verbal description was very different. The stronger incumbents lobbied vigorously for a "small change" to the design—that the price be determined when the numbers dropped from five to four, rather than from four to three.

This is the "standard" way of running an ascending auction, and it recreates the standard problem that entry is deterred because strong players can bid aggressively in the knowledge that the winners will only pay a loser's bid (the fifth bid) and not have to pay one of the winners' bids.

Revealingly, one of the strong players that, it is said, lobbied so strongly for changing the proposal was at the same time a weaker player (a potential entrant) in the Danish market and, it is said, professed itself entirely happy with the fourth-price sealed-bid rules for *that* market.

The lobbyists' arguments that their suggested change was "small" and made the auction more "standard", and also that it was "unfair" to have the bidders continue to "bid against themselves" when there were just four left, were politically salient points, even though they are irrelevant or meaningless from a strictly game-theoretic viewpoint.[48] Since the academic consultants who proposed the original design had very little influence at the higher political levels at which the final decision was taken, and since perhaps not all the ultimate decision-makers understood—or wanted to understand—the full significance of the change, the government gave way and made it.[49]

The result? Just the four strongest bidders entered and paid the reserve price—a major disappointment for the government, and yielding perhaps one-third to one-half the revenue that had been anticipated (allowing for market conditions). Whether other potential bidders gave up altogether, or whether they made collusive agreements with stronger bidders not to enter (as was rumored in the press), is unknown. But what is certain is that the design finally chosen made entry much harder and collusion much easier.

It is not clear what the economic theorists advising should have recommended. Perhaps they should have stuck to a (fourth-price) sealed-bid auction run in the standard way, but used computer technology that could determine the price to be paid while making it impossible for anyone other than the bidders to know the other bids made.

---

[48] The lobbyists also successfully ridiculed the original design, calling it the "dark auction", arguing that it "perversely" hid information when "everyone knows that transparent markets are more efficient", and claiming it was an "unfair tax" since bidders "paid more than if they had all the information".

[49] The highly sophisticated security arrangements that had been made to ensure secrecy of the dropouts (removal of bidding teams to separate top-secret locations in army camps, etc.) were not altered even though they had become much less relevant; there was no need to lobby against these.

The moral, however, is clear. Auction designs that seem similar to economic theorists may seem very different to politicians, bureaucrats and the public, and vice versa. And political and lobbying pressures need to be predicted and planned for in advance.

When the designers of the UK 3G auction proposed a design—the Anglo-Dutch—that was very unattractive to the incumbent operators, it probably helped that two alternative versions of the design were initially offered. Whilst the incumbent operators hated the overall design and lobbied furiously against it,[50] they also had strong preferences between its two versions, and much of their lobbying efforts therefore focused on the choice between them. When the government selected the version the operators preferred (the designers actually preferred this version too) the operators felt they had got a part of what they had asked for, and it proved politically possible for the government to stick to the Anglo-Dutch design until the circumstances changed radically.[51]

Another notorious "political failure" was the design of the 1998 Netherlands 2G spectrum auction. The EU Commission objected to the Netherlands government's rules for the auction shortly before the (EU imposed) deadline for the allocation of the licenses. The rules were therefore quickly rewritten by a high-ranking civil servant on a Friday afternoon. The result was an auction that sold similar properties at prices that differed by a factor of about two, and almost certainly allocated the licenses inefficiently.[52]

Economists are now waking up to the importance of these issues: Wilson (2002) addresses political constraints in the design of auction markets for electricity, and Roth (2002) also discusses political aspects of market design. But the politics of design remains understudied by economic theorists, and underappreciated by them in their role as practitioners.

---

[50] It is rumored that a single bidder's budget for economic advice for lobbying against the design exceeded the UK government's expenditure on economic advice during the entire three-year design process; the lobbying effort included hiring two Nobel prize winners in the hope of finding arguments against the design. See section 6.5.1 for details of the two versions of the design.

[51] When it became possible to offer an additional fifth license in the United Kingdom the design changed—as had been planned for this circumstance—to a pure ascending one (see section 4.3.1).

[52] See van Damme (1999). This auction also illustrates the potential importance of bidders' errors: although high stakes were involved (the revenues were over 800 million euros) it seems that the outcome, and perhaps also the efficiency of the license allocation, was critically affected by a bidder unintentionally losing its eligibility to bid on additional properties later in the auction; it has been suggested that the bidder's behavior can only be explained by the fact that it happened on "Carnival Monday", a day of celebrations and drinking in the south of the Netherlands where the bidder is based (van Damme, 1999)! (The German 3G auction described below provides another example of the large role that bidder error can play.)

4.5 UNDERSTANDING THE WIDER CONTEXT

Any consultant new to a situation must beware of overlooking issues that are well understood by those with more experience of the environment. The danger is perhaps particularly acute for economic theorists who are used to seeing the world through models that, while very elegant, are often lacking in real-world detail and context.

The German 3G auction illustrates the importance of the wider context. As we described in section 4.3.2, in Germany's 1999 DCS-1800 auction Mannesman used its bids to signal to T-Mobil how the two firms should divide the blocks between them and end the auction at a comparatively low price. T-Mobil then cut back its demand in exactly the way Mannesman suggested, and Mannesman followed through with its half of the "bargain" by also cutting back its demand, so the auction ended with the two firms winning similar amounts of spectrum very cheaply.

It seems that Mannesman used the same advisors in the 3G auction that it had used in the GSM auction. Although the rules for the 3G auction were not identical, it was another simultaneous ascending auction in which individual bidders were permitted to win multiple blocks. After the number of bidders had fallen to six competing for a total of twelve blocks, and when it was clear that the other four bidders would be content with two blocks each, Mannesman apparently signaled to T-Mobil to cut back its demand to just two blocks.[53] If T-Mobil and Mannesman had both done this the auction would have ended at modest prices. Instead T-Mobil seemingly ignored Mannesman's signals, and drove up the total price 15 billion euros before cutting back demand. Once T-Mobil did cut back its demand, Mannesman followed, so the auction ended with the allocation that Mannesman had originally signaled but with each of the six firms paying an additional 2.5 billion euros!

It seems that Mannesman's advisors saw the GSM auction as a template for the 3G auction; they took the view that, following previous practice, Mannesman would signal when to reduce demand, T-Mobil would acquiesce, and Mannesman would then follow through on its half of the bargain.[54] The bargain would be enforced by firms not wishing to jeopardize their future cooperation in subsequent auctions (including 3G auctions in other countries) and in negotiating with regulators, etc. (and the short-run advantage that could

[53] According to the *Financial Times* (3 November 2000, p. 21), "One operator has privately admitted to altering the last digit of its bid ... to signal to other participants that it was willing to accept a small license."

[54] It seems that another reason why Mannesman expected the firms to coordinate by T-Mobil reducing demand first in response to Mannesman's signals was that Mannesman saw itself as the leading firm in the market. However, T-Mobil may not have seen Mannesman as the leading firm—the two firms were closely matched—and this seems to have contributed to the problem.

be gained by failing to cooperate was anyway probably small; see Klemperer, 2002 and sections 7.5–7.8). But given their expectation that T-Mobil would cut back demand first, Mannesman's advisors were unwilling to reduce demand when T-Mobil did not.

Clearly, T-Mobil's advisors saw things differently. It seems that their main advisors had not been involved in the GSM auction and the example of the previous auction was certainly not in the forefront of their minds. Instead they mistrusted Mannesman's intentions, and were very unwilling to cut back demand without proof that Mannesman had already done so. True the 3G auction was a much more complicated game than the GSM auction because of the other parties involved, and sections 5.4.1 and 7.5–7.8 discusses other factors that may have contributed to the firms' failure to reduce demand.[55] But T-Mobil's refusal to cut back demand very likely stemmed partly from viewing the 3G auction in a different, and narrower, context than Mannesman did.

Just as previous auctions within any country might have been an important part of the wider context, auctions in other countries are also relevant parts of the broader environment: the sequencing of the 3G auctions across countries was crucial. Countries that auctioned earlier had more entrants, because weaker bidders had not yet worked out that they were weaker and quit the auctions, because stronger bidders had not yet worked out how and with whom to do joint ventures, and because complementarities between the values of licenses in different countries reinforced these effects—the number of entrants in the nine western European auctions were (in order) 13, 6, 7, 6, 6, 4, 3, 3, and 5 respectively.[56] Countries that auctioned earlier also suffered less from "collusive" behavior, because bidders had had less practice in learning how best to play the game. For example, when the Austrian 3G auction followed the German 3G auction that we have just described, using almost the same design, all the bidders very quickly saw the mutual advantage of coordinating a demand reduction (see section 4.3.2).[57]

The UK government's advisers anticipated this pattern of declining competition, and chose to run its auction first; indeed we persisted in the policy of running the first auction even when others were advising us to delay. Yet in more than one country auction theorists advising on 3G auction design seemed either unaware of (!), or at least unaffected in their thinking by, the fact that

---

[55] In particular, the firms might have been concerned about their relative performances (see also Grimm, Riedel, and Wolfstetter, 2002; Jehiel and Moldovanu, 2002; Ewerhart and Moldovanu, 2002).

[56] Furthermore, the number (6) achieved in the second auction (Netherlands) was perhaps lowered by the peculiarly incompetent design; the number (5) achieved in the last auction (Denmark) was raised by its design, which was very skillful except in its timing (see section 4.3.1). Of course, other factors, in particular the fall in the telecoms stock price index, may have contributed to the fall in the number of entrants.

[57] Chapter 5 develops the arguments in this paragraph in much more detail.

there was to be a sequence of auctions across Europe. Clearly these designers had far too narrow a view of the problem.[58]

Of course, other auctions are only the most obvious aspects of the wider context that auction designers need to consider. There are many other ways in which designers showed themselves very poor at thinking about the wider game. For example, many of the 3G auction designers had a very limited understanding of how the auction process affected, and was affected by, the series of telecom mergers and alliances that the advent of 3G engendered—in the United Kingdom alone, there were no fewer than *five* mergers involving the four incumbent 2G operators, in less than a year around the auction.[59]

4.6 USING ECONOMIC THEORY

I have argued that while a good understanding of elementary undergraduate economic theory is essential to successful auction design, advanced graduate auction theory is often less important. It is important to emphasize, therefore, the crucially important role that advanced formal theory plays in developing our economic understanding. In particular, advanced theory often develops deeper connections between apparently distinct economic questions than are superficially apparent.

For example, chapter 2 demonstrates that auction-theoretic tools provide useful arguments in a broad range of mainstream economic contexts. As a further illustration, I will discuss how a part of the received auction theory— the effect of affiliation—that was, I have argued, not central to the auctions of 3G licenses, can develop useful insights about the economics of the "m-Commerce" industry that 3G will create.[60]

4.6.1 Do e-Commerce and m-Commerce Raise Consumer Prices?

Some commentators and regulators have expressed concern that e-commerce and m-commerce ("mobile commerce" in which people purchase through

[58] Some of the incumbent bidders, by contrast, may possibly have had a clearer understanding. In an interesting example of the importance of political pressures, the Dutch operators successfully lobbied to delay the Netherlands auction and the clear gap that was thereby created between the British and Dutch auctions may have been a contributory factor to the Dutch fiasco.

[59] Section 7.3 gives another illustration of how real-world context that was non-obvious to outsiders was important to the UK 3G auction.

[60] Section 2.2 uses the other main piece of the received auction theory—the revenue equivalence theorem—to solve a war of attrition between several technologies competing to become an industry standard in, for example, 3G (see also Bulow and Klemperer, 1999) and to compute the value of new customers to firms when consumers have switching costs as they do for, for example, 3G phones (see also Bulow and Klemperer, 1998). Section 2.3.1 also uses auction theory to address how e-commerce (and likewise m-commerce) affects pricing.

their mobile phones, and which is predicted to expand rapidly as a result of 3G technology) allow firms to easily identify and collect information about their customers which they can use to "rip them off".[61]

A simple analysis realizes that each consumer is analogous to an auctioneer, while firms are bidders competing to sell to that consumer. As we discussed in section 4.2, bidders' expected profits derive from their private information, and the auctioneer generally gains by reducing the amount of bidders' private information. So if all firms learn the same piece of information about a given consumer, this (weakly) reduces the private information that any bidder has relative to the other bidders, and so often benefits the auctioneer, that is, lowers the consumer's expected transaction price.

Although this result is a good start, it is neither very novel,[62] nor does it address the bigger concern that e-and m-commerce allow different firms to learn different information about any given consumer. However, Bulow and Klemperer (forthcoming) show how to use the mathematics of affiliation to address this issue too; in our model, even if firms learn different information about the consumers, this makes the market more competitive. In other words, a quick application of Milgrom and Weber's (1982a) analysis suggests that the "loss of privacy" caused by 3G and the internet is actually *good* for consumers.

Of course, having been cautious about the practical significance of affiliation in auction design, we should also be cautious about asserting that Bulow and Klemperer's argument shows that 3G is not as valuable to firms as some people once thought.[63] However, our model suggests a possibility which needs further study—including considering any empirical evidence and the plausibility of the intuitions—to confirm or disconfirm. Moreover, it certainly demonstrates that just because firms learn more about consumers, it does not follow that they can exploit them better—just as the RET refutes any simple presumption that one form of auction is always the most profitable. Our analysis therefore shows that firms' learning has other effects in addition to the very obvious one that firms can price-discriminate more effectively, and it helps us to see what these effects are[64]—we can then consider further whether these effects are plausibly significant. It also provides a structure which suggests

[61] The US Federal Trade Commission has held hearings on this issue, and the European Commission is currently studying it. Amazon has admitted charging different prices to different consumers.

[62] Thisse and Vives (1988), Ulph and Vulkan (2001), and Esteves (forthcoming), for example, have developed similar results.

[63] Of course, there are more important reasons why 3G is no longer thought as valuable as it once was (see section 5.5).

[64] In this case, while a firm may raise prices against consumers who particularly value its product, in a competitive environment it will also lower prices to other consumers who like it less—and other firms will then have to respond.

what other factors not in the simplest model might in fact be important, and might perhaps yield the originally hypothesized result.[65] And it very quickly and efficiently yields results that provide a good starting point for such further analysis.

Bulow and Klemperer pursue these issues in the context of this specific application. Chapter 2 considers a range of other applications, including some that at first glance seem quite distant from auctions. The moral is that the "received auction theory" *is* of great value in developing our understanding of practical issues. But it needs to be used in conjunction with developing intuition and gathering empirical evidence to check its applicability to specific situations.

4.7 CONCLUSION

This chapter is *not* attacking the value of economic theory. I have argued that elementary economic theory is essential to successful economic policy. Furthermore, the methods of thinking that undergraduate economics teaches are very valuable, for example, in understanding the important distinction between Hong Kong's two superficially similar auction designs (the one proposed and the one actually implemented). I have focused on examples from auctions, but the more I have been involved in public policy (for example, as a UK Competition Commissioner), the more I have been impressed by the importance of elementary undergraduate economics.

Nor is this chapter intended as an attack on modern, or sophisticated, or graduate economics. True, the emphasis of some graduate courses is misleading, and the relative importance of different parts of the theory is not always well understood, but almost all of it is useful when appropriately applied; it is *not* true that all economic problems can be tackled using undergraduate economics alone.[66]

Policy errors are also less likely when expertise is not too narrowly focused in one subdiscipline—for example, auction designers should remember their industrial economics and political economy (at least) in addition to pure auction theory.

---

[65] For example, the analysis shows that even though it may be no bad thing for consumers if different firms learn different pieces of information about them, the result depends on firms learning the same amount of information about any given consumer. It probably is costly for a consumer to "lose his privacy" to only one firm, just as having asymmetrically informed bidders may be a bad thing for an auctioneer. Furthermore, even when firms learn the same amount of information about consumers' tastes, this information may sometimes lead to inefficient price-discrimination which reduces total welfare, in which case consumers may be made worse off even though firms' profits are lowered, just as inefficient auctions may be bad for both auctioneers and bidders. Learning information may also affect firms' abilities to collude, and the ease of new entry.

[66] Furthermore, it is often only the process of thinking through the sophisticated graduate theory that puts the elementary undergraduate theory in proper perspective.

While advanced theory can be misapplied, the correct answer is not to shy away from it, but rather to develop it further to bring in the important issues that have been omitted. It may sometimes be true that "a little bit too much economics is a dangerous thing", but it is surely also true that a great deal of economic knowledge is best of all. Moreover auction theory also illustrates that when a subdiscipline of economics becomes more widely used in practical policy making, its development becomes more heavily influenced by the practical problems that really matter. Like a rapidly growing bush, theory may sometimes sprout and develop in unhelpful directions, but when pruned with the shears of practical experience it will quickly bear fruit!

Furthermore, advanced economic theory is of practical importance in developing our economic understanding of the world, even when it cannot be directly applied to an immediate practical problem. To recapitulate only the incomplete list of its merits that was illustrated by our example in section 4.6, it refutes over-simple arguments, makes precise and quantifies other arguments, allows us to see the relationship between superficially unconnected problems, organizes our ideas, brings out the important features of problems, shows possibilities, and quickly develops general results which, even when they are not final answers, provide good starting points for further analysis.

Nevertheless, the main lesson of this chapter is that the blinkered use of economic theory can be dangerous. Policy advisers need to learn from Marshall's example to beware of the wider context, anticipate political pressures, and, above all, remember that the most sophisticated theory may not be the most relevant.

Case Study:
The "3G" Mobile-Phone Auctions

CHAPTER FIVE

Overview of the European Auctions*

There were enormous differences in the revenues from the European "third generation" ("3G", or "UMTS") mobile-phone license auctions, from 20 euros per capita in Switzerland to 650 euros per capita in the United Kingdom, though the values of the licenses sold were similar. Poor auction designs in some countries facilitated collusion between firms and failed to attract entrants. The sequencing of the auctions was also crucial. We discuss the auctions in the United Kingdom, Netherlands, Germany, Italy, Austria, Switzerland, Belgium, Greece, and Denmark.

5.1 INTRODUCTION

The 2000–2001 European auctions of "third generation" (3G) mobile tele-communication (or UMTS) licenses were some of the largest in history. But table 5.1 shows that although the auctions cumulatively raised over \$100 billion (or over 1.5 percent of GDP) there was enormous variation between countries.[1] This chapter discusses why.

The blocks of spectrum sold were very similar in the different countries, and most analysts assumed a roughly constant per capita value across Western Europe. Smaller countries were said to be worth a little less, centrally located countries were worth a little more (because of the possibilities of expansion to neighbors, and cost savings from sharing fixed costs with them), and richer countries were, of course, worth more.[2] So the last two effects favor Switzerland, for example, and none of this can explain much of the discrepancies in prices.

The dates of the auctions mattered more, since market sentiment towards 3G cooled dramatically over the period of the auctions. For example, analysts'

* This chapter was originally published under the title "How (Not) to Run Auctions: the European 3G Telecom Auctions", in the *European Economic Review* 2002, 46, 829–845. (It is also reprinted in *Spectrum Auctions and Competition in Telecommunications*, Illing, G. and Klüh, U. (eds.), MIT Press, 2004.) I am very grateful to the referees and to many colleagues including Bruno Bosco, Jeremy Bulow, Tim Harford, Paul Hofer, Emiel Maasland, Roland Meeks, Margaret Meyer, David Salant, Tommaso Valletti, Mark Williams, and especially Marco Pagnozzi, for helpful advice on this chapter.

[1] Other major European countries used "beauty contest" administrative procedures, with generally dismal results (Klemperer, 2000c).

[2] Other issues affecting license values were population densities, regulatory regimes, and the coverage requirements imposed on the licenses.

TABLE 5.1
Revenues (in euros per capita) from European 3G Mobile Spectrum Auctions

	Year 2000		*Year 2001*
Austria	100	Belgium	45
Germany	615	Denmark	95
Italy	240	Greece	45
Netherlands	170		
Switzerland	20		
United Kingdom	650		

estimates of the proceeds from the Swiss auction fell from as high as 1000 euros per capita after the UK auction was held, to 400–600 euros per capita in the week before the Swiss auction was due to begin—but this was still a very far cry from the actual outcome of 20 euros per capita, as was underlined by the enthusiasm with which the lucky winners greeted the Swiss result.

Probably the bidders' valuations of the licenses at the dates of the auctions should have implied proceeds above 300 euros per capita in all the year 2000 auctions (see section 5.5). The lower revenues in the year 2001 auctions can be explained by changed valuations (and Denmark should be counted a success). (See figure 7.1 and section 7.4.) But much of the variation in the year 2000 outcomes is due to flawed auction designs.

5.2 WHAT REALLY MATTERS IN AUCTION DESIGN?

Good auction design is really good undergraduate industrial organization; the two issues that really matter are attracting entry and preventing collusion.[3]

An important consequence is that choosing an *ascending auction*[4] is often a mistake for an auctioneer. Ascending auctions allow bidders to use the early rounds to signal to each other how they might "collusively" divide the spoils and, if necessary, use later rounds to punish any rivals who fail to cooperate. Ascending auctions can also deter entry into the bidding since a weaker potential bidder knows that a stronger bidder can always rebid to top any bid he makes.

[3] See Klemperer (2000b) and chapters 3 and 4. By contrast, a graduate knowledge of modern auction theory is at best of lesser importance and at worst distracting from the main concerns (see chapter 4).

[4] An ascending auction is the kind of auction typically used to sell an art object or antique. The price starts low and competing bidders raise the price until nobody is prepared to bid any higher, and the final bidder wins the prize at the final price he bid. Mobile-phone licenses are often sold in *simultaneous* ascending auctions which are much the same except that several licenses are sold at the same time with the price rising on each of them independently, and none of the licenses is finally sold until no one wishes to bid again on any of them.

By contrast, a (first-price) *sealed-bid auction*[5] provides no opportunity for either signaling or punishment to support collusion. Furthermore, entry is promoted because a weaker bidder knows he has a better chance of victory. (A stronger bidder does not know how much he needs to bid to win, and does not want to bid too much because he wants to make a good profit when he does win, so the weaker bidder might win at a price that the stronger bidder would have been willing to bid, but did not.)

Of course, sealed-bid auctions are not perfect either. The biggest disadvantage of the sealed-bid auction is the flip-side of one of its advantages—because it allows bidders with lower values to sometimes beat opponents with higher values (and so encourages entry) it is more likely to lead to inefficient outcomes than is an ascending auction.[6] So an auction's design must be tailored both to its environment and to the designer's objectives.[7] Auction design is not "one size fits all".

Klemperer (2000b) provided a detailed development of these arguments. The European 3G auctions subsequently illustrated their validity.[8]

5.3 The Year 2000 Simple Ascending Auctions: the United Kingdom, Netherlands, Italy, and Switzerland

5.3.1 The UK Auction (March–April 2000)[9]

The United Kingdom ran the world's first 3G auction. It originally planned to sell just four licenses. The problem we faced was that there were also exactly four incumbent "2G" mobile-phone operators who had the advantages over

---

[5] In a first-price sealed-bid auction every bidder makes a single "best-and-final" bid, and the winner pays the price he bid.

[6] Of course it is not necessarily socially inefficient to allocate a license to a bidder with a lower value, for example, if that bidder is a new entrant who will increase competition and hence consumer and social welfare.

Allowing resale is not a perfect substitute for an efficient initial allocation, because resale does not resolve all inefficiencies (Cai, 2000; Myerson and Satterthwaite, 1983; Cramton, Gibbons, and Klemperer, 1987).

[7] We assume governments auctioning spectrum licenses care both about efficiency and revenue, because of the substantial deadweight losses of raising government funds by alternative means. (Typical estimates are that deadweight losses are between 17 and 56 cents for every extra $1 raised in taxes (Ballard, Shoven, and Whalley, 1985).) The United Kingdom and Switzerland, at least, were explicit that revenue mattered even though efficiency was the main objective (see section 6.3; Wolfstetter, 2003).

[8] Klemperer (2000b) was revised as chapter 3. It also discusses applications to auctions of commodities other than spectrum.

[9] I was the principal auction theorist advising the Radiocommunications Agency which designed and ran the UK auction. Ken Binmore led the team and supervised experiments testing the proposed designs. Other academic advisors included Tilman Börgers, Jeremy Bulow, Philippe Jehiel, and Joe Swierzbinski.

any other bidders of existing 2G brand names and customer bases to exploit, and lower costs of building 3G networks (because of the ability to piggyback on their 2G infrastructure). We were therefore very concerned that an ascending auction might deter other firms from bidding strongly, or even from entering the auction at all. So the government planned to run a hybrid of the ascending ("English") and sealed-bid ("Dutch") auctions, what we called an "Anglo-Dutch" auction. An ascending auction would have continued until just five bidders remained, after which the five survivors would have made sealed bids (required to be no lower than the current price level) for the four licenses.[10] The idea was that the sealed-bid stage would induce some uncertainty about which four of the five "finalists" would win, and entrants would be attracted by the knowledge that they had a chance to make it to the final stage. So the sealed-bid stage would attract entry and so also raise revenue, while the ascending stage would mean less loss of efficiency than might result from a pure sealed-bid auction. The sealed-bid stage would also make collusion harder (see chapters 3 and 4). The design performed extremely well in laboratory experiments.

However, when it became possible to sell five licenses, a straightforward ascending auction made more sense. Because no bidder was permitted to win more than one license and licenses could not be divided, there was no simple way to share the spoils, so "tacit" collusion would be hard. Even more important, the fact that at least one license had to go to a new entrant was a sufficient carrot to attract new entrants. In this respect, it was also crucial that the United Kingdom was the first in the world to auction the 3G spectrum so that it was very unclear which new entrant(s) might be successful, and this made it possible to persuade a large number to play the game (see section 5.7). Going to market first was a deliberate strategy of the UK auction team,[11] and the fact that planning had begun in 1997 for a 2000 auction also meant that there was time for a sustained (and very successful) marketing campaign to attract entrants.

So the problems of collusion and entry deterrence emphasized in section 5.2 were minimal in the UK context, and efficiency considerations pointed towards an ascending design.[12]

Therefore a version of an ascending auction was actually used, and was widely judged a success; nine new entrants bid strongly against the incumbents, creating intense competition and record-breaking revenues of 39 billion euros ($34 billion). For a full account of the auction process, see chapter 6.

---

[10] All four winners would pay the fourth-highest sealed bid and, since the licenses were not quite identical, a final simultaneous ascending stage would follow to allocate the licenses more efficiently among the winners (see sections 3.5.3 and 6.5.1).

[11] We deliberately maintained this strategy even when the complications engendered by the Vodafone-Mannesman takeover battle led many to suggest that the UK auction be postponed.

[12] In particular, the five licenses were of very unequal sizes. A sealed-bid component to the design might have resulted in an inefficient allocation of licenses among winners.

5.3.2 The Netherlands Auction (July 2000)

The Netherlands' blunder was to follow the actual British design when they had five incumbent operators and five licenses. The equal numbers of incumbents and licenses created exactly the situation in which it could be predicted that very few entrants would bother to show up to an ascending auction. Indeed Klemperer (2000b), quoted in the Dutch press prior to the auction, and Maasland (2000) did predict exactly this.

Recognizing their weak positions, the strongest potential new entrants made deals with incumbents, and Netherlands competition policy was as dysfunctional as its auction design, allowing firms such as Deutsche Telekom, DoCoMo, and Hutchison, who were all strong established players in other markets than the Netherlands, to partner with the local incumbents.[13]

In the end just one weak entrant (Versatel) competed with the incumbents, and stopped bidding after receiving a letter from an incumbent (Telfort) threatening legal action for damages if Versatel continued to bid.[14] Although Versatel complained to the government, the government took no action, perhaps because excluding Telfort would have ended the auction immediately, and it might have been hard to impose a meaningful fine. (Hundreds of millions or even billions of euros would have been required.) The result was that the auction raised less than 3 billion euros rather than the almost 10 billion euros the Dutch government had forecast based on the UK experience.[15]

A version of the Anglo-Dutch design would surely have worked better. There are reasons to believe Versatel would have bid higher in the sealed-bid stage than the price at which it quit the ascending auction. And of course the fear of this would have made the incumbents bid higher. Furthermore, the sealed-bid stage would have given weaker bidders a chance (a "hope and dream" in the words of one frustrated potential entrant) which might have attracted more bidders and discouraged the joint bidding. Most likely the

[13] A slightly different view is that there may not initially have been a problem because one of the incumbents (Ben) was weak. But after Ben strengthened its hand by joining with Deutsche Telekom there was definitely the same number of strong bidders as licenses, and no hope for entrants in an ascending auction. This view places more of the blame for the auction's failure on weak anti-trust policy, although the ascending design increased the incentive to joint venture (see section 5.3.4).

[14] Telfort claimed Versatel "believes that its bids will always be surpassed by bids of the other participants in the auction" so it "must be that Versatel is attempting to either raise its competitors' costs or to get access to their 2G or future 3G networks", and said it "will hold Versatel liable for all damages as a result of this" (see van Damme, 2002).

[15] The auction's problems were aggravated by the government's belief that it could not legally set binding minimum prices. The rules therefore specified that lots that received no bids at the beginning of the auction would have their minimum prices reduced. Since bidders were permitted to sit out some rounds of bidding, all but one did this at the start of the auction driving the minimum prices down towards zero and making the government look ridiculous. (Starting the prices at zero would have been functionally equivalent and reduced political embarrassment.) Setting a binding reserve price based on the information revealed by the UK auction would clearly have improved the outcome.

incumbents would still have been the winners, but the revenues would have been much closer to the UK levels that the government had predicted.

Six months later the Dutch parliament began an investigation into the entire auction process.

5.3.3 The Italian Auction (October 2000)

The Italian government thought it had learned from the Netherlands fiasco. It also chose roughly the UK design, with the additional rule that if there were not more "serious" bidders (as tested by various prequalification conditions) than licenses, then the number of licenses could (and probably would) be reduced. At first glance this seemed a clever way to avoid an embarrassingly uncompetitive auction à la Netherlands, but (as I and others argued) the plan was badly flawed. It would be "putting the cart before the horse" to withdraw a license and so create an unnecessarily concentrated mobile-phone market just in order to make an auction look good. And the Netherlands auction had anyway made it clear that guaranteeing just one more bidder than license does not guarantee that an ascending auction will be competitive!

By the time of the Italian sale the situation was dramatically different from the one the United Kingdom had faced. Most importantly, firms had learned from the earlier auctions who were the strongest bidders, and hence the likely winners, at least in an ascending auction. So weak bidders would not show up or would bid jointly in such an auction (see section 5.7), and the number of entrants would be much lower than the 13 who had entered the UK auction.[16] Furthermore, an ascending auction makes collusive or predatory behavior much easier if the number of contestants is low (see chapters 3 and 4). An ascending auction was therefore a much riskier proposition than for the United Kingdom.

In the event only six bidders entered the auction to compete for five licenses and one (Blu) then quit after less than two days of bidding and only just above the reserve price.[17] Although this price was not as absurdly low as in some other countries, it still did not seem to have been set using the information from the UK and German auctions. So the result was per capita revenues below 40 percent of the UK level, or less than 14 billion euros instead of the more than 25 billion euros that the government had estimated.

While the precise nature of the Italian disaster could not have been predicted, it was clear in advance that the design was not robust. Although

[16] Two losers in the UK auction (Sonera and Telefonica) formed a joint venture and several weak bidders quit the auction process altogether. Curiously, the Italian government also eliminated two weak bidders prior to the main auction in a "beauty contest" phase.

[17] Government officials claimed there had been "collusion" by which Blu entered simply to avoid invoking the rule reducing the number of licenses, thus allowing every other bidder to win a cheap license. But an investigation found no evidence. Blu was a joint venture between British Telecom and Italian-based firms whose main business was not in telecoms, and perhaps they were unable to agree terms for competing seriously.

the reasons why attracting entry was hard were a little different from the Netherlands, the implication was the same—a sealed-bid or Anglo-Dutch design would have performed better.[18]

5.3.4 The Swiss Auction (November/December 2000)

Switzerland again copied the UK design and achieved the most embarrassing result of all. The Swiss ran an ascending auction for four licenses, and attracted considerable initial interest from potential bidders. But just as in Italy weaker bidders were put off by the auction form—at least one company hired bidding consultants and then gave up after learning that the ascending-bidding rules would give the company very little chance against stronger rivals. And the government permitted last-minute joint-bidding agree-ments—essentially officially sanctioned collusion—so the field shrank from nine bidders to just four (!) in the week before the auction was due to begin. Unfortunately the reserve price had been set ludicrously low given the infor-mation available from the preceding European 3G auctions. The government postponed the auction for a month while it tried to change the rules, but this was furiously opposed by the remaining bidders who successfully argued that it was legally obliged to stick to the original rules.[19] So the bidders had just to pay the reserve price—one-thirtieth per capita of the UK and German prices, and one-fiftieth of what the government had once hoped for.[20]

By contrast, in a sealed-bid (or Anglo-Dutch) design joint bidding is less attractive because if strong firms bid jointly they increase the opportunity for weaker competitors, so may simply attract other firms into the bidding. For example, Deutsche Telekom or Hutchison who had both won licenses in Germany, Austria, Netherlands, United Kingdom, and elsewhere, and who had quit the Swiss auction just one week earlier, might perhaps have re-entered a sealed-bid contest.[21] So strong firms would have been more likely to bid independently in a sealed-bid auction, and Switzerland might have had a much more competitive auction.

[18] Note that firms in a sealed-bid auction want their rivals to think them weak, so other bidders would probably not have gambled on Blu being genuinely weak. Even in the ascending auction they seemed surprised when Blu quit at such a low price. And, of course, in a sealed-bid contest Blu might have bid more, or other firms might have entered. The two weak bidders that the Italian government eliminated prior to the auction (note 16) might also have scared the stronger bidders into more aggressive bidding if they had been permitted to compete in a sealed-bid contest.

[19] By contrast, the United Kingdom retained the right to cancel its auction in circumstances like these. This also reduced the incentive to joint ventures in the United Kingdom.

[20] Actually the auction yielded 2.5 percent more than the reserve price because slight differences between the licenses led to a little competition for the best license.

[21] Although there were also rumors (investigated by the regulator) that Deutsche Telekom "collusively" agreed not to participate in the auction in return for subsequently being able to buy in to one of the winners.

5.4 THE YEAR 2000 "VARIABLE-PRIZE" ASCENDING AUCTIONS: GERMANY AND AUSTRIA

5.4.1 The German Auction (July–August 2000)

The Germans conformed to national habits (or at least to British stereotypes of them) by choosing a more complex design: Germany auctioned twelve blocks of spectrum from which bidders could create licenses of either two or three blocks, for example, four firms could win large three-block licenses or six firms could win smaller two-block licenses. This contrasted with the auctions discussed previously in which all the licenses were of predetermined (though not always identical) sizes. As always, firms could win at most one license each. The twelve blocks were sold by a simultaneous ascending auction, much like the auctions discussed previously.

The point of the design was to let the number of winners be determined by the bidders who might have information unavailable to the government about, for example, the engineering advantages of large versus small licenses. But such an auction's outcome is driven by bidders' profits, not by consumers' or social welfare. Klemperer (2000b), Jehiel and Moldovanu (2001b), and section 3.4.5 discuss the different distortions that can result. Since the bidding in the British auction had already revealed a lot about bidders' relative valuations of different licenses,[22] it would have been wiser to fix the number of licenses in advance.[23]

The auction also proved vulnerable to collusion and entry problems: only seven bidders participated. (The entry of weaker bidders was perhaps discouraged by the ascending design, as in other auctions after the UK auction, see section 5.7.) Early on, one bidder (MobilCom) made what looked like a collusive offer to another (Debitel), telling a newspaper that "should [Debitel] fail to secure a license [it could] become a 'virtual network operator' using MobilCom's network while saving on the cost of the license" (*Financial Times*, 2 August 2000, p. 28). Shares in Debitel rose 12 percent in response

[22] The United Kingdom auctioned two large (roughly three-block) and three small (roughly two-block) licenses, and the bidding showed that the strongest new entrants, and probably also the two smaller incumbents, valued small licenses almost as much as large ones, but the two larger incumbents valued large licenses considerably more than small ones, so five or six winners was probably socially correct in the United Kingdom. The correct number also depends on the likely competitiveness of the market, which the German regulator is best qualified to judge for Germany.

[23] Not only were consumers' interests unrepresented in the choice of the number of winners, but the auction's complexity generated other potential problems. A bidder might have stayed in the auction in the hope of being one of five winners, but suddenly found itself one of six winners, and been quite unhappy and even tried to default. Also, the possibility that the auction would end with a bidder being the high bidder on just one block, in which case the block would be re-auctioned, created both considerable uncertainty for bidders and the possibility of an inefficient allocation, since the price in the re-auction could be very different from that in the original auction. The government was lucky that these problems did not arise.

to the remarks which, if taken literally, would be similar to the offer of a side payment for quitting the auction. But, as in the Netherlands case, and probably for similar reasons, the government did not punish MobilCom; in particular, excluding MobilCom would have risked ending the auction almost immediately when the price level was about 3 percent of what the auction finally achieved.[24]

Although Debitel did not quit immediately, MobilCom's suggestion might have made dropping out of the auction seem less unattractive, and Debitel did stop bidding at a relatively low level—just 55 percent of the per capita revenue achieved by the UK auction. There were then two natural outcomes, depending on the strategies followed by the two dominant incumbents, Deutsche Telekom and Vodafone-Mannesman, each of whom had about 40 percent of the existing German mobile market. Either these dominant firms could raise the price to force the weaker firms among the remaining six to quit, which would yield high revenue for the government but a concentrated industry. Or they could lead all six remaining firms to tacitly "collude" to reduce their demands to two blocks each, thus ending the auction quickly and giving the government a lowish revenue but a more competitive industry. (A problem with the German approach of auctioning many small blocks is that it is often easy for firms to see how to collusively divide them.)

Vodafone-Mannesman ended a number of its bids with the digit "6" which, it was thought, was a signal that its preference was to end the auction quickly with six remaining bidders.[25]

Surprisingly, however, Deutsche Telekom first continued to push up the price while it was well below the levels that the weaker firms had shown themselves willing to pay in the UK auction, but then ended the auction before pushing any of the weaker firms out, giving up just when the price approached the level at which the weaker players had quit the UK auction.[26] Some observers wondered whether Deutsche Telekom's objectives were affected by the fact that it was majority-owned by the German government.[27] In any case, the government ended up with both high revenues (94 percent of the UK revenues

---

[24] The government had failed to set a meaningful reserve price.

[25] According to the *Financial Times* 3 November 2000, p. 21, "One operator has privately admitted" to this kind of behavior. A weaker player behaved similarly. It is also understood that Mannesman (successfully) signaled a desire to cooperate with Deutsche Telekom in the 1999 2G auction, and Mannesman may have seen the earlier auction as setting a precedent for behavior in the 3G auction. (See sections 3.2, 4.5, and 7.5–7.8.)

[26] The two weakest bidders in Germany both quit the UK auction very close to its end. One announced in advance of the German auction that it was willing to pay the UK price.

[27] Deutsche Telekom's behavior reminds me of my father-in-law whom I often see join a queue but quit in frustration before the front of the line. Rational behavior generally involves sizing up the queue first, and then either quitting quickly (cf. ending the auction quickly) or gritting one's teeth and waiting to the end (cf. waiting for another firm to quit the auction.) In fact my father-in-law's behavior might be more rational than Deutsche Telekom's, since he might learn about the queue's behavior. Deutsche Telekom learnt nothing new after Debitel quit (except that no one else

per capita) and an unconcentrated mobile-phones market! But the fragility of the design was emphasized by the Austrian sequel.

5.4.2 The Austrian Auction (November 2000)

Austria mimicked the German design (again conforming to national habits?). Again interest in entering an ascending auction was limited, and just six firms competed for the twelve blocks available. Because the government had set a very low reserve price—just one-eighth of the per capita price that the identical German 3G auction had achieved three months earlier—there was an obvious incentive for the six firms to tacitly agree to divide up the market to obtain two lots each.[28] Any bidder who might have been inclined to compete for a third unit knew he would have to push the price up a very long way to drive out another bidder (and he would then have to pay this high price on all three units). So the bidding stopped very soon after starting at the reserve price. It is rumored that the bidding only lasted the few rounds it did in order to create some public perception of genuine competition and reduce the risk of the government changing the rules. The final price was less than one-sixth of the per capita revenue raised in the United Kingdom and Germany, and the only reason that Austria did any better than Switzerland was that its reserve price was not quite so ridiculously low.

was quitting), although it might have felt pressured by the stock market response to the climbing auction prices.

(Put more technically, the cost to Deutsche Telekom of allowing the price to rise a small bid increment, Δ, before ending the auction approximated 2Δ, while the benefit was the probability of a weaker bidder quitting in the interval Δ times the value of that outcome. So it cannot have maximized Deutsche Telekom's expected profits for Deutsche Telekom to end the auction when the probability of a weaker bidder quitting in the next increment was increasing—as it surely was. Grimm, Riedel, and Wolfstetter (2002) argue the behavior may have been rational, but they use a model that abstracts from this issue, see sections 7.5 and 7.6.)

Given that Deutsche Telekom had pushed up the price so far, should Vodafone-Mannesman now have changed its strategy and continued pushing the price up further? Not if it retained pessimistic views about the cost of driving out a weaker firm. Furthermore, if Vodafone-Mannesman, only, had successfully continued to demand three blocks and driven a weaker bidder out, the rules would then have required the re-auction of a block (see note 23) with unpredictable results, and Deutsche Telekom might have ended up with three blocks at a much lower price than Vodafone-Mannesman, an outcome which Vodafone-Mannesman's management probably wished to avoid. (Grimm, Riedel, and Wolfstetter (2002) also abstract from this concern.) In any case, Vodafone-Mannesman cooperated with Deutsche Telekom in ending the auction.

See also sections 4.5 and 7.5–7.8.

[28] The agreement may not have been completely tacit. In the week before the auction, the largest incumbent, Telekom Austria, was reported as saying it "would be satisfied with just two of the 12 blocks of frequency on offer and if the [five other bidders] behaved similarly, 'it should be possible to get the frequencies on sensible terms'... but that it would bid for a third block if one of its rivals did" (*Reuters* 31 October 2000, *Austrian UMTS Auction Unlikely to Scale Peaks*). If taken literally, this could be interpreted as both offering a "collusive" deal, and threatening "punishment" if its rivals failed to accept the offer.

5.5 BIDDERS' VALUATIONS OF LICENSES

The available evidence about firms' and the wider market's valuations of the licenses sold in the year 2000 auctions suggests revenues could probably have been in the range of 400–650 euros per capita, and certainly above 300 euros per capita, in all these countries.

The Netherlands government cancelled its July bond issue in anticipation of receiving over 600 euros per capita, while the Italian government expected around 450, and the Swiss telecom regulator predicted revenues of around 400 euros per capita just five days before the auction. Analysts' estimates were consistent with these numbers, or higher, right up to the auction in Italy and Switzerland, and until a month before the Netherlands and Austrian auctions.[29]

It is also clear that the winners of all these four "failed" auctions were delighted—some reports said "euphoric"— about the outcomes. Some non-winners also valued the licenses at higher prices than the winners paid, but were deterred by the auction designs. And when the denouement of the Swiss auction became clear and the government tried to revise the rules, a winner (Swisscom) threatened legal action to preserve the status quo.[30]

Meeks (2001) studies the jumps in Swisscom's share price when the number of bidders in the Swiss auction fell from five to four (for four licenses, thus crippling the auction), and again when the Swiss government dropped its attempt to rewrite the rules. The share-price changes are highly statistically significant and, controlling for general market movements, correspond to the market expecting that bidders would pay several hundred euros per capita less in the auction than was earlier anticipated.[31]

---

[29] Later estimates for Austria and the Netherlands reflected these auctions' obvious design flaws.

[30] Even in the United Kingdom where the high revenues took commentators by surprise, several losing bidders seem to have secured funding in advance of the auction to levels that implied revenues of 300 euros per capita (and all the losers bid at least that far), one winner claimed to have predicted the final price to within 10 percent, a second winner was said to have guessed the final price to within 20 percent, and another winner resold a fraction of its license at a profit shortly after the auction. And before the UK bidding had gone very high, a new entrant in Germany announced a willingness to pay up to a price that would imply proceeds of around 660 euros per head from the German auction.

Furthermore Cable, Henley, and Holland (2002) analyze share price movements around the UK auction and argue that the market was neither surprised by the prices paid in the United Kingdom (the evidence is from movements of the share prices of the incumbents, whose winning was not news, but whose payments were news) nor felt that the winners overpaid (the evidence comes from the share prices of entrants whose winning or losing was news).

[31] The excess returns beyond general European telecom and Swiss market movements correspond to 570 euros per head at the first event and (after intermediate ups and downs) 190 euros per head at the second event. A 95 percent confidence interval is ±320 euros per head so the first event, at least, suggests a change of at least 250 euros per head in the expected revenues from the auction hence that expected revenues from the auction had been (well) over 250 euros per head.

However, perceptions of the values of 3G licenses did fall dramatically over the course of the auctions. For example, some analysts marked down expectations of the Swiss proceeds from 1000 euros per capita to 400–600 euros per capita between the end of the UK auction and the planned beginning of the Swiss auction (the last of the year 2000 auctions). License values fell even further after the Swiss auction.

In part valuations were caught up in what now seems to have been a dotcom and technology bubble. The Dow Jones European telecom stock price index fell by over one-third between the UK and Swiss auctions, and then fell even more precipitously by almost another 50 percent—to less than one-third its level during the UK auction—by the time of the Danish auction. In part there were a number of negative "shocks" about both the development of the 3G technology itself, and likely consumer interest in it. And the values are highly leveraged since they reflect the difference between the (large) expected revenues and the (also large) expected costs of developing the required network infrastructures.[32] So a small reduction in expected revenues has a proportionally much larger effect on license values. Furthermore the option values of licenses are not necessarily high since the licenses come with "roll-out" investment requirements attached to them.

In 2001, valuations collapsed.[33] Typical analysts' estimates prior to all the year 2001 auctions were around one-tenth of the levels predicted the year before, or about 50 euros per capita.

5.6 THE YEAR 2001 AUCTIONS

5.6.1 The Belgian and Greek Auctions (March and July 2001)

Not only were valuations low by Spring 2001, but Belgium and Greece seemed particularly unattractive to new entrants. In Belgium a very dominant incumbent (Belgacom's Proximus) had two-thirds of the existing mobile market and was substantially owned, and many people thought favored, by the state. Greece is not a rich country. So probably little more could be done in these countries than set an appropriate reserve price to the incumbent operators who had established second-generation customer bases and therefore still valued 3G.

Both countries held auctions for four licenses—and in each case attracted only the three incumbents, who therefore obtained licenses at the reserve prices which yielded about 45 euros per capita in each case.

---

[32] The costs of building infrastructure were estimated to be far more than was paid for licenses.

[33] The collapse seems to have been gradual. The French beauty contest in late January 2001 suggested valuations were still one-third to one-half the previous summer's levels. (Two firms agreed to pay the French government a price corresponding to total proceeds of 330 euros per capita, while others probably valued licenses this highly but refused to pay so much in the hope of negotiating a lower price.)

It is very hard to argue plausibly that an auction design deterred much entry when a license goes unsold,[34] and there is also no obvious reason to criticize the reserve prices that these governments chose. Indeed their auctions yielded more than twice the per capita revenue of the Swiss farce, even though, as discussed, their timing was much less propitious and their markets are much less profitable.[35]

5.6.2 The Danish Auction (September 2001)

The Danes, who ran the last of the western European auctions, were in a particularly tricky position. Not only were valuations still very low,[36] but Denmark planned to sell the same number of licenses (four) as it had incumbent operators—exactly the situation that the Netherlands had fumbled so spectacularly. But the Danish designers had in fact read Klemperer (2000b), and they took its arguments seriously. Denmark chose a sealed-bid auction to give weaker bidders a chance of winning, in the hope both of attracting new entrants and of scaring the incumbent operators into making higher bids.[37]

It was a resounding success, attracting a serious bid from a new entrant and shocking analysts with revenues of 95 euros per capita, or almost double most expectations.[38-40]

---

[34] Furthermore, although the Belgians just copied the UK design, the Greek rules made the payment terms much easier (effectively lowering the reserve price) if a fourth bidder appeared—so the government was willing to sacrifice revenue to attract an additional entrant and create a more competitive market for 3G services. And if five or more bidders had appeared, the Greek auction would have used sealed bids—making entry yet more attractive.

[35] In particular, Greece's GDP per head is less than one-third of Switzerland's, and its neighbors—Albania, Macedonia, Bulgaria, Turkey—do not quite stack up against Switzerland's—Germany, France, Austria, Italy (and of course Liechtenstein)—or make it a key piece of the European puzzle.

[36] In a defining moment in the 3G process, shortly before the Danish auction, a new entrant in Norway (Sonera) handed the license it had won in the previous year's beauty contest back to the government for free, completely writing off its investment. Admittedly Norway is an unattractive market and the licensees must pay annual fees but "In spite of Sonera splashing out 4 billion euros on licenses, most analysts now value them at zero" (*Financial Times* 11/12 August 2001, p.1).

[37] The designers saw little point in running an Anglo-Dutch auction, since the chance of attracting many new entrants was very tiny in the Danish context, and with just one new entrant (the actual outcome) a sealed-bid auction is equivalent. The auction was a sealed-bid auction in which all bidders paid the fourth-highest bid (and only this bid was revealed), and the government pre-committed to keeping the number of bidders secret in the hope of scaring better bids from the incumbents even if no new entrant actually bid.

[38] Some semi-formal support for our views about the relative successes of different auctions is provided by a simple OLS regression of price per capita on the Dow Jones European telecom stock price index (a measure of market sentiment). The United Kingdom, Denmark, and Germany performed much better than the model predicted, while Austria, Switzerland, and the Netherlands were the worst performers. Italy also appears among the worst performers if population is also included in the regression (small countries are said to be worth less per capita). Otherwise including population, GDP per head, mobile usage, or internet usage makes little difference, as do several other natural specifications.

5.7 How Did the Sequencing Matter?

The entry and collusion problems of the later auctions were exacerbated by the very fact that they were later.

5.7.1 Learning to Play the Game

It is notable that the only successful auctions (from the seller's viewpoint) were the first of their type; there was enough time between plays of the European game for bidders to learn from the early auctions and adjust their strategies for the later ones.

The United Kingdom's successful simple ascending auction design was closely copied by the Netherlands, Italy, and Switzerland, with results that, we have seen, went from bad (Netherlands and Italy), to worse (Switzerland). The UK sale taught firms the costs of participating in a competitive auction, and they became increasingly successful at forming joint ventures that ensured the subsequent auctions were less competitive.[41]

We also saw that the German auction followed the UK and Netherlands auctions, but was a more complex ("variable-prize") ascending design. The dominant firms clearly misplayed their hands, with excellent results from the government's viewpoint. But when the Austrians copied the German design three months later, the firms had learnt to coordinate their behavior during the auction, and it was the firms that won the Austrian round.

Finally the Danes pulled off a success with a sealed-bid design. We have argued that this kind of design may prove more robust to future gaming by firms but that, of course, remains to be seen.

5.7.2 Learning Opponents' Valuations

Section 5.7.1 assumes firms need to learn because they are boundedly rational, rather than because they lack information. But firms also learn about their

---

[39] In fact the entrant was one of the winners, squeezing out an incumbent. The losing incumbent will presumably pursue 3G as a virtual network operator (the Danish government mandates licensees to rent spectrum to VNOs). So the new entrant has probably increased the competitiveness of the ultimate 3G market.

[40] At almost the same time as the Danish auction, Hong Kong also planned to sell four licenses. Hong Kong originally planned a design similar to Denmark's but the strong incumbents successfully lobbied to change to a simple ascending auction—and there were just four entrants for the four licenses, even though Hong Kong was thought to be an attractive market.

[41] And while the firms became more sophisticated, the governments became less sophisticated, leaving out safeguards that were in the UK auction (see, e.g., note 19) and using the UK design in inappropriate contexts; unlike the UK auction, which spent three years in planning and development, some subsequent auctions were rushed, last-minute affairs.

rivals, and this was critical to why the first auction, in the United Kingdom, had 13 bidders while no subsequent auction had more than seven.

Firms learnt from the UK auction whether they had any realistic chance of victory, and companies that recognized they were clearly outgunned did not want to invest their time and effort in bidding in later auctions.[42] Certainly they did not want to bid in ascending auctions which pretty much guarantee the strongest bidders will win.

Furthermore, a bidder who learnt that others' valuations were somewhat higher than its own might have figured that its best hope was to buy or lease part of a license after the auctions. In this case the bidder might have stayed out of the later auctions to keep its valuation private and so strengthen its bargaining position in the aftermarket. Again, this may be a particular problem in ascending auctions since they make losers' valuations more transparent.[43]

The elimination of some firms, and the fact that the remainder had learnt something about each other's valuations for the licenses, may both have been important factors in making bargaining between the bidders easier, facilitating the joint ventures and "collusion" that emerged in the later auctions.[44]

---

[42] The effects in this subsection might be mitigated if firms recognized that their opponents might bid aggressively in order to persuade them not to enter subsequent auctions, although this would be a further reason for higher prices in early auctions. Pagnozzi (forthcoming) is exploring the issues in this section.

[43] With private values and straightforward bidding up to one's value, the losers' values are perfectly revealed. (Bidders who foresee this will not bid so straightforwardly—this is just another version of our point—but entering the auction may still reveal information that could be damaging later.) Managerial incentives and compensation mechanisms may also mean that resale could not easily be at a lower price than in the original auction. And tacit collusion that rewards a non-bidder with a lower resale price would also encourage non-participation (see note 21). Of course these issues are only significant when sharing a license is (privately) efficient and renting or partial resale is easy.

[44] To illustrate why a tighter distribution of beliefs about opponents' valuations facilitates bargaining, imagine two firms with privately known values for a single license, independently drawn from a distribution with lower-bound zero, and decreasing hazard rate. Then bargaining is "very hard" in the sense that the expected ex-ante joint surplus (before knowing either firm's value) from competing in an ascending auction exceeds the joint surplus from colluding to divide the prize equally at price zero. (If bidders' values, v, are independently drawn from distribution $F(v) = 1 - \exp(-\lambda v)$, that is, constant hazard rate λ, the winner's profits from an auction equals the expected distance between the values, $1/\lambda$, which equals the expected average value.)

With increasing hazard rates, bargaining is not "very hard" in this sense. For example, with values uniformly distributed on $[0, 1]$, bidders' expected joint surplus from the auction is $1/3$, but is $1/2$ from agreeing to divide the pie at a price of zero. So successful bargaining seems more likely, at least before bidders have invested to determine their own values.

But even in the latter case, bargaining is still "hard" in the sense that a bidder who knows he has the highest possible value expects the same private surplus, $1/2$, from the auction as from collusion at a price of zero. So, with even a tiny cost of negotiating, opening negotiations might be taken to be the bad signal that one's value is not very high, and—depending on the model—neither player may be willing to make the first offer. "Easy" bargaining, in this sense, requires a still tighter distribution of valuations.

5.7.3 Complementarities

Markets that were auctioned later were more valuable to those who had won earlier ones that fitted well with them in a network, and an early win also allowed a firm to influence suppliers about the development of the technology in ways that would help the firm in later markets. These "real" complementarities reinforced the learning effects discussed in section 5.7.2, and further discouraged losers of early auctions from entering later auctions, especially ascending ones.[45,46]

5.7.4 Budget Constraints

It is hard to believe that capital market constraints mean many very profitable investments are foregone. However, if some bidders faced higher financing costs than others then, as above, even a slight relative weakness could have encouraged them to quit the auction process, at least as long as ascending auctions were being used. It is certainly clear that many firms were caught by surprise by the change in market sentiment towards telecoms, and some firms faced difficulties in borrowing.

The issues in this section clearly need more careful analysis; the area seems ripe for research.[47]

5.8 CONCLUSION

A key determinant of success of the European telecom auctions was how well their designs attracted entry and discouraged collusion (as is true for most auctions; see chapters 3 and 4). The sequencing of the auctions exacerbated the entry and collusion problems.

The organizers of most of the auctions after the UK's, and of the Netherlands and Swiss auctions in particular, failed to give enough attention to attracting entry, and magnified their problems by permitting joint-bidding

---

[45] Bikhchandani (1988), Bulow and Klemperer (2002), Bulow, Huang, and Klemperer (1999), Klemperer (1998), and Klemperer and Pagnozzi (forthcoming) emphasize how small differences in bidders' valuations can have dramatic effects on prices achieved by ascending auctions.

[46] Awareness of these effects probably encouraged more aggressive bidding in the earlier auctions, further accentuating the downward trend in prices. The effects were mitigated by budget constraints.

[47] A "declining price anomaly" is often observed in the sequential auction of identical objects such as art, wine, real estate, radio transponders (Ashenfelter, 1989; Beggs and Graddy, 1997; Harford, 1998; Milgrom and Weber, 2000, and chapter 1). But the issues in sections 5.7.1 and 5.7.2 are probably more important than the explanations usually given for this. I also know no evidence of bidders colluding by taking turns to win the auctions; most likely there were too many players with different strengths and interests. And the auction in any given country was probably too large a one-off event to be treated as a single play in a repeated game of some kind in that country.

agreements prior to the auctions. The German and Austrian auctions demonstrated the vulnerability of ascending auctions to "collusive" behavior during the auctions, and there were also rumors of collusion in the ascending auctions in Italy, the Netherlands, and Switzerland. All these problems were aggravated by most later auctioneers' failure to use the information from the UK auction to set sensible reserve prices.

The auctions also showed that auction design is not "one size fits all". The ascending design that worked very well for the United Kingdom worked very badly in the Netherlands, Italy, and Switzerland because of entry problems, and this was predictable (and predicted) in advance. These other countries would clearly have done better if they had included a sealed-bid component in their auctions, as Denmark did, and as the United Kingdom would have done if entry had been a concern there.

We have emphasized the revenues generated by the different auctions because they differed so greatly. "Assigning the spectrum efficiently", interpreted roughly to mean maximizing the sum of the valuations of those awarded licenses, was most governments' main objective, but we cannot assess whether the auctions achieved this.[48] There was no obvious inefficiency, but there also seems to be no reason to believe that alternative designs (such as the Anglo-Dutch) would have been much less efficient, and they would have yielded higher revenues from some of the sales. Whether it would have been better to run a single grand European auction is beyond our scope.[49] But there was no appetite for a coordinated process at the time and, as we saw, the United Kingdom did well to steal a march on its rivals by going it alone and auctioning first.

---

[48] See Börgers and Dustmann (2002b), Plott and Salmon (forthcoming), and section 7.2.

[49] A simultaneous auction of all the continent's spectrum might have alleviated the entry problems that some countries faced, and helped companies build the particular networks of licenses that most interested them (in the actual process companies had to bid in early auctions without knowing what they would win later on). On the other hand, it would have been harder to prevent collusion. An auction for *all* radio spectrum including TV and radio, etc., might also allocate the spectrum more efficiently between different uses.

CHAPTER SIX

Designing the UK Auction*

This chapter reviews the part played by economists in organizing the British third-generation mobile-phone license auction that concluded on 27 April 2000. It raised £22.5 billion ($34 billion or 2.5 percent of GNP) and was widely described at the time as the biggest auction ever. We discuss the merits of auctions versus "beauty contests", the aims of the auction, the problems we faced, the auction designs we considered, and the mistakes that were made.

Twenty-two and a half billion pounds (34 billion dollars) is a great deal of money to raise for selling air, but that is what the British government raised in an auction for five telecom licenses.[1] The auction ran from 6 March to 27 April 2000, and was frequently described as the "biggest ever"—not since the Praetorian Guard knocked down the entire Roman Empire to Didius Julianus in AD 195 had there been an auction quite as large.[2] We led the team that advised on the design of the British auction (the "third-generation mobile spectrum license auction", or "3G auction", or "UMTS auction").[3] This chapter summarizes our experience.[4]

* This chapter was originally published under the title "The Biggest Auction Ever: The Sale of the British 3G Telecom Licences", in the *Economic Journal* 2002, 112, C74–C96. It is jointly authored with Ken Binmore. We led the academic team advising the UK government's Radiocommunications Agency, which designed and ran the UK mobile-phone license auction. The views expressed in this chapter are ours alone. Many colleagues, especially Tilman Börgers, Jeremy Bulow, Tim Harford, Margaret Meyer, Marco Pagnozzi, Carol Propper, Mark Williams, and two anonymous referees made very helpful comments. Ken Binmore gratefully acknowledges the support of the Leverhulme Foundation and the Economic and Social Research Council through the Centre for Economic Learning and Social Evolution.

[1] The exact total raised was £22,477.4 million (or about £22,477.3 million after deducting the cost of the economic consultants—primarily for programming simulations, running experiments, etc.).

[2] See Gibbon (1776). The German telecom auction subsequently raised even more in cash terms (although less per head of population) and takeover battles often reduce to a kind of auction with even higher prices.

[3] The ESRC Centre for Economic Learning and Social Evolution (ELSE) successfully tendered to the UK Radiocommunications Agency for the contract. The other economists on the team were Tilman Börgers, Jeremy Bulow, Philippe Jehiel, and Joe Swierzbinski. The laboratory work was conducted by Geoff Miller, Chris Tomlinson, and John McCarthy.

[4] Readers seeking more detail should consult the British Radiocommunications Agency website (www.spectrumauctions.gov.uk). Another useful source is the independent report of the National Audit Office (2001) on the auction, available at www.nao.gov.uk. (The NAO is "totally independent of Government" but "report(s) to Parliament on the economy, efficiency, and effectiveness [of Government] departments and other bodies"—see the NAO website.)

6.1 BACKGROUND

In 1997, when our advice was first sought, four mobile-phone companies operated in Britain using "second-generation" (2G) technology. The incumbents were Cellnet, One-2-One, Orange, and Vodafone. (British Telecom (BT), the erstwhile state-owned monopolist privatized under Mrs. Thatcher, held a 60 percent stake in Cellnet which it increased to 100 percent in 1999.) The proportion of the population using a portable phone was rising rapidly.[5] And, as in other parts of the world, the cellular telephone industry was regarded as a runaway success; the industry was set to become even more important with the introduction of the "third generation" of portable telephones that would allow high-speed data access to the internet.

How "third-generation" technology will work, and what the final products of the industry will be, remains uncertain even today. In 1997, three years before the auction, predictions were even more fluid. This was of major importance in planning for the auction, because the engineering and the commercial advice received towards the end of the planning period was very different from the advice received at the beginning of the period. It was therefore necessary to keep urging the importance of retailoring the auction design to fit the changing circumstances since, as we shall see, "one size fits all" is a very bad principle in auction design.

Economists had been advocating auctioning radio spectrum at least since Ronald Coase (1959). William Vickrey, in particular, had been pushing the use of auctions in such contexts for many years, but had been left to sing unheard for most of his career. However, the US Federal Communications Commission (FCC) eventually turned to auctioning radio spectrum for phone licenses in 1994. The FCC used the "simultaneous ascending auction" design that had first been sketched by Vickrey (1976) and whose details were independently developed by McAfee, Milgrom, and Wilson. This auction is much like a standard "ascending" auction used to sell a painting in Sotheby's or Christies,[6] except that several objects are sold at the same time, with the price rising on each of them independently, and none of the objects is finally sold until no one wishes to bid again on any of the objects.[7] The FCC auctions worked fairly well in practice (McAfee and MacMillan, 1996; Milgrom, 2004; Klemperer, 1998; although see sections 3.2 and 3.3), and the fact that $20 billion was raised in the initial series of auctions—twice the original estimate—attracted much favorable media attention.

The United Kingdom embraced auctions later than the United States, and the United Kingdom's current "second-generation" mobile-phone licenses were

[5] The number of cellular mobile phones subscribers grew from 1 million to 10 million between 1992 and 1998, and leapt to 35 million—60 percent of the population—by 2000, according to Oftel.
[6] In an ascending auction, the price starts low and competing bidders raise the price until no one is prepared to bid any higher, at which point the final bidder then wins the prize at the final price he bid.
[7] The design allows a bidder to switch his interest between objects as relative price levels change.

awarded using a "beauty contest", in which firms submitted business plans to a government committee which awarded the licenses to those candidates it judged best met a set of published criteria. But by the late 1990s, economists' arguments for the use of auctions were beginning to make headway in Britain.

6.2 AUCTIONS VS. BEAUTY CONTESTS[8]

6.2.1 Arguments for Auctions

Most importantly, a well-designed auction is the method most likely to allocate resources to those who can use them most valuably.[9] Rather than relying on government bureaucrats to assess the merits of competing firms' business plans, an auction forces businessmen to put their "money where their mouths are" when they make their bids. An auction can therefore extract and use information otherwise unavailable to the government.[10]

Secondly, the difficulty of specifying and evaluating criteria for a beauty contest[11] makes this a time-consuming and opaque process that leads to political and legal controversy, and the perception, if not the reality, of favoritism and corruption.[12] Indeed, some governments make no secret of choosing beauty contests precisely because of the possibilities for favoring their

---

[8] This section is based on Klemperer (2000c).

[9] Allowing resale is not a perfect substitute for an efficient initial allocation, because resale does not resolve all inefficiencies (Cai, 2000; Myerson and Satterthwaite, 1983; Cramton, Gibbons, and Klemperer, 1987). Milgrom (2004) argues that the resale of phone licenses has been only imperfectly efficient in the United States where it has been permitted.

[10] For example, we were advised during the auction development that one of the three smaller licenses sold was worth a little less than the other two. But the auction demonstrated otherwise. We have seen exactly the same—firms ranking licenses differently from government expectations—in other countries.

[11] Nicholas Negroponte (the technology guru who is one of the most prominent advocates of beauty contests), for example, argues that 3G licenses should be allocated to those who would guarantee the lowest prices to consumers, invest the most in infrastructure, stimulate most creativity, etc. But how can firms guarantee consumer prices for 5–20 years in the future for products that we may not yet even be able to imagine? Infrastructure investment can be costed, but will it all be useful? How can the government possibly decide who will be most creative? And how could the government monitor and enforce any commitments made by firms? How should the government penalize a firm that turns out to be insufficiently creative? What should the government's response be to a firm that is creative and develops a product with valuable unforeseen features but above the previously guaranteed price? It is hard to think of a more serious drag on innovation than prespecifying future prices for products that do not yet exist! Note that we are not arguing that the government should not specify quality criteria for the licenses, merely that these should be clearly thought out in advance (as, e.g., was the UK government's requirement that 3G licensees roll out a network covering 80 percent of the UK population by 2007).

[12] The Spanish and Swedish 3G beauty contests, for example, provoked litigation and substantial and still-continuing political debate. By contrast, several losing bidders complimented the United Kingdom on its auction process.

"national champions" over foreign firms. But such protectionism is unlikely to benefit consumers or taxpayers.

Thirdly, of course, an auction can raise staggering sums of money to support the public finances—the UK auction yielded about 2.5 percent of GNP, or enough money to build 400 new hospitals. A beauty contest, by contrast, can give away valuable assets at a fraction of what they are worth. The winners of the United Kingdom's previous "second-generation" licenses made original payments in the region of just £40,000.[13] Economists argued that those who advocated beauty contests should say how they would prefer to fund the government. Did they want higher income taxes?[14]

6.2.2 Popular Objections to Auctions

There are several common objections to auctions. They are said to be unfair to firms, to raise consumer prices, and to reduce investment. But all of these complaints are based on misperceptions.

First consider the argument that auctions are unfair to firms who are "forced to bid". It is true that incumbent mobile-phone operators might feel forced to win a new license, or see the value of their previous investments sharply reduced. But in no European 3G auction have there been fewer licenses than incumbents, and the prices of licenses were set by the marginal bidders who were therefore new entrants who had nothing to lose if they failed to win a license. And in the United Kingdom, Germany, Italy, and elsewhere, some licenses were won by companies who had no previous presence in those markets, further proving that companies who were under no pressure to compete—and would find it far harder than incumbents to exploit 3G (see section 6.4.1)—saw the risks as worth taking.[15] Of course, the companies are taking huge risks in bidding in an auction, just as, for example, firms take huge risks when they invest in developing a new aircraft, a new drug, or a Channel Tunnel. They know that they are buying into a lottery that might result in huge losses or huge gains. Although 3G's prospects look a lot less rosy a year after the auction, and many people now believe that the winners of the British 3G

[13] The operators also pay annual license fees which had risen to £300,000 per MHz by 2000–2001, or about 1 percent of the annual rental value of the spectrum implied by the UK third-generation auction prices.

[14] Martin Feldstein (1999) recently estimated that every extra $1 of income tax raised in the United States costs the economy an additional $2 in deadweight losses caused through the disincentives to earn, and the misallocation of resources to avoid taxes. True, Feldstein's estimates may be overstated—33 cents in deadweight loss would be a more typical estimate (see, e.g., Ballard, Shoven, and Whalley, 1985)—but charging companies for spectrum incurs none of these additional costs.

[15] Indeed in the UK case, one winner quickly re-sold shares of its license to two other new entrants at a profit! See section 6.7.1. Also in the United Kingdom. two incumbents, but no entrants, competed to offer £2 billion more for a larger license; no one has ever suggested that any incumbent needed a larger rather than a smaller license to protect its previous investments.

auction "paid too much", only time will tell whether their gamble was a good one. [16]

PRICE EFFECTS

The most common fear about auctions seems to be that firms' costs in an auction will be passed on to consumers in the form of higher prices. This would be at least partly true for an auction in which firms bid royalties (see section 6.4.2). But the argument is generally mistaken in an auction in which firms make once-and-for-all lump sum payments. Like any other firms, telecom companies will charge the prices that maximize their profits, independently of what the spectrum cost them in the past.

One way to explain how sunk costs work to non-economists is to imagine we are now in 2010 and the new cellular telephone services are being sold at whatever prices maximize their profits. If the government were suddenly to refund the license fees (with interest, so that it was as though the licenses had initially been given away), how would these prices change? Other things being equal, the prices would remain exactly the same, because it would be irrational for a company to lower its price below what the market will bear; the only result of the refund would be to increase the profit of the shareholders of the operating companies.

To take a more familiar example, consider housing prices. The price of new housing is no lower when the developer had the good fortune to obtain the land below its current market value (e.g., because it was obtained free through inheritance or was bought before planning permission was available) than when the developer has paid the full market value. In either case, the price is determined by the housing market at the time the new housing is sold. There is no more sense in handing out free spectrum to the telecom companies than in failing to charge developers for land in the belief that this will lead to cheaper houses.

Of course, telecom companies (and land developers) have enormous incentives to argue the opposite, because they obtain large windfall profits if they can obtain a scarce resource for free. And it is true that consumer prices can be affected (even by past lump sum payments). For example, paying auction fees could potentially create "focal points" that allow firms to tacitly coordinate on charging higher prices. Paying auction fees also makes firms poorer, so perhaps more willing to risk collusion, especially if they believe they are too poor to afford any fines. An auction will, in principle, select those firms that are better able to collude (hence are more profitable). But all these effects seem small, and certainly avoidable, with good competition policy.

---

[16] It is because entrepreneurs take such risks that caution must be exercised in taxing away their profits when things turn out well.

Much more worrying is that companies' specious arguments may fool politicians and regulators into agreeing that the auction is a reason for allowing artificially high prices.[17] If we do see higher prices in countries that ran auctions, it will probably be because of these political effects.

INVESTMENT EFFECTS

A final concern is that large auction fees may slow investment because of capital-market constraints. Of course this is theoretically possible,[18] but it seems unlikely that very many highly profitable investments are being foregone because of difficulty raising funding for them.[19] Giving licenses away to firms at discounted prices would certainly relax firms' capital-market constraints, just as any other state handouts would. There may perhaps be good grounds for subsidizing this industry, but advocates of giveaways need to explain quite a lot: Why subsidize this industry rather than others? Why subsidize the mobile-phone operators (rather than, e.g., providers of content to be transmitted over the mobile-phone networks)? Why subsidize them to this extent?

Furthermore, even a government that accepted (as the British government did not) that auctions would slow investment (or raise prices to consumers) might find it in its own national interest to run an auction, because the auction revenues accrue only to the country itself while any investment effects apply to other countries too—the fact that Telefonica's consortium spent over $7 billion on a license in Germany and almost nothing on its Spanish license is obviously not an argument for Telefonica to invest less in Germany than in Spain.[20] (In fact some commentators have suggested the opposite, arguing that internal organizational incentives will drive firms to launch their services faster in Germany to demonstrate that they can quickly recoup their auction costs.[21])

Occasionally—for example, when there are too few potential bidders, or large costs of supplying necessary information to bidders—a form of struc-

---

[17] There are some signs that this might happen in the United Kingdom and Germany. For example, Oftel (the United Kingdom's telecoms regulator) will be doing just this if it accepts operators' arguments that it should permit firms to set higher call-termination fees to "reflect" firms' sunk auction costs.

[18] For example, the "pecking order" theory of funding suggests that depleting a firm's cash by upfront payments raises the firm's cost of capital, and the finance literature is replete with examples where capital structure matters for firm efficiency (see, e.g., Wruck, 1994).

[19] In fact, by summer 2001, at least four of the five winners of the UK 3G licenses, including the new entrant, had arranged the necessary funding for their new UK networks.

[20] The Spanish government may have noticed this. It is belatedly trying to levy large fees on the winners of its beauty contest.

[21] Indeed two of the winners of the UK licenses have said that the high price they paid for the licenses in the auction encouraged them to develop 3G services faster than if the spectrum had been given away.

tured negotiations may be better.[22] However the general rule is that auctions treat firms fairly and transparently, and yield the greatest possible benefits for consumers and taxpayers.

In the autumn of 1997 therefore, the UK government asked us to help design a 3G auction.

6.3 AIMS OF THE AUCTION

Unlike some governments, the British were honest in pursuing their published aims. An originally fuzzy set of aspirations, reflecting various different interests and constrained by European Commission directives, were gradually refined into the following set of objectives:

- to assign the spectrum efficiently;
- to promote competition;
- to "realize the full economic value" (subject to the other objectives).[23]

In the event, the competition aim was addressed by permitting no bidder to hold more than one license, and auctioning the maximum number of licenses given the available spectrum and the need to make them large enough for viable businesses.

As for the other objectives, our clear instructions were that efficiency considerations were to take priority over revenue considerations.

Efficiency was understood as putting the licenses into the hands of the bidders with the best business plans. Since a bidder with a better business plan will generally value a license more,[24] this aim roughly reduces to seeking to maximize the sum of the valuations of the bidders who are awarded licenses.[25]

But how does one find out the bidders' valuations? There is no point in simply asking the bidders. If asked, each bidder will earnestly insist that his

[22] See Bulow and Klemperer (1996).

[23] In a written answer to a Parliamentary Question, Barbara Roche, then Minister for Small Firms, Trade and Industry, said "In offering through an auction licenses to use specified frequencies for the delivery of UMTS, the Government's overall aim is to secure, for the long term benefit of UK consumers and the national economy, the timely and economically advantageous development and sustained provision of UMTS services in the UK. Subject to this overall aim the Government's objectives are to (i) utilize the available UMTS spectrum with optimum efficiency; (ii) promote effective and sustainable competition for the provision of UMTS services; and (iii) subject to the above objectives, design an auction which is best judged to realize the full economic value to consumers, industry and the taxpayer of the spectrum." See *Hansard*, 18 May 1998.

[24] Of course, there are reasons why this need not be true.

[25] Note that the government was unwilling to permit resale (see section 6.4.1), but resale cannot in any case be guaranteed to achieve efficiency (see note 9). Note also that while some commentators have argued that more spectrum should have been sold off, that possibility was beyond our control: the amount of spectrum to be used for 3G licenses had been pre-determined by international treaty.

value is the highest. An auction gets around this problem by making bidders back their plans with their money. So promoting efficiency necessarily involves raising revenue which, happily, fits with the government's last objective of "realizing economic value".

In view of the £22.48 billion that the auction raised, the media expressed profound skepticism about revenue being genuinely last on the list of priorities, but the British government could obviously have made substantially more money by selling fewer licenses.[26] How much money it would have made by creating a monopoly by selling just one license beggars the imagination!

6.4 MAIN ISSUES

Our first task was to assess the economic and legal environment in which the auction would take place, and offer a menu of auction designs from which the Radiocommuncations Agency could make an initial choice.

6.4.1 The Problem of Entry

We felt strongly that questions of market structure were substantially more important than the informational issues on which orthodox auction theory focuses.[27] Events were to show that we were even more right in this judgment than we knew.

The essential structural problem in auctioning 3G telecom licenses is that the incumbents who are already operating in the 2G telecom industry enjoy a major advantage over potential new entrants, so it may be hard to persuade potential entrants to bid. Not only are the incumbents' 2G businesses complementary to 3G, but their costs of rolling out the infrastructure (radio masts and the like) necessary to operate a 3G industry are very substantially less than those of a new entrant, because they can piggyback on their 2G infrastructure.[28] Incumbents also have the advantage of established customer bases and brand-name recognition. These considerations loomed even larger in the early planning stages, because market research indicated that the more obvious potential entrants were not yet showing any great interest in the coming British

---

[26] Not only would reducing the number of licenses reduce competition in 3G services and so increase the total profits in the industry, but reducing below four licenses would exclude an incumbent operator.

[27] Jehiel and Moldovanu's (1996) and Jehiel, Moldovanu, and Stacchetti's (1996) work on "externalities" was a notable exception, as is Jehiel and Moldovanu's (2001b) recent model concerning market structure considerations inspired by the 3G auctions. See chapter 1 and Klemperer (2000a) for summaries of the extensive auctions literature.

[28] Furthermore, there is the possibility that the regulations might in some circumstances be altered so that the spectrum licensed for 2G purposes can be "refarmed" for 3G purposes (though the Government made clear that no commitments could be made on how and when refarming would be implemented).

3G industry, and so there were no good reasons for being optimistic about entry to the auction.

Our initial report therefore emphasized the importance of encouraging entry to the auction in pursuit of the aim of promoting competition. Two of the measures we suggested, allowing resale and making bidding credits available to the entrants, were ruled out for various reasons. But we were successful in advocating that the government mandate "roaming", which would allow an entrant access to the incumbents' 2G network at a regulated price.[29]

6.4.2 Royalties or Lump Sum Payments?

Payment for licenses using a royalty rather than a lump sum fee is another way of promoting entry, both because it allows the government to share the risk with an operator, and because new entrants are likely to make smaller payments for any given royalty rate, but we were unenthusiastic about using royalties. They must necessarily be levied on some genuinely observable variable, which profit is not. So they are usually based on some correlate of revenue. For example, in some American oil-tract auctions, the royalty is based on an independent metering of the oil pumped to the well-head, valued at that day's market price.

However, a royalty based on revenue corresponds to a "value added tax" and so creates deadweight losses in an oligopolistic industry such as telecoms, for exactly the same reason that a sales tax makes a monopoly or oligopoly worse. Moreover, a royalty of the form x cents per phone call corresponds to a specific tax and is even more distortionary.[30] By contrast oil has, roughly speaking, a competitive price set in the world market that is largely unaffected by any one country levying a royalty.

Royalty payments also allow bidders to default, or to attempt renegotiation if optimistic predictions of demand turn out to be mistaken. One therefore faces the risk that a buyer may treat his purchase only as an "option to buy". Many of the US spectrum auctions suffered from this kind of behavior—winners were not required to make payments upfront and some simply never paid—which caused the FCC administrative difficulty and political embarrassment.

All these problems arise when royalties are pre-set by the government. If firms bid royalties, the problems are even worse: the US Department of the Interior ran a very unsuccessful experiment with royalty-based auctions for oil-tracts about 20 years ago, in which the government fixed a relatively small

---

[29] See section 6.6.1. We were of course not alone in our concern to attract entry. Advice from Oftel and N. M. Rothschild and Sons Ltd. was also important.

[30] To see that a proportional tax (or royalty) on revenue is less distortionary than a per-unit (specific) tax, observe that the former corresponds to the sum of (i) a non-distortionary proportional tax on profits (= revenues − costs) plus (ii) a distortionary proportional tax on costs. For a given amount of tax raised, this is less distortionary than a per-unit tax. See Bulow and Klemperer (1998) for further discussion.

up-front "bonus" payment, and the companies bid percentages of their revenues. The result was that many speculators bid enormous royalty rates in order to win licenses. If the oil fields turned out to be highly productive they could make money even at the high royalty rates, but most fields were simply not developed, even when it was economically efficient to do so. (For example, a winner paying an 80 percent royalty would develop a field only if it yielded a return more than five times the production cost.)

And, of course, further distortions would be created in an oligopolistic market like telecoms if different winners paid different royalty rates.

In spite of these problems, we considered schemes in which payment would involve both royalties and a lump sum fee. However, such schemes were ruled out by various technical and other considerations and given a straight choice between royalties and lump sum fees it was clearly right to recommend the latter. Although economically efficient, this choice attracted considerable criticism from commentators unable to distinguish between the impact of a sunk cost and a variable cost on pricing decisions (see section 6.2.2).[31]

6.4.3 How Many Licenses?

We were also anxious that engineering concerns about the higher quality of service made possible by issuing large licenses should be properly balanced by an appreciation of the benefits to consumers of the increased competition made possible by issuing a larger number of smaller licenses.

Many officials are attracted by the idea pushed by incumbent firms that the "market" should decide how many licenses there should be. But this confuses two different markets; the interests of the consumers who participate in the phone market created by the auction are not represented in the auction "market" for licenses. We considered a number of possible designs in which the number and size of the licenses would be determined endogenously in the auction, but advised that an efficient allocation of licenses across bidders could not be guaranteed, and that only unacceptably complex designs would provide reasonable protection against the emergence of an anticompetitive industry.[32]

So in the end the UK government chose to auction a fixed number of licenses, permitting no bidder to win more than one license.

---

[31] With some honorable exceptions, much of the media seemed very slow in catching on to the significance of the auction, and singularly ill-informed on economic realities when they did. This was disappointing, since although we personally were not allowed to talk to the media about events in the auction while it was going on, the government put extensive effort into media briefing.

[32] We also wanted to avoid any risk of a "sorry winner" who bid rationally to maximize expected profit but ended up losing money because of the particular behavior of other bidders (see Pagnozzi, 2002). Such a sorry winner may litigate, or default, and so embarrass the government. For example, the German and Austrian 3G auctions, which determined the number of licenses within the auction, ran the risk of creating sorry winners (see, e.g., note 23 to chapter 5 and note 34 to chapter 7), even though this turned out not to be the biggest problem of these auctions (see, especially, section 5.4).

6.4.4 Legal Issues

On several occasions we had to get involved with the legal fine print.

We had to argue more than once that bids must be binding. Permitting bidders to withdraw them later would have reduced the bids to cheap talk and made a mockery of the process.

We also had to insist that any reserve price should be a clear commitment not to sell if the bidding did not meet the price. If bidders expected that the government would immediately turn around and re-auction any unsold license at a lower price, then the reserve prices would have no meaning. We won this point in the end, but reserve prices actually played little role in the auction because the information available to the government was limited so it was appropriate to set reserves very cautiously.[33]

Awkwardness in the wording of the relevant Telecommunication Act required us to develop special implementations of some of the auction formats we were proposing. While we could always find an implementation of our ideas that circumvented the problems, considerable care was sometimes required. Changing the wording of the Act would have risked delaying the auction and was probably not politically viable.

It would be easy to underestimate the difficulty of ensuring that the small print does not somehow undermine the principles of an auction design.

6.5 AUCTION DESIGNS

6.5.1 The Anglo-Dutch Design

Our preliminary analysis considered the implications of various different numbers of licenses being put up for sale. The worst case for the success of an auction was that only four licenses would be available—one for each of the four 2G incumbents. Given that the incumbents would be bidding from an advantaged position, why would a potential new entrant spend any money preparing to bid in an auction?

So when it seemed that engineering considerations made it impossible to provide more than four licenses, each of roughly equal size, we felt that our major problem was to promote entry to the auction. The design of the auction could not be expected to have the same sort of effect on entry as matters like the provision of roaming rights, but we nevertheless thought it important to do what could be done.

Where entry is a concern, an ascending-price auction is not ideal. An example of the problem was the sale of the Los Angeles license in the big American telecom auction run by the FCC. The license was acquired cheaply by the incumbent, Pacific Bell, which faced little risk in implementing its

---

[33] Reserve prices should have played a larger role in the subsequent European 3G auctions (see section 6.7.3).

widely advertised strategy of not being beaten in Los Angeles. All it had to do was to persistently make the minimum overbid if an entrant challenged, until the entrant gave up the hopeless struggle (Klemperer, 1998). Under these circumstances, the FCC were lucky that Pacific Bell faced any challenge at all.[34] For similar reasons, some recent ascending-price telecoms auctions, notably the Swiss 3G auction, have been fiascos in which there were no more bidders than licenses (see, especially, sections 4.4 and 5.3.4).[35]

Sealed-bid auctions do better at promoting entry because they give entrants a better chance of winning against strong incumbents (see, especially, chapters 3 and 4). However, sealed-bid auctions do not allow bidders to gather information on the business plans of their rivals by observing who is staying in and who is getting out as the price rises. They therefore make it impossible for bidders to refine their valuations of the licenses on the basis of this information. In an attempt to capture the desirable features of both auction types, we proposed what we called an Anglo-Dutch design.[36]

In an Anglo-Dutch auction for one object, the price rises until all but two bidders quit and the last two bidders then make "best and final" sealed bids with the winner paying the price he bid in this final round. So an Anglo-Dutch auction resembles the process by which houses are sometimes sold; the fact that we could describe it in terms of this very familiar institution was important for our ability to sell the proposal to government officials, who in turn had to explain the proposal to their political masters.

In our case we had *four* licenses to sell, so the price would rise until only *five* bidders remained. The surviving bidders would then be committed to bid at or above this price in a sealed-bid auction in which the four highest bidders are awarded a license.

We considered two versions of the Anglo-Dutch; one in which each winner is committed to paying his own bid, and one in which each winner is committed to paying the fourth-highest winning bid. The prospective bidders preferred the latter design, as did we.[37]

---

[34] The activity rules for the auction meant that some bidders placed (low) bids on licenses they had no expectations of winning in order to maintain eligibility to win other licenses later in the auction.

[35] See also Bulow and Klemperer (2002); Bulow, Huang, and Klemperer (1999); Gilbert and Klemperer (2000); and Klemperer and Pagnozzi (forthcoming).

[36] A Dutch auction is equivalent to a first-price, sealed-bid auction. An English auction is the prototype of an ascending-price auction. The Anglo-Dutch auction was first proposed and described in Klemperer (1998). See also sections 2.3.2 and 3.5.3.

[37] The latter (uniform-price) design is likely to be more efficient given the need for the third, simultaneous-ascending stage discussed in the next paragraph.

  If desired, it can be run without revealing the winners' bids by isolating the five bidders from each other and running an ascending auction, keeping the first quit secret from the other bidders, stopping the auction only when the second quit is announced to the auctioneer, and then selling to the four winners (including the second quitter) at the final price. From the bidders' point of view this procedure is equivalent to a uniform-price sealed-bid auction, that is, the second quit-price in this procedure would equal the fourth-highest sealed-bid price.

Finally, although the four licenses that were to be offered were close substitutes, they were not sufficiently similar that they could be assigned arbitrarily. A third stage, modeled on the standard simultaneous ascending design used by the US FCC, was therefore introduced to determine who got which license and at what price.

Since the three stages of an Anglo-Dutch auction are quite complicated, we thought it especially important to test its efficiency in the laboratory. The short deadlines with which one is typically faced in consulting work are particularly troublesome in experimental work, since one is left with very little time to sort out the teething problems that always turn up after running a few pilots. In this case, the original pilots seemed to indicate that the design was hopelessly inefficient. However, the amount that subjects are paid for their time and attention can sometimes be critical in laboratory experiments, and so it proved here. Subjects were paid a flat attendance fee and an amount proportional to the profit they made for the company on whose behalf they were told they were bidding. After doubling the latter rate of payment (so that subjects left with an average of £50 ($75)), the experimental results became close to efficient. We used two rough-and-ready criteria to judge efficiency in a variety of scenarios about relative valuations that market research rendered plausible. In terms of money, we found that the sum of the valuations of the allocated licenses was always within 2 or 3 percent of the theoretical maximum. In terms of an ordering of all possible allocations of the licenses, the experimental allocation usually achieved the social optimum, sometimes achieved the second most efficient allocation, and was only occasionally worse.[38]

The Radiocommunications Agency therefore bravely decided to go ahead with the proposed Anglo-Dutch design, in spite of fierce criticism from the incumbents, who could not be expected to welcome a design intended to promote entry.[39] We think that their experience in playing the roles of bidders within our experimental software had a significant effect in bolstering the confidence of non-economists on the auction team in the workability of the design. (By contrast, mathematical equations have very little persuasive power.)

However, all the work developing and testing the Anglo-Dutch design proved unnecessary when the engineering advice changed and we were informed that it would be possible to make five licenses available instead of four.

---

[38] A bidder commissioned experiments (Abbink, Irlenbusch, Pezanis-Christou, Rockenbach, Sadrieh, and Selten, 2001a) that found that the Anglo-Dutch design did not necessarily promote more entry than does a uniform price auction, but the setting it tested was one in which (unlike ours) entry is relatively easy in either case.

[39] One major bidder employed two Nobel prizewinners in the hope of finding arguments to oppose the design.

6.5.2 *The Simultaneous Ascending Design*

The five licenses that we were now advised could be fitted into the available spectrum were of different sizes (because of the need to observe the international UMTS standard for third-generation mobile that required spectrum to be bundled in 5 MHz chunks). Some licenses would therefore be valued very differently from others by the bidders in an auction. License A is the largest, comprising 2 × 15 MHz of paired spectrum plus 5 MHz of less-valuable unpaired spectrum. License B is a little smaller, comprising 2 × 15 MHz of paired spectrum, but no unpaired spectrum. Licenses C, D, and E are all roughly the same, each comprising 2 × 10 MHz of paired plus 5 MHz of unpaired spectrum, but these three licenses were thought substantially less valuable than the other two.[40]

The existence of five licenses solved the overall entry problem, especially when it was decided to restrict the incumbents in the 2G industry to licenses B, C, D, and E, so ensuring that one of the two large licenses would go to a new entrant. (There was concern about whether new entrants would be interested in the smaller licenses.) The raison d'être for the Anglo-Dutch design therefore vanished. Furthermore, it might not have worked as well for licenses of very different sizes as it would have worked when the licenses were of very similar values.

So with five licenses and only four incumbents, we advised abandoning the Anglo-Dutch design in favor of a modified version of the simultaneous ascending design pioneered by the FCC. We believed that the design would work even better for us, since the fact that each bidder was restricted to getting at most one license insulated us against the problems with collusion that arose in America.[41]

Our design entailed multiple rounds of simultaneous bids. In the first round, each bidder makes a bid on one license of its own choice. To remain in the auction, a bidder must be "active" in every subsequent round. An active bidder either currently holds the top bid on a particular license, or else raises the bid on a license of the bidder's choice by at least the minimum bid increment.[42] A bidder

[40] With six licenses, there was thought to be a substantial risk that no license would be large enough to attract an entrant.

Each license was to last until the end of 2021, and included an obligation to roll out a network covering at least 80 percent of the UK population by 2007.

[41] If the spectrum was divided into many small blocks, with bidders allowed to win multiple blocks, bidders might try to collude to divide the blocks between them; roughly this seems to have happened in some of the US auctions (Engelbrecht-Wiggans and Kahn, 1998c; Brusco and Lopomo, 2002a; Cramton and Schwartz, 2000, 2002; and section 3.2). If bidders can win just one license each, every bidder is either a winner or a loser—there is no middle ground—and collusion is much harder.

[42] A bidder could also remain "active" by using one of three waivers allowed per bidder or, when eight or fewer bidders remained, by calling for one of two recesses allowed per bidder. Each recess would stop all bidding for a day.

who is inactive in any round is eliminated from the rest of the auction. A bidder who currently holds the top bid on a license cannot raise or withdraw its bid, nor bid on another license in the current round. At the end of every round all bidders' bids are revealed, the current top bidder for each license is determined,[43] and minimum bid increments are set for the next round. The auction concludes when only five bidders remain. They are each then allocated the license on which they are the current top bidder at the price they have currently bid for that license.

This design ensured that even if new entrants had only been interested in the two large licenses, the competition for these would have spilt over to the smaller licenses too. The incumbents would engage in arbitrage, switching their bids to whichever license seemed best value to them, so as the prices of the large licenses were driven up, the prices of the smaller ones would have had to follow, and the price of every license would have been determined by real competition.

Apart from its transparency, and from generating competitive prices, the design has two important advantages, which we explain on the assumption that the minimum raise is always negligible. The first is the simplicity of bidders' strategies. Consider the case of "private values", that is, when every bidder is completely confident of the exact value to himself of each object, and these values are independent of who wins the other objects and at what prices. Assume bidding is costless, and that at every point of time every bidder assigns a positive probability (which may be arbitrarily small) to the possibility that each rival will be willing to make no further bid, so each bid may possibly be the last one.[44] In each round, a bidder should then simply make the bid that would maximize his profit if that bid were the last. A bidder should therefore never make more than the minimum raise, and always choose the license with the greatest gap between the minimum required bid and his value for the license. In the general case, relaxing the assumption of "private-values", things are a little harder; in particular, a bidder must adjust his valuations for the licenses if the previous bidding of his rivals shakes his confidence in his business case but, having done that, bidding as described previously is still a reasonable strategy to recommend.[45]

A second advantage is that the design generates an efficient outcome when bidders with "private values" who are not budget constrained behave as described above. To see why, note that at the end of the auction the prices

---

[43] In the event of a tie on a license the "top bidder" for that license was designated randomly. (The rules allowed the auctioneer to instead ask the tied bidders to each rebid at least as high on the license in question, and the intention was as far as possible to use whatever tiebreaking rule made the bidders happiest. In the event, the bidders proved to be as unconcerned as we were about this detail.)

[44] These assumptions exclude the case in which a bidder quits before reaching his value for a license (or even fails to enter the auction) because he knows he cannot win the license.

[45] The precise conditions under which such bidding behavior is optimal remain a subject for debate among both theorists and practitioners.

are such that every bidder, including every loser, would choose to buy exactly what he ends up with, given the prices. Therefore no reallocation of licenses among bidders, given the prices, could raise the surplus of any individual bidder. So since prices are just a transfer between the buyers and the seller, the total surplus of the buyers and the seller cannot be increased by first reallocating the licenses in any way and then changing the prices in any way. So even if different prices were used the auction's outcome must maximize the sum of the values of the winning bidders, which is what we understood by "efficiency" (see section 6.3).[46]

Of course, these advantages need not apply under other assumptions, in particular the case in which a bidder may quit early or fail to enter the auction because bidding is not costless and he believes he has very little chance of winning a license. So only when a fifth license was available to attract new entrants did we feel comfortable recommending the simultaneous ascending design.

In early 1999 the decision was made to proceed with the simultaneous ascending design.

6.6 OTHER ISSUES

6.6.1 Roaming

At a late stage, One-2-One and Orange mounted a successful legal challenge against mandated "roaming", throwing our plans into disarray since it was unclear whether any entrants would bid without guaranteed roaming onto an existing 2G network.

However, new entrants needed only one incumbent network to roam on, and one incumbent was prepared to offer roaming, conditional on itself winning a 3G license. So new entrants would be prepared to bid if they were permitted to withdraw any winning bids in the event that this incumbent failed to win, with the government then re-auctioning the corresponding licenses in this event.

The difficulty was that this incumbent might then strategically avoid winning, deliberately triggering the withdrawal of the winning entrants so that it could win a cheap license in the re-auction. We overcame this danger by inserting an extra stage into the game. If this incumbent failed to win a license, the other 2G incumbents would then be asked whether they were now, after all, prepared to permit roaming. If any of them were, the auction result

---

[46] To illustrate the point mathematically, imagine that an auction for only two licenses ends with bidder 1 obtaining license A for £a and bidder 2 obtaining license B for £b. Using Greek letters for bidders' valuations and assuming the minimum allowable raise is negligible, we have that $\alpha_1 - a \geq \beta_1 - b$ and $\beta_2 - b \geq \alpha_2 - a$. Adding the two inequalities yields $\alpha_1 + \beta_2 \geq \alpha_2 + \beta_1$. The outcome is therefore efficient insofar as the winners are concerned. It is obviously also efficient in respect of losers, because losers' valuations cannot be above a and b, and hence must be lower than winners' valuations.

would stand. The point is that the other incumbents would likely see this as an unmissable opportunity to exclude a strong competitor from 3G. The first incumbent would therefore be most unlikely to run the risk of strategically avoiding winning in the original auction.

In the end, two incumbents, BT and Vodafone agreed to offer roaming voluntarily, so this scheme was not needed.[47]

6.6.2 Associated Bidders

The European telecom industry is rather incestuous, with potentially many pairs of "associated bidders" whose ownership is sufficiently shared that both could not be allowed to win licenses without damaging the competitiveness of the UK 3G market we were creating. For example, Cellnet was jointly owned by BT and Securicor at the time, so not more than one these three firms could be permitted to win. We saw no very satisfactory way of modifying the auction rules to guarantee that only one of any associated pair won a license. Instead, therefore, we made provision for a pre-auction in which it could be decided which of two or more closely associated bidders should go forward to the main auction.[48]

As we hoped, the pre-auction was not used in practice. We saw the pre-auction as a stopgap measure designed to provide a clear status quo for the bargaining between associated bidders when they sort out their cross-ownership problems themselves. The pre-auction would also have disadvantaged associated bidders relative to the other bidders, so gave them an incentive to sort out their common ownership problem in advance of the auction. In the event, BT bought out Securicor's share of Cellnet in July 1999 and then bid only as BT3G, thereby resolving the most pressing association problem.

We do not believe that actually running pre-auctions of this kind is a good way of solving problems with associated bidders, even though it might make the best of a bad job. So we hope that such pre-auctions will not be seen as a standard preliminary to a telecom auction. When associations begin to be even a little bit complex, there is no guarantee that their outcomes will be efficient.

In our case, the pre-auction fulfilled its function by providing some encouragement for the bidders to work out their problems themselves.

[47] Furthermore, the Court judgment in favor of One-2-One and Orange was subsequently overturned on appeal in favor of the government.

[48] The pre-auction would have consisted of every associated bidder bidding in an ascending auction on a price per MHz basis until it either quit, or all those associated with it had quit. Once all associations had been broken, bidders who had quit would have been considered for re-entry in the reverse order in which they quit; each bidder who had quit would have been re-entered at the price at which it had quit if this was possible without recreating any association. Finally, each survivor would have been required to begin the main auction with a bid at the price per MHz at which it become unassociated, or at which it rejoined the pre-auction. Of course, these rules are very rough and ready, and we did not expect them to be needed in practice.

6.6.3 The Vodafone-Mannesmann Takeover

In October 1999, one of Germany's two largest mobile-phone operators, Mannesmann, took over Orange for almost $35 billion. This left Vodafone in a quandary, since it had been contemplating an alliance with Mannesmann, but this was no longer possible as Orange was one of its strongest 2G competitors in the United Kingdom. In the event, Vodafone decided to attempt the biggest takeover ever, and the first hostile takeover in modern history of a German company, by making a bid for Mannesmann-Orange. Vodafone simultaneously appealed that both Orange and Vodafone should be allowed to bid in the British 3G auction if the takeover were successful, pending the divestment of Orange after the auction.

This appeal left the British government in a difficult position.

The situation was not an ordinary "associated bidders" problem since Vodafone was committed to divesting Orange, so allowing both to win licenses caused no competition-policy problems, and indeed would very likely be efficient. And (by contrast with BT-Cellnet-Securicor) the common-ownership problem could not necessarily be quickly resolved, because complex provisions of German law meant that Vodafone could not guarantee divesting Orange until several months after the conclusion of a successful takeover of Mannesmann.

Denying the appeal and proceeding with the 3G auction could seriously interfere with Vodafone's chances of success in its takeover bid. Even if Vodafone did, nevertheless, successfully take over Mannesmann-Orange, denying one or both of Vodafone and Orange the chance to compete in the auction would have seriously damaged the excluded business(es), and most likely have generated an inefficient allocation of licenses.

One option was to delay the auction, but this would have risked creating market uncertainty and delaying the introduction of 3G. The auction team was also very keen to maintain the advantage of being the first of the 3G auctions. We thought subsequent 3G auctions might attract less entry since bidders would work out from the first auction who the likely winners were in future auctions. The later auctions would also be less competitive if bidders formed more alliances. Furthermore prices in the first auction might be driven higher if bidders thought that winning that auction gave them a competitive advantage in future auctions. The decision not to delay proved very wise. There was in fact much less entry and competition in later 3G auctions (Netherlands, Germany, Italy, Austria, Switzerland, Belgium, Greece, Denmark) and much lower prices in most of them (see section 6.7.3, and chapter 5).

In deciding whether to grant the appeal, a major concern for the British government was the extent to which joint ownership of Orange and Vodafone would injure the aim of allocating the licenses efficiently, if both were allowed to bid with appropriate "Chinese wall" requirements, forbidding the exchange of relevant information and the coordination of bids. The point is that Voda-fone, as temporary owner of Orange, would have an interest in maximizing the sum of Vodafone and Orange's profit in the auction, rather than simply maxi-mizing its own profit. Advising on the efficiency implications of this at short notice was the most stressful event in the whole auction design process. However, some simple theoretical calculations and our computer simulations both indicated that, within the range of likely relative valuations of the licenses, the effect on efficiency would be negligibly small.

Since it was a finely balanced decision whether to permit both Orange and Vodafone to bid in the British 3G auction if Vodafone's takeover of Mannes-mann were successful, our report may have tipped the scales in favor of both being allowed to bid with appropriate legal safeguards. In the event, Vodafone took over Mannesmann for about $175 billion. There is no evidence that this led to any inefficiency in the auction bidding. After the auction, Orange was bought by France Telecom for over $40 billion.

6.7 ASSESSMENT

6.7.1 The Auction Outcome

Beginning the planning so far in advance of the auction (almost three years in advance as it turned out) proved a shrewd move by the UK government. It allowed us plenty of time to develop and test our ideas and, just as importantly, it allowed for a sustained marketing campaign[49] without Britain being over-taken in the race to be first on the European scene (indeed worldwide) with a 3G auction.

By 15 February 2000, interest in acquiring a license had reached boiling point. Thirteen serious candidates had qualified to bid in the auction, with the media that took notice predicting that licenses would sell for a total of about £2–5 billion (or about $3–7 billion). The first round of the auction took place on 6 March 2000, when a little more than the sum of the reserve prices, £500 million ($750 million), was bid. The first withdrawal came in round 94 as the price of the cheapest license passed £2 billion ($3 billion), and four more withdrawals followed almost immediately.[50] However the last three withdrawals took longer. The final bid took the cheapest license price past £4 billion ($6 billion), and after 150 rounds of bidding the auction

---

[49] The investment bankers advising the government (N.M. Rothschild and Sons Ltd.) were paid a fee that depended on the number of bidders who participated in the auction. By attracting 13 bidders, Rothschilds earned £4,770,000, or over forty times the total expenditure on economic consultancy (see note 1).

[50] The rush of dropouts can be interpreted either as agreement among this group of bidders about the values, or as agency problems that meant that no management wished to be seen to be the first to quit. The former seems to be the case: it became known afterwards that several bidders had secured funding up to £2 billion.

finished on 27 April 2000 with a total of about £22.5 billion ($34 billion) on the table—five to ten times the initial media estimates.[51]

The four incumbents won licenses, with Vodafone paying about £6 billion ($9 billion) for license B, compared with the £4 billion ($6 billion) or so paid by the other incumbents for each of licenses C, D, and E. The reserved license A was taken by the entrant TIW (largely owned by Hutchison Whampoa) for about £4.4 billion ($6.6 billion).

The final outcome cannot, of course, be proved to be efficient, but the evidence strongly suggests it was, in the sense of maximizing the sum of the valuations of the bidders who were awarded licenses, given the number and sizes of licenses that were sold (see section 6.3). See Börgers and Dustmann (2002b) and Plott and Salmon (forthcoming) for detailed analyses of the bidding.[52]

While the auction proceeded, our chief task was to advise on the size of the minimum percentage raise, which fell gradually from 5 percent to 1.5 percent largely in response to bidders' preferences. We also urged with only limited success that the auction be speeded up by running more rounds per day, lest some external event derailed the process by leading the bidders to adjust their valuations downwards. In fact, there was a major dip in share prices during the auction as the market corrected for over-optimistic investment in e-commerce companies, but this event seems to have had little impact on the bidders.

The arrangements for waivers and recess days (to allow consultation with financial backers) seemed to work out well, and the auction process was

---

[51] The British Treasury used the money towards paying off the National Debt.

[52] Bidders did not follow the simple bidding rule discussed in section 6.5.2 of always making the minimum raise possible on the license on which they bid (Börgers and Dustmann, 2002b). However, the deviations were not substantial and some deviations from this rule are optimal for a bidder and so to be expected when the minimum allowable raises are not negligible. Börgers and Dustmann also argue BT's bidding seems erratic, although it might be largely explained by common-value components to valuations and by BT wishing to push up the price Vodafone paid for a large license.

Furthermore, in the early stages of the contest, when it was clear that there was no realistic chance of the auction ending very quickly (even up to round 120, eight bidders still remained in the auction), some bids were probably slightly frivolous, or designed to attract media attention. For example, One-2-One raised their bid by slightly more than the minimum required in round 76 to bid £1,212,100,000! (Additional 1s and 2s were ruled out, because all bids were required to be multiples of £100,000.)

While Börgers and Dustmann's analysis makes clear that the behavior they document means that the auction ran the risk of a slightly inefficient conclusion, it also seems clear that the actual outcome was efficient or very close to efficient in the sense of section 6.3. (It seems clear after the fact—and after the other European auctions—that the four incumbents had the highest valuations, so were appropriate winners in the sense of section 6.3, and it is extremely implausible that any losing entrant quit the auction with a value for a license that exceeded TIW's. Furthermore, the evidence both during and subsequent to the auction suggests Vodafone had a higher incremental value for a large license than did any other incumbent, and therefore that the allocation of licenses among winners was also correct.)

sufficiently well organized as to provoke compliments from several bidders, including those who did not win licenses.

However, media criticism began immediately about the bidders being "forced" to pay too much for their licenses (see section 6.2.2). But Hutchison sold 35 percent of its holding in TIW to KPN and NTT DoCoMo, valuing the license it won for £4.4 billion in late April at about £6 billion in early July. Moreover, after Orange had won and committed to pay for a license, France Telecom paid £6 billion more for Orange in May than the price Mannesmann had paid for it in the previous October, before the auction. Neither event suggests that the firms or the market shared the concerns expressed by the media in the months immediately following the auction.[53]

Of course, confidence in hi-tech industries in general has waned since that time. But the auction design deserves neither praise nor blame if the values placed on the 3G licenses have now fallen because of a change in the capital market's view of 3G's prospects.

6.7.2 Mistakes

What could have been done better in organizing the British 3G auction?[54] Neither of the problems we mention next actually caused any disruption, but they might have done if circumstances had been adverse.

We think the chief problem was the inadequacy of the deposits that the bidders were required to put down. These began at £50 million (about $75 million), ratcheting up to £100 million when the bidding for any license reached £400 million. This might not provide an adequate disincentive for a winner in the auction who changed his mind about wanting a license after bidding several billions.[55] Fortunately, the winners were uninterested in

---

[53] Furthermore one winner claimed afterwards that it had predicted the final auction price to within 10 percent of the actual price, in advance of the auction. And when the prices in the UK auction had reached less than half their final levels, a new entrant in Germany announced a willingness to pay over £5 billion (18 billion DM) for a similar license in Germany.

More formal evidence is provided by Cable, Henley, and Holland (2002) whose analysis of share price movements using event-study methodology suggests that, at the time of the auction, the market did not feel that the winners overpaid. Cable et al. also "conclude there is no evidence that the outcome of the auction was anything but efficient".

[54] We restrict attention to issues within our terms of reference excluding, for example, grand issues like whether there should have been one single pan-European auction, or how the terms for any infrastructure sharing should have been determined.

[55] From a narrow economic perspective the deposits were clearly too small to ensure there were no defaults. From the perspective of a manager who might have to explain to others why he has given up £100 million for nothing, the deposit might suffice to persuade him to swallow any doubts he has about going through with the license purchase.

Note that the winning bidders were required to pay at least half their bids almost immediately after winning their licenses, and the repayment terms were such that every winner in fact chose to pay its full bid within days of receiving its license.

The losers' deposits were completely refundable.

defaulting and all quickly paid their entire bids. We should have been stouter in our resistance to the imposition of an upper bound on our original proposal that deposits should ratchet up with the amounts bid.

With such small deposits, the slow pace at which the auction was run became more significant. The reserve prices were very low (see section 6.4.4), and there was, in our view, an unnecessary maximum of 5 percent on the size of the minimum increment. The number of rounds per day was also much smaller than we would have liked and there were many recesses for holidays and weekends.[56] We were very concerned that some external event might occur during the auction that would lead the bidders to lower their valuations below what they had already bid. What would have happened if a very negative discovery about the health implications of mobile phones had been made and reported during the auction? We were much less comfortable during the 7.5 weeks of the auction than we pretended to be. There was in fact a substantial dip in technology share prices during the auction that looked as though it might create a confidence crisis, but this scare proved to be only a paper tiger at the time, although it looks more like a real tiger now.

6.7.3 Telecom Auctions Elsewhere

Subsequent telecom license auctions seem to justify some of our decisions, and reinforce our view that the officials we worked with had done an impressive job in managing the auction process.

FACILITATING ENTRY

Our emphasis on the importance of entry was richly confirmed by the miserable failure of the very next European 3G auction: the Netherlands used an ascending design even though they were selling exactly as many licenses as they had 2G incumbents—precisely the setting in which we had decided not to risk a pure ascending auction. As one of us predicted in advance, in the press and in Klemperer (2000b) in May, their July auction was a disaster.[57] Only one weak entrant showed up to compete with the 2G incumbents, and the auction raised just $2.5 billion instead of the $8.5 billion that the Dutch government had forecast based on the UK experience.

The Italian and Swiss 3G auction also had problems attracting entry, and we think that the Anglo-Dutch design—that the United Kingdom would have used if entry had been a concern there—would have worked better for these countries.

---

[56] On the other hand, some have argued that an auction of this size should be run slowly to give shareholders and directors adequate time to monitor and control their firms' bidding.

[57] See also *Billions from Auctions: Wishful Thinking* (Maasland, 2000).

CAREFULLY THINKING THROUGH AND TESTING THE RULES

A recent Turkish telecom auction illustrates the need to think through the implications of rules very carefully and often subject a design to careful experimental testing. The Turkish government auctioned two licenses sequentially, but set the reserve price for the second license equal to the price at which the first license was sold. One company then bid much more for the first license than the market thought it could be worth if the company had to compete with a rival holding the second license. But the company had rightly figured that no rival would be willing to bid that high for the second license, which therefore remained unsold, leaving the company without a rival operating the second license!

Either careful thought or a few laboratory trials would have exposed this problem.[58]

MARKET STRUCTURE

The Turkish fiasco illustrates another point too: if the choice of the number of licenses is left to "the market", the choice is likely to favor the industry. The sale of just one license in Turkey both increased industry profits and reduced social welfare relative to the sale of two. Other auction forms can yield different distortions, and it is hard to rule out distortions in any simple auction form that leaves the number of licenses endogenous to the auction. Though the German 3G endogenous-number-of-licenses auction worked well, this was probably due more to good luck than good design. The same design proved very vulnerable to collusion and yielded a very poor outcome when used in the Austrian 3G auction (see, especially, section 5.4.2).

OTHER ISSUES

The later European 3G auctions suffered from other problems too—in particular, firms' formation of joint-bidding agreements once they had seen how costly the competitive UK auction was. Ideally, auctioneers and/or antitrust agencies should prohibit such agreements.

Furthermore, although on the whole it was a disadvantage to go to market later, the later countries could have used the information from the earlier auctions to set more realistic reserve prices. Their failure to do this, combined with their other errors, led to embarrassing results, especially for the Austrian and Swiss governments.

The failure of most of the 3G auctions after the UK auction is often attributed to a turn-round in market sentiment about the likely profitability of 3G,

---

[58] The Turkish government has now trumped this move by making arrangements for a new sale of the unsold license, but who will believe that it will stand by its auction rules in the future?

and to the increase in firms' costs of capital to which this led. But the problem was severely exacerbated in most countries by their choice of auction designs that were inappropriate to their particular circumstances. One of us wrote shortly after the UK auction that other "European governments would be foolish not to copy the UK in auctioning the radio spectrum, but they would be equally foolish to blindly copy the UK design without attention to their local circumstances" (Klemperer, 2000b). We stand by that advice.

More detailed discussion of all nine 2000–2001 western European 3G auctions can be found in chapter 5.

6.8 CONCLUSION

We learnt a lot in advising on the telecom auction.

The auction confirmed our view that industrial-organization issues are more important than the informational issues on which the auction literature has mostly focused. In particular, the problems of attracting entrants and dealing with alliances and mergers are likely to remain major preoccupations of telecom-auction designers for the foreseeable future. Tackling such problems sensibly requires high-quality market research that keeps pace with developments in an industry that can change its clothes with bewildering rapidity. We also need more theoretical work on the industrial-organization implications of major auctions.

The really bad mistake in running an auction is just to take an auction design off the shelf, as shown by a comparison of the British and subsequent European 3G auctions. Auction design is a matter of "horses for courses", *not* "one size fits all"; each economic environment requires an auction design that is tailored to its special circumstances.

Starting the planning early was invaluable in giving us time to carefully think through and test our ideas. It was also important to start marketing the auction to potential entrants early; attracting bidders is not only about good auction design.

We learnt the need to widen our horizons to a whole range of legal and commercial issues. One cannot afford to defer to special experts in these fields, because they are frequently insensitive to the gaming opportunities that various measures may create for the bidders in a major auction. One must be ready to read the small print and to generate user-friendly examples of what might go wrong.

The value of computer simulations as an educational tool, and the persuasive power of laboratory experiments, was also brought home to us.

But perhaps the most important lesson of all is not to sell ourselves too cheap. Ideas that seem obvious to a trained economist are often quite new to lay folk. Our marginal product in preventing mistakes can therefore sometimes be surprisingly large.

CHAPTER SEVEN

Bidder Strategies*

I suggest explanations for the apparently puzzling bidding in the British and German 3G telecom auctions in 2000. Relative performance maximization may have been important, but the outcome of the British auction seems to have been efficient.

A. SOME OBSERVATIONS ON THE BRITISH 3G TELECOM AUCTION

7.1 INTRODUCTION

As discussed in chapters 5 and 6, and section B of this chapter, the UK auction was one of the most successful of the western European 3G auctions. Indeed in terms of revenue raised per capita it was *the* most successful of all the auctions, and it is therefore appropriate to examine, as Börgers and Dustmann (2002a) (henceforth B-D) do, whether the auction's outcome was also as efficient as is often claimed and whether the bidding in the auction fits well with standard theory.[1]

7.2 EFFICIENCY OF THE UK AUCTION

B-D's analysis makes clear that an ascending auction like that in the United Kingdom runs the risk of an at least slightly inefficient outcome arising in some circumstances. However, it also seems clear that the actual outcome of

---

* This chapter bundles my comments on two papers presented at the December 2001 CES Ifo conference on the telecom auctions, but the chapter can be read independently of those papers. It was originally published as "Some Observations on the British 3G Telecom Auction: Comments on Börgers and Dustmann", in *ifo Studien* 2002, 48, 115–120, and "Some Observations on the German 3G Telecom Auction: Comments on Grimm, Riedel, and Wolfstetter", in *ifo Studien* 2002, 48, 145–156. (This material is also reprinted in *Spectrum Auctions and Competition in Telecommunications*, Illing, G. and Klüh, U. (eds.), MIT Press, 2004.) I am grateful for helpful comments from Tilman Börgers, Elmar Wolfstetter and the representatives of some of the firms involved in the German auction to whom I showed an earlier draft; I am especially grateful to Marco Pagnozzi for our collaboration in the study of the 3G auctions and for his helpful suggestions about these essays.

[1] I learnt a lot from B-D's analysis. In what follows, I discuss just two issues where my interpretation is slightly different. I was the principal auction theorist advising the Radiocommunications Agency which designed and ran the UK auction, but the views expressed in this chapter are mine alone.

the UK auction was efficient, or very close to efficient, in the sense of maximizing the sum of the valuations of the license holders.

Klaus Schmidt's (2002) excellent comment explains that the evidence from the bidding in the auction itself suggests that the UK auction was probably efficient. Evidence subsequent to the auction supports the same claim. It seems clear after the fact—and especially after the other European auctions—that the four incumbents had the highest valuations,[2] so were efficient winners. There is no evidence that any losing entrant had a value for a license that exceeded TIW-Hutchison's. Finally, the evidence subsequent to the auction, as well as from within it (including the interpretation of the bidding offered below), suggests that Vodafone had a higher incremental value for a large license than did any other incumbent, and therefore that the allocation of licenses among winners was also correct.

In short, all the available evidence suggests that the UK auction's outcome was efficient in the sense claimed.[3]

7.3 BT's Bidding Behavior

B-D also suggest that some of the behavior they document is very hard to rationalize, but I conjecture that doing sufficient research into the environment in which the auction took place will yield good explanations; I illustrate this by examining the main "puzzle" of BT's bidding.[4]

BT's bidding was such that the prices bid for the large (2 × 15 MHz) "B" and small (2 × 10 MHz) "C", "D" and "E" licenses differed by roughly a constant in the early stages of the auction (phase 1 of the auction in B-D's terminology), and then switched to differing by roughly a fixed proportion (50 percent of the price level of the small licenses) in the later stages of the auction (phases 2 and 3 in B-D's terminology).[5] This pattern seems unusual, but reviewing analysts' reports provides a clue: some analysts assumed the value of the large license must be 1.5 times the value of a small license (reflecting an assumption that 1.5 times the amount of spectrum would

---

[2] See van Damme (2002) and Fortis (2000) for evidence and discussion of these value differences. (Indirect evidence is also provided by the fact that only one out of the 30 incumbent bidders in the eight western European ascending auctions failed to win a license—and even this single failure was attributed to collusion or organizational strife within the bidder, rather than to the incumbent having a low value, see section 5.3.3.)

[3] Cable, Henley, and Holland (2002) use stockmarket data to argue that 'there is no evidence that the outcome of the auction was anything but efficient'.

[4] However, B-D are to be congratulated on having already explained so much; they also looked at evidence from outside the auction to explain behavior within it.

[5] That BT's behavior in the later stages of the auction can be described in this way was observed independently, by B-D and myself, after the conference in Munich to which their paper was contributed. The details are reported in B-D's companion paper, Börgers and Dustmann (2002b).

allow 1.5 times the service to be offered[6]), while several other analysts insisted that the large license was worth a fixed sum more than a small one (reflecting the additional costs—base stations, etc.—required to run the same service with a smaller license), and it was clearly well understood in the industry that different bidders might make different choices between these two different valuation models.

Of course, if one or more bidder valued the large license at 1.5 times the value of the small license, this cannot on its own explain the price difference being a fixed proportion of the value of the small license. For example, if BT's private valuations for small and large licenses were £4 billion and £6 billion, respectively, while Vodafone's were £6 billion and £9 billion, respectively, and other bidders were closer to indifference between small and large licenses, then with "straightforward bidding" (in B-D's terminology) the absolute value of the price difference would quickly move to equal £2 billion (since whenever the price difference was less than £2 billion, both BT and Vodafone would regard the large license as the best deal, and so would bid on it).[7]

However, it seems plausible that BT intrinsically valued a large license more than a smaller license by a fixed value that was considerably below 50 percent of the final price of a small license. BT may also have become very confident that Vodafone valued a large license at 50 percent more than a small one. (Apart from any information from outside the auction, Vodafone never placed a bid on any license other than the large license in the auction.) Furthermore, BT may have wished to make Vodafone pay as much as possible for its license[8] for at least two reasons. First, this would reduce Vodafone's budget and so make Vodafone a weaker competitor in subsequent auctions (the British auction was the first of nine western European 3G auctions, and was also followed by others elsewhere in the world). Second, making Vodafone pay more would make "the market" think Vodafone had not done better than BT in the auction. There is anecdotal evidence that BT was very concerned both about the stock market's perceptions of its performance, and about the wider market's view of its position relative to Vodafone. Allowing Vodafone to win the larger license at a lower per MHz price than BT was paying might suggest BT's managers had got a bad deal. Or it might suggest that BT was not able to make effective use of a larger license in the way that Vodafone could, and hence that BT thought it was in a weak market position,

---

[6] The technology might actually allow offering slightly more than 1.5 times the service, hence the value ratio might be slightly more than 1.5.

[7] Even if, as I will argue, some of the early bidding was non-serious, the price difference would move to the fixed amount, £2 billion, as soon as the bidding became serious.

[8] After the auction BT claimed it had deliberately pushed up the price that Vodafone had paid, and this was reported in the press (see Cane and Owen 2000). (At the time, this claim was dismissed by auction theorists as implausible, since it was hard to reconcile with the evidence without realizing that BT and Vodafone might both have had different valuation models and also have had a reasonably clear idea of the other's valuation model.)

while Vodafone was clearly "number one".[9] So bidding up the large license's price to 50 percent more than the current small license price may have seemed a reasonable risk to take, even given the small chance of ending up winning the large license at hundreds of millions of pounds more than BT valued it.[10]

Of course, even a small risk of winning the large license might seem to have a significant expected cost. But it was also possible that if BT did end up winning the large license, it might have been able to resell part of it at little or no loss, given that the auction prices would then have established a clear price per MHz. (The possibilities for resale were unclear, but Hutchison did in effect resell a fraction of the license it won, very shortly after the auction, to KPN and Docomo at almost exactly the price per MHz that BT and Vodafone paid in the auction.[11]) In any event, observers might not think BT's managers had made a bad decision, even if BT did end up winning (and keeping) the large license for 50 percent more than the price of a small license.[12]

This theory leaves an important question unanswered. Why did BT not push up the price of the large license in the early stages of the auction? One reason is that much of the bidding in the early stages of the contest, when it was clear that there was no realistic chance of the auction ending very quickly (B-D's phase 1) does not seem to have been very serious.[13] In fact, some bids were probably slightly frivolous, or designed to attract media attention. For example, One-2-One raised its bid by slightly more than the minimum required in round 76 to bid £1,212,100,000![14] And BT did start pushing up the price difference between the large and small licenses in round 99 when there

---

[9] Section 7.8 and Abbink et al. (2001b, section 4) discuss the importance of bidders' concerns about relative performance in two other auctions in which BT's and Vodafone's subsidiaries both competed, the German 3G auction and the previous year's German DCS-1800 spectrum auction. (Strictly, Vodafone was not involved in the earlier auction, but Mannesman, which was a subsidiary of Vodafone by the time of the UK auction, did compete in the earlier auction.)

[10] If BT was correct in its assessment that Vodafone's valuation of a large license was (at least) 50 percent more than that for a small license, the (only) risk that BT faced was that Vodafone would quit the auction altogether. But this outcome was completely implausible, since it would imply that Vodafone's valuation for a small license was below that of Orange and One-2-One (which were both weaker incumbents) and at least one new entrant. The real risk would have been that BT had misjudged Vodafone's valuation difference between the licenses, and BT perhaps knew this risk was small.

[11] The UK Government now seems likely to make resale relatively easy, but this was unclear at the time of the auction, and actual resale of part of a license may in any case be unattractive since bringing a new competitor into the industry makes the remaining spectrum less valuable. Bringing new partners into a joint venture as Hutchison did therefore seems the most relevant form of resale.

[12] Of course, the arguments of this paragraph are in effect postulating that there may have been important common value elements to valuations. Note that with common value elements, it is plausible that the large license might be worth a fixed amount (say £500 million to £1 billion) more than a small license at low prices, but a constant fraction (say 150 percent) of the small license at large prices.

[13] Four bidders have informally confirmed this.

[14] Additional 1's and 2's were ruled out, because all bids were required to be multiples of £100,000.

were still nine bidders left (so four more dropouts were still required to end the auction), and did not then stop pushing up the price difference until round 112 when the large license was more than 50 percent (and more than £1.5 billion) more expensive than the small licenses.

A more serious reason why BT did not push up the price difference earlier is that BT may not have wanted to influence other bidders too early to think that license values were very high (since these other bidders might need time to adjust their views, and get extra money approved by their Boards, etc.). For example, if BT's valuation for a small license was £5 billion, it might have been confident that Vodafone's value exceeded £4 billion for a small license, and therefore that Vodafone would pay at least £2 billion more for a large license. But pushing the price difference up to £2 billion immediately would have sent a very clear signal about what the ultimate prices might be at a time at which the auction prices for the smaller licenses were still very low, and this could only have been damaging to BT's interests.

A final possible reason why BT did not push up the price difference early on is that BT may not have become confident that Vodafone's valuation of the large license was 1.5 times its valuation of the small license until later in the auction.

Most likely BT thought that the early bidding was probably not very important but that its best strategy was to roughly mimic what straightforward bidding would have been if it had had low valuations and a correspondingly low difference in valuations. Certainly this is consistent with the evidence.[15]

So it seems possible to give a reasonable explanation for BT's bidding. Of course, this may not be the only possible explanation.[16] However, the moral is that understanding bidding in auctions often requires knowing a lot of real-world detail about the players and the context in which they are operating. Facts from outside the bidding itself—in this case knowing the differing valuation models that different analysts used—may be the key to explaining behavior. In understanding auctions, as well as in designing them, "the devil is in the details".[17]

B. SOME OBSERVATIONS ON THE GERMAN 3G TELECOM AUCTION

7.4 INTRODUCTION

The German 3G spectrum auction was undoubtedly a success from the government's viewpoint. Indeed, it was probably one of only three successes among the nine western European 3G auctions. The measure of success most

[15] Although Vodafone only bid on the large license, it is very plausible that Vodafone was following a similar strategy, but mimicking a bidder with slightly lower valuations.

[16] For example, there may have been much stronger common value components to valuations than usually assumed.

[17] See chapters 3, 4, and 5 for more discussion of the importance of understanding the wider context, and of apparently small details, in auction design.

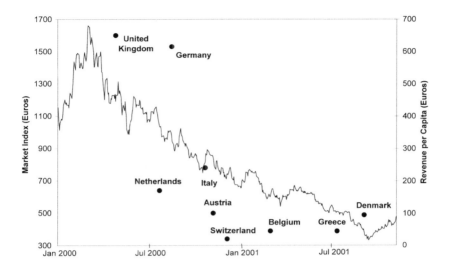

Figure 7.1 European 2000–2001 3G Mobile Spectrum Auctions.
Note: Per capita revenues, by country ● are given by the right-hand scale; auctions are shown on the dates at which they finished. Dow Jones European Telecom Stock Price Index is given by the left-hand scale.

commonly used is total revenue raised per capita, with some adjustments for the level of the telecoms stock index as a reflection of sentiment towards 3G's prospects.[18] (We assume governments have no ability to time the market, and therefore deserve neither credit nor blame for selling when market sentiment is unusually positive or negative.) Based on this, the figure suggests the UK, German, and Danish auctions were successes, while the Dutch, Austrian, and Swiss auctions were the biggest failures (figure 7.1).

Figure 7.1 flatters larger countries (especially Germany, conversely it underrates tiny Denmark), flatters centrally located countries (Germany, again, and also Austria and Switzerland), flatters countries with lightly regulated telecom industries (Germany, again, among others)—since larger, centrally located, lightly regulated markets are worth more—but it also ignores the fact that Germany and Austria sold more licenses than other countries, reducing the total profitability of those markets. However, the more systematic discussion of the relative performance of the different auctions in chapter 5 comes to very similar conclusions.

Since the German auction was a success and was of a novel and complex design, it clearly deserves study, and Grimm, Riedel, and Wolfstetter's (2002) paper (henceforth GRW) would be welcome for that

[18] Although efficiency was generally the primary objective, there is no evidence that efficiency differed much across the different countries' auctions; hence the focus on revenues.

reason alone; their paper gives very valuable detail about the auction and will be a key reference for anyone studying it. But more than that, the paper is extremely interesting and makes acute observations about both the German and other 3G auctions.

I have learned a lot from the paper, and agree with much of it. However, these comments will naturally focus on the disagreements. Section 7.5 summarizes why I think GRW's explanation of the bidding in the German auction is not fully satisfactory, and section 7.6 develops this point more fully (the latter section can be omitted by readers who do not want too much detail). Section 7.7 suggests other explanations for the bidding, and section 7.8 develops a relative performance maximizing theory for it. Sections 7.9 and 7.10 briefly comment on some other 3G auctions, and stress (as GRW also do) the importance of attracting entry into an auction.

7.5 THE GERMAN AUCTION

In particular, I disagree with GRW's central claim that their model, as it stands, rationalizes the behavior of the two strongest bidders, T-Mobil and Mannesman, or "T" and "M", in GRW's terminology.[19] These bidders initially pushed up the price in the hope of driving out the sixth-strongest bidder, "bidder 6" in GRW's terminology, but then gave up pushing the price up so that the auction did actually end with six winners but at a much higher price than was necessary to end the auction with this number of winners. This seems bizarre. To put the point simply, consider T's and M's decision about whether to end the auction with six winners at some given price, or whether to push the price up further. Raising the per-block price by 1 euro costs T and M 2 euros each, since they would each win two blocks in a six-winner outcome. Their gain is the probability that bidder 6 quits, times their benefit from bidder 6 quitting. If it is worthwhile for T and M to push the price up in one round, but to stop pushing the price up in the next round, then the perceived probability of bidder 6 quitting in the next round must be both low, and also lower than it was in the last round. However, most observers thought the probability of bidder 6 quitting in the next round, conditional on not having previously quit, was high and increasing around the time T and M ended the auction (when per capita price levels were approaching those achieved in the United Kingdom) and was much lower earlier (a six-player conclusion for the auction became possible at 55 percent of the UK price levels). So any rationalization of T and M's behavior must explain this apparently irrational behavior of theirs. But GRW's model side steps this basic issue, as I now explain.

---

[19] T-Mobil and Mannesman were subsidiaries of Deutsche Telekom and Vodafone, respectively.

7.6 GRW'S ANALYSIS OF THE GERMAN AUCTION

[This sub-section can be omitted by readers who do not want too much detail.]

To understand GRW's argument—and why I believe it is incomplete in this context—consider the preferences of either one of the two strong bidders, M and T. At any point in time, it would like to end the auction only if it prefers this to waiting until the price has risen a small further amount, $\Delta price$, before the auction ends.

The gain from waiting is the probability, ρ_6, that bidder 6 will quit in the price interval, $\Delta price$, times the value of driving bidder 6 out. This value is itself the benefit, β, of winning a third block, including the benefits from excluding bidder 6 from the industry (leading to a more concentrated, and hence more profitable, market), less the current price of buying an additional block. That is, the total gain from waiting equals $\rho_6[\beta - price]$.

The cost of waiting is the extra price, $\Delta price$, paid on the two units that the bidder will win anyway, that is, $2(\Delta price)$. That is, the bidder would prefer to plan to end the auction if a further price rise of $\Delta price$ fails to drive out bidder 6, rather than end it now if

$$\rho_6[\beta - price] > 2[\Delta price]. \tag{1}$$

The bidder would prefer to end the auction now if

$$\rho_6[\beta - price] < 2[\Delta price]. \tag{2}$$

In GRW's model, bidder 6's value can only take one of two possible values, v_6' (strong type) and v_6 (weak type), and the auction cannot be ended before price p ($< v_6$), so the only conceivably sensible strategies for the strong bidders are:

(a) to end the auction as soon as possible at p, or
(b) to push the price up a further $\Delta price = v_6 - p$ to v_6 to drive out the weaker type of bidder 6, but then to end the auction, or
(c) to push the price up further still, by an additional $\Delta price = v_6' - v_6$ more to v_6', to drive out both types of bidder 6.

The observed behavior in the actual auction corresponded to case (b) of GRW's model.

The condition for (b) to be preferred to (a) is the appropriate version of (1) or equivalently is GRW's equation (9).[20] The condition for (b) to be preferred to (c) is the appropriate version of (2), or equivalently GRW's equation (6).[21] So these are the key conditions in GRW's Theorem.[22] If (6) holds there is an equilibrium in which outcome (b) arises. (If (6) fails, both strong bidders prefer (c), and either

---

[20] In GRW's notation, $\beta = v_{13} + b$ for the case of successfully driving out bidder 6 at price v_6.

[21] In GRW's notation, $\beta = v_{13}' + b$ for the case of driving out bidder 6 at price v_6', but $\rho_6 = 1$ in GRW's model at stage (c).

[22] GRW rename (6) as "$\Delta_{pr}^2 \leq 0$" in their statement of Theorem 1.

can unilaterally implement it.) If (9) holds, the equilibrium is unique. If (9) fails, outcome (b) can still be an equilibrium of the model if (6) holds, since neither strong bidder can unilaterally end the auction, but the equilibrium is neither unique, nor plausible.[23] So for the observed play to correspond to a plausible equilibrium of GRW's model, both (9) and (6) are required.[24]

Noting that (9) and (6) are just my equations (1) and (2) suggests why GRW's theory seems unlikely to describe reality. Of course, (9) and (6) correspond to (1) and (2) evaluated at different values of ρ_6, β, price and $\Delta price$, reflecting the different stages of the game at which (9) and (6) are computed. So the observed play can correspond to an equilibrium of GRW's model. But this requires that $[\rho_6/(\Delta price)]$ not be too much lower when the strong bidders could first have ended the auction (when (1) must be satisfied) than at the actual end of the auction (when (2) must be satisfied).[25]

Furthermore, the tension between conditions (9) and (6) is more severe when the game is generalized to many small stages since the values of $[\rho_6/(\Delta price)]$, β, and price to be substituted into (1) and (2) cannot then vary much between stages, and related conditions must then hold at all the stages—an issue that GRW do not address.[26] In particular, (1) must hold just

---

[23] This equilibrium is not plausible if (9) fails because in this equilibrium both strong players prefer outcome (a) to outcome (b), but both follow the strategy corresponding to (b) because each expects the other to do this. This logic can only hold in the two-stage model: with more stages, each strong player would know that if it followed the strategy corresponding to (a), then the other strong player would follow just one round of the auction later (if (9) fails)—that is, the players could trivially coordinate on strategy (a) in the actual multi-round auction, which eliminates this equilibrium. This equilibrium is, of course, also Pareto dominated by the more natural equilibrium for the players in GRW's two-stage model, and GRW also eliminate this equilibrium in their limited extension to multiple rounds (see note 26). However, an equilibrium of this kind becomes more plausible if M and T are each uncertain that its rival shares its assessment of the parameters, or are uncertain about the rival's objectives (see section 7.8).

[24] GRW note that Theorem 1 also requires other conditions.

[25] It does not seem likely that $(\beta - price)$ ever became very small because β includes both the value of a third block to a strong bidder and the value, b in GRW's terminology, of excluding bidder 6 from the industry, leading to a more concentrated and hence more profitable market. Therefore, β must be greater than $p_2 + b$, where p_2 is the expected maximum of the value of a fourth block to a strong bidder and a third block to a less strong bidder. And, as GRW point out, p_2 must itself be quite high for the GRW equilibrium to make sense—the logic of GRW's equilibrium requires p_2 to be at least equal to the final German auction price. (The very limited anecdotal evidence suggests that p_2 might have been, very roughly, in the region of the final German auction price.)

[26] GRW do briefly consider extending their model to many rounds of bidding, but when they do this they maintain the extreme assumption that bidder 6's valuation can take only two possible values, v_6 and v'_6. Thus, in their extension there is no possibility of bidder 6 quitting before v_6, or between v_6 and v'_6, so the additional rounds of bidding are mostly irrelevant and (1) and (2) are relevant only at the same points at which they matter in the two-stage game, i.e., GRW's conditions (9) and (6) suffice as before. In a proper many-round extension of GRW's game in which it is also recognized that bidder 6's valuation is not restricted to just two possible values, conditions related to (1) or (2) must hold at each round of the game. (One difference that arises even in GRW's simplified many-round version is that (9) and (6) are both required for GRW's result to be an equilibrium.)

before the auction ends, and (2) must hold at the price at which the auction ends. If the price is changing only slowly between rounds (as was the case in the actual auction), it is required that $[\rho_6/(\Delta price)]$ is falling (or at least not increasing much) at the end of the auction.

Summarizing the two previous paragraphs, GRW's equilibrium requires that, at the end of the auction, the probability of bidder 6 quitting conditional on not yet having done so is *both* not much increasing, *and* not much larger than at the lower prices at which the strong bidders could earlier, if they had both wished, have ended the auction.

These two conditions seem implausible. A six-player conclusion to the auction became possible when Debitel quit at prices that were just 55 percent of the final UK prices (per capita).[27] The German auction actually finished at 94 percent of the final UK prices. The weakest of the six remaining bidders was generally thought to be either Mobilcom or "Group 3G", the joint venture between Telefonica and Sonera, so ρ_6 represents the probability that one of these would quit in the next round, conditional on their not yet having quit. But Telefonica and Mobilcom had quit the UK auction when the price levels reached 94 percent and 100 percent of the final UK price level, respectively.[28] Mobilcom (at least) had made public statements that suggested that it was likely it would bid as far as it had in the UK auction,[29] and outside observers also thought that these bidders would probably go a lot further than 55 percent of the UK auction price, but might quit at around the final UK price levels. Certainly, most plausible distributions of valuations implied that at the end of the auction the probability of bidder 6 quitting was both much higher than earlier, and increasing, and either of these implications is sufficient to rule out GRW's equilibrium.[30]

In brief, GRW's equilibrium requires, roughly, that the strong bidders thought it relatively likely that Mobilcom or Group 3G would quit while prices were well below UK levels but then, having seen that Mobilcom and Group 3G did not quit at such low prices, the strong bidders thought it both relatively

[27] Ending the auction at these prices would have required the cooperation of all six bidders, but this could probably have been obtained. Even if this seemed hard, M and T could together have ended the auction once the other four bidders had stopped bidding for three blocks; none of the other bidders had high bids for three blocks beyond round 136 when the prices were 70 percent of the final UK price, and all could be proved to have lost eligibility for three blocks shortly thereafter.

[28] Mobilcom was owned in large part by France Telecom which was also part owner of NTL Mobile, the last bidder to quit the UK auction.

[29] It may be said that such statements were cheap talk. But following through on them may be necessary to maintain management credibility; they probably reflected an availability of finance, and—what matters—they seemed credible to observers at the time.

[30] Although GRW argue (in the last paragraph of their section V) that it was reasonable to expect that bidder 6 might quit at some point before the final German auction price, they fail to consider the crucial questions about the relative likelihoods of bidder 6 quitting at a very low price, or at close to the final UK prices.

unlikely, and increasingly unlikely, that they would quit while prices were close to UK levels. This seems unreasonable.

7.7 WHAT ACTUALLY HAPPENED IN THE GERMAN AUCTION?

Whilst no one can be certain, it seems that other factors are required to explain the behavior of T-Mobil and Mannesman in the German auction. Some of these factors are discussed in sections 4.5 and 5.4.1.[31]

They include the complexity of the rules and the opacity of the information available to bidders about others' bids, which made it hard for bidders to figure out optimal strategies (T may simply have made a mistake in failing to heed M's signal suggesting that they both reduce demand early on) or to understand their rivals' thinking. Section 4.5 stresses the apparent lack of trust and understanding between the two strong bidders, and discusses why this mistrust might have arisen.

Furthermore, the strong bidders may not simply have been maximizing expected profits. M and T may have focused more on their performances *relative* to each other, as might be rational behavior for managers who had private career concerns, or were concerned that their firm seemed well managed and deserving of further investment, etc. Relative performance concerns may explain the auction's outcome, especially in conjunction with the mistrust between the bidders, as we explain in more detail in the next section.

Other contributory factors to T's behavior that have been suggested include that T felt pressured by the stock market's response to the rising auction prices (and that T had not fully anticipated this), and even that T's objectives were affected by the fact that it was majority owned by the German government.

7.8 A RELATIVE PERFORMANCE MAXIMIZING THEORY OF THE GERMAN AUCTION

GRW explain that if, for example, M reduced demand to two blocks while T did not, and T then won three blocks by driving out bidder 6, there would then have been a second auction for the remaining block which would most probably have been won by M at an expected price p_2 (in GRW's terminology) so both M and T would have ended up with three blocks but having paid different prices for them.

[31] Ewerhart and Moldovanu (2001) make interesting points about the German design but in a model in which there is only a single strong bidder, so they cannot address why initially both strong bidders pushed up the price, and then both stopped doing so. Also they do not model the second auction that would have taken place if just one strong bidder had pushed up the price and subsequently driven a weak bidder out, and this possible second auction may have played an important role in the behavior in the main auction, as we discuss in section 7.8.

Recall also from our discussion above that when prices are still low (e.g., around 55 percent of the final UK auction price) the probability of bidder 6 quitting is low, so it probably maximizes both firms' expected profits to reduce demand to two blocks and end the auction at low prices. However, if one firm, say M, reduces demand while T fails to do so and continues to push the price up, there is some—perhaps small—probability that bidder 6 will be driven out at a price $\tilde{p} < p_2$, in which case T and M will both end up with three blocks (assuming that M wins the block in the second auction), but T will on average pay less for its blocks than M (since T pays $3\tilde{p}$, but M expects to pay $2\tilde{p} + p_2$). Even in this case T and M may both be worse off in absolute terms than if T and M had both reduced demand to win two blocks at low prices. Because the chance of driving out bidder 6 at a low price is not that high, the more probable result would simply be that T would eventually reduce its own demand to two blocks later on, in which case both T and M would be much worse off than if they had both reduced demand earlier. But note that T always improves its performance relative to M by failing to reduce demand at prices below p_2.

Furthermore, even if each firm is actually an ordinary profit maximizer, but each firm expects that the other is likely to maximize relative performance, then neither firm will reduce demand first (since being the only firm to reduce demand when prices are low risks paying $2\tilde{p} + p_2$ rather than $3\tilde{p}$).[32]

Similarly, when prices are higher (e.g., close to the final UK levels), it may maximize both M's and T's expected profits to push up the price to drive out bidder 6. But if one of the firms, say T, reduces demand to two blocks and lets M push up the price on its own to drive out bidder 6 at a price $p^* > p_2$, then again T and M will both end up with three blocks (assuming that T wins the block in the second auction) but T will pay less on average for its blocks than M pays (since T expects to pay $2p^* + p_2$, but M pays $3p^*$. So T would improve both its relative and its absolute performance if it could reduce demand alone, and M would then improve its relative performance by reducing demand along with T, even though M might increase its (and T's) absolute profits by continuing to raise the price to drive out bidder 6.

The story told thus far is extreme. True, there is anecdotal evidence that firms' managers cared about relative performance, and concerns about relative performance also seem to have played at least some role in other European 3G auctions (see, e.g., section 7.3).[33] But M and T were surely not concerned only with relative performance. So one might have expected M and T to attempt to coordinate their behavior to reduce their demands at low prices to maximize both of their absolute profits. Indeed it seems that M did initially try to signal to T that they should do

---

[32] A similar argument is that if all firms are known to be ordinary profit maximizers, but firms are unsure that their rival has the same estimates of parameters such as ρ_6, then firms may be unwilling to reduce demand first.

[33] Abbink et al. (2001b, section 4), provides some evidence that relative performance issues were important to these bidders in the German DCS-1800 auction.

just this (see GRW and sections 4.5 and 5.4.1). But T could not know whether M was sincere, and the firms apparently mistrusted each other's intentions (see section 4.5) and, as we have seen, there are very strong relative performance arguments (it suffices that each feared that the other might maximize relative performance) why neither was prepared to be the first to reduce demand while prices were still low.

T then reduced demand later when prices were higher, perhaps for relative performance reasons,[34] and/or because this could also improve its absolute performance if M failed (or was unable) to follow its demand reduction.[35,36] Once T had reduced demand, there are several possible reasons why M followed straight away. First, M had a strong relative performance incentive to follow immediately, as explained above. Second, M may have wanted to develop a reputation for cooperative behavior in which M and T parallel each other's behavior—a kind of 'relative performance' effect but strictly driven by M's long-run absolute performance goals (see section 4.5). Third, M might have been concerned only with its (short-term) absolute performance, but it might all along have taken the view that this would be maximized by M and T both reducing demand, and it might have stuck to this view (i.e., M may have been extremely pessimistic about driving out bidder 6 at low prices and, even though driving out bidder 6 seemed more likely at high prices, remained fairly pessimistic—see section 5.4.1); this is consistent with M's early behavior (signaling T to reduce demand but not unilaterally reducing demand) if it feared that T might place a large weight on relative performance.

---

[34] It might seem that a firm could protect its relative performance by following a strategy of quitting only if its rival quits when prices are above p_2. However, it takes time to be sure the rival has quit (because the auctioneer gave the bidders only limited information about their rivals' bidding), and it also takes time to respond. Furthermore, some of the weaker players may have been staying in the auction in the hope of being a winner in a five-firm industry, which would have been the outcome if M and T had successfully driven one of them out—in particular, each of Mobilcom and Group 3G might have hoped that the other (or possibly E-plus or Viag) was the 'bidder 6' who might have been driven out. In this case, when one of M and T quits bidding for a third block, these weaker players may expect the other of M and T to try to follow suit and may therefore try to quit first rather than find themselves stuck as winners in a much less profitable six-firm industry. So if either M or T failed to quit first when prices became high, it might have risked being stranded buying a third block at a higher price than its opponent, and achieving a very poor relative-performance.

[35] If T thought M was not too concerned with relative performance, T could improve both its relative and absolute performance by reducing demand once the price exceeded p_2, and free-riding on M continuing to push price up to drive out bidder 6. Even if M was concerned with relative performance, there was the possibility that M would have been unable to follow T (see note 34).

[36] Of course, there may be other reasons, such as T being influenced by stock market pressure or its government ownership (see section 7.7). It might be argued that another possibility was that β was not in fact that high. However, this seems less likely since β must have substantially exceeded p_2 (see note 25) and if p_2 were low then both firms would have been willing to reduce demand early on for relative, as well as absolute, performance reasons.

Of course, there may be other reasons for the observed behavior in the auction. For example, fear that one's rival has very different perceptions from one's own about the chance of driving out bidder 6 can have similar effects to fear that one's rival is a relative performance maximizer,[37] and section 4.5 emphasizes the mistrust and misunderstanding between the bidders. But the point is that the apparently puzzling behavior can be explained by postulating only a limited concern with relative performance. To explain why M and T failed to reduce demand early on, it suffices that each firm thought its rival put some weight on relative performance; it is not necessary that either firm actually did so, and even the conjectured weights on relative performance need not have been large if firms were also uncertain about their rivals' perceptions about bidder 6's behavior, etc. Not much more concern with relative performance is needed to explain the firms' later behavior in the auction.

7.9 THE AUSTRIAN AND SWISS AUCTIONS

Turning to other 3G auctions, I disagree with GRW's assertion that the Austrian auction design was superior to the Swiss, except to the extent that the Austrian reserve price was somewhat more realistically chosen than the Swiss reserve. Neither auction attracted more bidders than there were winners, and neither involved any significant bidding. (Although there was a semblance of serious bidding in the Austrian auction, the bidders there were put under considerable pressure from the authorities to continue the bidding, and it was widely believed that the bidding only lasted the few rounds it did in order to create some public perception of genuine competition and reduce the risk of the government changing the rules.) Neither auction achieved more than 11 percent more than the reserve price that had been set. The only important difference is that the Swiss reserve price had been set ludicrously low at 20 euros per capita, while the Austrian reserve price, although still far lower than it should have been, was 90 euros per capita.[38] But revenues in excess of 300 euros per capita should probably have been attainable in both auctions (see section 5.5). So both of these auctions were failures, and both were intensely embarrassing to their respective governments. Indeed there was no successful European 3G auction after the UK and German auctions until the Danes switched to a sealed-bid design. I have discussed all these auctions in more detail in chapter 5.

---

[37] In particular, fear can make a bidder unwilling to reduce demand first when prices are low, because of the perceived risk that the rival will not follow (see note 32).

[38] Of course, Switzerland sold four licenses while Austria sold six, but the Swiss could obviously have used the same design to sell six licenses if they had preferred that outcome.

7.10 THE IMPORTANCE OF ENTRY, AND THE UK AUCTION

Where I do agree very strongly with GRW is on the importance of attracting entry into an auction.[39] As GRW say, "competition is not a free good" and auctions must be designed with this in mind. However, this does not imply that there is any single best design. Often a sealed-bid design is best for attracting entry, as is suggested by the Danish example in the previous paragraph. But this need not be the case. The UK design was appropriate in its context, because the UK auction was the first 3G auction and was therefore unlikely to suffer from entry problems. (See sections 4.5, 5.3.1, and 5.7 for more discussion of why being first was so important.) Indeed the UK auction attracted 13 bidders compared with the seven that entered the German auction. It seems improbable that the German design would have usefully increased competition in the British auction, and the British design had other advantages over the German design,[40] see chapter 5 and section 6.4.3 (though my view may be colored by my having been the principal auction theorist for the UK auction[41]). In another context, when Peter Cramton, Eric Maskin, and I advised on the UK's 2002 auction for greenhouse gas emission reductions, we chose a uniform price ascending design as being most likely to attract "small" bidders who did not have the resources to work out how to bid correctly in a discriminatory price auction (see Klemperer et al., forthcoming).[42] Nor, of course, is entry always the key issue. As I discussed in chapters 3–6, good auction design is not "one size fits all", but must always be tailored to its context.

---

[39] I emphasized this in Bulow and Klemperer (1996), Klemperer (1998), and chapters 3–6.

[40] One advantage is identified in note 34: in the German design a bidder might rationally follow a strategy that could mean that it felt sorry to have won as soon as the auction finished.

[41] I was the principal auction theorist advising the Radiocommunications Agency which designed and ran the UK auction. Ken Binmore led the team and supervised experiments testing the proposed designs. Other academic advisors included Tilman Börgers, Jeremy Bulow, Philippe Jehiel and Joe Swierzbinski.

[42] Larry Ausubel and Jeremy Bulow were also involved in the implementation of this auction. This was strictly a descending auction, since the auctioneer was buying reductions in emissions rather than selling permits to emit, but the auction corresponded to an ascending auction to sell emissions.

CHAPTER EIGHT

Were Auctions a Good Idea?*

I briefly review the effects of the 3G auctions on the telecom industry. (The general question of auctions vs. beauty contests is the topic of section 6.2.)

The wrong culprit for telecom trouble

European telecommunications companies are now worth about $700bn (£443bn) less than when the UK began the world's first "third generation" (3G) auction in March 2000. These auctions are now routinely blamed for the travails of the telecoms industry and even – by extension – the world economy.

President Jacques Chirac recently protested to the European Union about the 3G auctions, the head of the United Nations telecommunica-

* This chapter was originally published under the title "The Wrong Culprit for Telecom Trouble", in the *Financial Times*, 26 November 2002, p. 21.

:

tions agency claimed that they "helped drive the telecoms industry into its crisis", and a Finnish minister even called them "the biggest industrial political failure since the second world war".

The critics assume three things: that the telecoms companies paid more for the licenses than they thought the licenses were worth; that this expenditure has reduced investment in 3G; and that it destroyed the telecoms companies' market value.

Sustaining these views requires little more than a fallible memory. There has now been so much bad news about the technology and about the lack of consumer interest in 3G services that it is hard to imagine any company voluntarily paid billions of dollars for a 3G license. But volunteer they all did. Not only that but they celebrated their victories. The stock market was happy, and shortly after the UK auction Hutchison even resold part of its license at a profit.

It is hard now to imagine any company voluntarily paid billions for a 3G license. But volunteer they all did— and they celebrated their victories

In retrospect, of course, the licenses look expensive. But in retrospect, shares or houses sometimes look expensive. Like any other market, an auction simply matches willing buyers and willing sellers—it cannot protect them against their own mistakes.

A more subtle complaint is that incumbent operators had to win 3G licenses to protect their existing 2G businesses, so were "forced" to overbid.

But all the main 3G auctions were ascending bid auctions, in which the price stops rising when the losers give up; so the price was set by losers who were new entrants with no existing 2G businesses to protect. Were these entrants – including Hutchison, France Telecom, Telefonica and Sonera – all naively bidding more than the helpless incumbents thought the licenses were worth? It seems unlikely: incumbents, with their established brands and infrastructure, could make much better use of 3G licenses. Entrants would have had to bid a long way north of their valuations before any incumbent could be hurt by matching them. Even if the incumbents did think the entrants were overbidding, they always had the option of dropping out, and buying the entrants later when valuations had settled down.

Furthermore, in the UK, two incumbents, but no entrants, competed to offer £2bn more for a larger license – hardly a sign that the entrants had backed them into a corner. And no one has ever suggested that any incumbent needed a larger rather than a smaller license to protect its 2G business!

Some opponents of the auctions concede the bids were voluntary but argue they were damaging nevertheless: because the licenses were so expensive, investment in 3G is lower and slower than it should be. This is odd: the auction fees are history; they have (almost) all been paid in full, cannot be recouped by cutting investment, and make no difference to its profitability.

It is conceivable that capital markets are so inefficient that obviously highly profitable investment is being forgone because no one wants to fund it. It is more likely that the same bad news that now makes the licenses look overvalued is also making further investment look unwise.

It is even possible that investment may now be too rapid. Two license winners told the UK government that high license costs would spur investment – perhaps because companies would be keen to prove that they could recoup their license costs. And if high license fees persuade governments to regulate companies more lightly and permit them to raise prices, investment will become attractive for all the wrong reasons. Probably none of these effects is critical. Investment in 3G, as in anything else, is primarily motivated by attractive returns in the future – not by money spent in the past.

Then there is the final claim: that 3G license fees wiped hundreds of billions off the value of European telecoms companies. Before accepting that view too quickly, look across the Atlantic. The United States held no 3G auctions, yet telecoms companies lost just as much: in fact, they lost more. Even setting aside the collapses of Global Crossing and WorldCom, wireless companies such as Nextel and Sprint PCS each lost more than $50bn in valuation. In the United Kingdom, the most distressed telecoms companies are not the license winners but firms such as NTL – the disappointed runner-up – which has recently been restructured. All in all, it seems a stretch to blame $700bn of shareholder misery on $100bn of 3G license fees.

None of the complaints really hold water. Why do we keep hearing them? It is obviously convenient for embarrassed company executives to be able to blame the government. They may even persuade the governments to return the $100 billion to them – if not in whole and in cash, then at least in part and by the back door through more lenient regulation. But for governments to do this would be a huge mistake.

There is nothing special about an auction: it is just another market. Buying houses or shares at the peak of a housing or stock-market boom does not entitle anyone to compensation. Why should we make an exception for the phone companies?

If governments wish to subsidize the telecoms or any other industry, that has nothing to do with auctions. Furthermore, governments' past use of public funds to subsidize "key" industries has rarely inspired confidence, and if they do insist on paying subsidies, why pick the telecoms sector (and the telecoms operators within this sector) in particular? Any case for subsidies is completely separate from who paid what for 3G licenses.

The main effect of the license fees was simply to transfer $100bn from shareholders around the world to certain European governments. This was both equitable, since the companies were buying a public asset that they valued this highly at the time, and efficient, since such a lump sum transfer is much more efficient than most forms of taxation. Efficient, equitable and voluntary government funding is not easy to find: perhaps we should be more enthusiastic about it.

The writer is a professor of economics at the University of Oxford, and advised the UK government on its 3G license auction www.paulklemperer.org

Suggestions for Course Outlines

While the independent **general reader** would find it most straightforward to read each part separately (though the parts may be taken in any order), an instructor of a **graduate course** might teach the material in the following order:

(i) *Basic Auction Forms and the Revenue Equivalence Theorem*:

> Part A: Appendix 1.A, first part of Appendix 1.D, sections 1.1–1.4
> Exercises 1–3
> Further reading: Vickrey (1961), Myerson (1981)

(ii) *Applications of the Revenue Equivalence Theorem*:

> Part B: sections 2.2, 2.5.2
> Exercises 4–6
> Further reading: Bulow and Klemperer (1994, 1999)

(iii) *The Analysis of Optimal Auctions, Including Marginal Revenues*:

> Part A: Appendix 1.B, section 1.4
> Exercises 7–8
> Further reading: Myerson (1981), Bulow and Roberts (1989)

(iv) *Applications of Marginal Revenue Analysis*:

> Part B: section 2.4
> Part A: section 1.7.1
> Further reading: Bulow and Klemperer (1996)

(v) *Common Values, and the Winner's Curse*:

> Part A: Appendix 1.D (continued), section 1.7.2
> Exercises 9–10
> Further reading: Klemperer (1998)

(vi) *Affiliation*:

> Part A: Appendices 1.C, 1.D (continued), section 1.6
> Further reading: Milgrom and Weber (1982a)

(vii) *Other Theory (Risk-Aversion, Asymmetries, Budget Constraints, etc.)*:

    Part A: sections 1.5, 1.7, 1.11–1.14
    Part B: section 2.5.1
    Exercise 11

(viii) *Multi-Unit Issues, and Introduction to Entry, Collusion* (these topics will be a focus of segments (ix)–(x)):

    Part A: sections 1.8–1.10, Afterword
    Part D: section 6.5.2
    Part B: section 2.3

(ix) *Practical Auction Design*:

    Part C

(x) *Case Study: the European 3G Auctions*:

    Part D

Each of these ten segments might use about 1–1.5 hours of class time. All of the further readings are reprinted in Klemperer (2000a), and many can also be found at www.paulklemperer.org. Optional additional readings are described in Part A, and are also reprinted in Klemperer (2000a).

UNDERGRADUATE COURSE

Undergraduate lectures might comprise:

(a) *Introduction to the Basic Auction Forms, Private and Common Values*: brief statements and explanations of the Winner's Curse, and the Revenue Equivalence Theorem:

    Part A: sections 1.1–1.4
    Further reading: Part A: sections 1.5–1.7, first two parts of Appendix 1.D

(b) *Practical Auction Design*, including Case Study: the European 3G Auctions:

    Part C
    Part D (except chapter 7)

Each of these two lectures might take about 2 hours of class time.

MBA COURSE

An MBA course segment might be similar to the undergraduate lectures, but probably with less time devoted to (a), more time devoted to (b), and excluding the "further reading".

Solutions to Exercises[1]

1. (i) See Appendix 1.A.

(ii) It is a dominant strategy for each bidder to bid up to her value. Hence, conditional on winning, bidder i expects to pay the expected highest of the other $n - 1$ bidders' values, conditional on her own value, v_i, being highest, that is, $[(n - 1)/n]v_i$.[2]

(iii) Bidder i wins with probability $(F(v_i))^{n-1} = (v_i/\bar{v})^{n-1}$. So in an ascending auction, her unconditional expected payment is $[(n - 1)/n](v_i^n/\bar{v}^{n-1})$. By revenue equivalence, this is her (unconditional) expected payment in the "all-pay" auction, and, hence, her bid.

(iv) Assuming the other $n - 1$ bidders bid according to the equilibrium bidding strategy $b(v)$, i's surplus from bidding as type $\tilde{v}$ is $S_i = v_i(F(\tilde{v}))^{n-1} - b(\tilde{v})$. Bidder i's optimal choice of $\tilde{v}$ satisfies

$$\frac{\partial S_i}{\partial \tilde{v}} = 0 \quad \Rightarrow \quad v_i(n - 1)(F(\tilde{v}))^{n-2}f(\tilde{v}) - b'(\tilde{v}) = 0.$$

In equilibrium, each bidder behaves as her own type, that is, $\tilde{v} = v_i$, so $b'(v_i) = v_i(n - 1)(F(v_i))^{n-2}f(v_i)$. For $F(v)$ uniform on $[0, \bar{v}]$, we have

$$b'(v) = (n - 1)\frac{v^{n-1}}{\bar{v}^{n-1}},$$

which, since $b(0) = 0$, has solution

$$b(v) = \frac{(n - 1)}{n}\frac{v^n}{\bar{v}^{n-1}}.$$

(See chapter 1, note 121 for a more detailed explanation of applying a similar procedure to a first-price auction.)

2. (i) Type Ls always reject, because their value is less than a. For Hs, given that an H opponent accepts

$$S(H \mid \text{reject}) = \tfrac{1}{2}(0) + \tfrac{1}{2}\tfrac{1}{2}(1) = \tfrac{1}{4}$$

---

[1] I am very grateful for the assistance of Eric Budish and Marco Pagnozzi in preparing these solutions.

[2] Recall from Appendix 1.D that the expected value of the kth highest among n values independently drawn from a uniform distribution on $[0, \bar{v}]$ is $[(n + 1 - k)/(n + 1)]\bar{v}$.

$$S(H \mid \text{accept}) = \tfrac{1}{2}(1-a) + \tfrac{1}{2}\tfrac{1}{2}(1-a) = \tfrac{3}{4}(1-a) > \tfrac{1}{4}.$$

So Hs always accept, and

$$S(H) = \tfrac{3}{4}(1-a), \quad S(L) = 0, \quad \pi(\text{seller}) = \tfrac{3}{4}a$$

[In fact, if $a \in [\tfrac{1}{2}, \tfrac{2}{3})$ it is also an equilibrium for Hs always to reject, and there is also a mixed strategy equilibrium in which Hs accept a fraction $q = (4 - \tfrac{2}{a})$ of the time.]

(ii) The distribution of types is not strictly increasing and atomless. So types' relative surpluses are not pinned down as they are in Appendix 1.A, figure 1.1—in terms of that analysis, equation (4) is not well defined (see part (iii) of this question). [The relative surpluses would be pinned down, and so revenue equivalence would apply, if the distribution of types were *either* strictly increasing *or* atomless; in our context a more restricted set of auction forms satisfies revenue equivalence; see, e.g., Maskin and Riley (1985).]

(iii) Type Hs win with probability $p_H = \tfrac{3}{4}$, and type Ls win with probability $p_L = \tfrac{1}{4}$. The incentive compatibility constraints are:

$$S(H) \geq S(L) + p_L(v_H - v_L) \quad \Rightarrow \quad S(H) \geq S(L) + \tfrac{1}{4},$$

$$S(L) \geq S(H) + p_H(v_L - v_H) \quad \Rightarrow \quad S(H) \leq S(L) + \tfrac{3}{4}.$$

Since L's individual rationality constraint requires $S(L) \geq 0$, an optimal mechanism has $S(L) = 0$, $S(H) = \tfrac{1}{4}$. The mechanism in (i), with $a = \tfrac{2}{3}$, is one such mechanism.

(iv) A take-it-or-leave-it offer of 1 to both buyers (with a lottery if both accept, and a commitment not to sell if neither does) is accepted by Hs and captures the entire surplus.

3. (i) See Appendix 1.A. (The fact that a bidder's probability of winning an object, $P_i(v)$, is different in a multi-unit context does not affect the standard argument.)

(ii) If after the first sealed-bid auction the second unit were unexpectedly sold by ascending auction (with the five remaining bidders), the expected payment, conditional on winning, of a bidder with value v would be $E(v_2{}^5 \mid v_1{}^5 = v)$. Since the other four bidders' values, conditional on being below v, are uniformly distributed below v, this expectation equals $\tfrac{4}{5}v$ (see note 2). By revenue equivalence this must be the player's bid in the second sealed-bid auction.

(iii) If both objects are sold simultaneously in an ascending auction, a bidder with value v wins if she has one of the two highest values, and pays the third-highest actual value when she wins. Her expected payment is then

$$P(v \text{ is highest}) E(v_3{}^6 \mid v \text{ is highest})$$

$$+P(v \text{ is second highest}) E(v_3{}^6 \mid v \text{ is second highest}).$$

If the objects are sold in sequential sealed-bid auctions, the bidder still wins an object if her value is in the top two, and her expected payment is

$$P(v \text{ is highest})(v\text{'s bid in 1st auction})$$

$$+P(v \text{ is second highest})(v\text{'s bid in 2nd auction}).$$

By revenue equivalence, the expected payments from these two different two-unit auctions are equal. Furthermore, from part (ii) her bid in the second sealed-bid auction is $\frac{4}{5}v$, which equals $E(v_3{}^6 \mid v_2{}^6 = v)$. Therefore, v's bid in the first sealed-bid auction is $E(v_3{}^6 \mid v_1{}^6 = v)$ which equals $\frac{4}{6}v$.

(iv) Extending the argument, when $(m + 4)$ bidders remain for m objects, v's bid is $[4/(m + 4)]v$. Since the winner of the rth auction has the actual value v_r^{n+4}, and $m = n + 1 - r$, the actual winning bid in the rth auction is $[4/(m + 4)]v_r^{n+4} = [4/(n + 5 - r)]v_r^{n+4}$. But $E(v_r^{n+4}) = [(n + 5 - r)/(n + 5)]\bar{v}$, so the ex-ante expected price in the rth auction equals $[4/(n + 5)]\bar{v}$, which is constant. [It is not hard to check the price is a martingale.]

(v) See section 1.10.3.

4. (i) In an ascending auction, bidder i's unconditional expected payment is

$$\Pr(v_i > v_j) E[v_j \mid v_i > v_j] = F(v_i) \int_{\underline{v}}^{v_i} x \frac{f(x)}{F(v_i)} \, dx = \int_{\underline{v}}^{v_i} x f(x) dx$$

(or, integrating by parts, $v_i F(v_i) - \int_{\underline{v}}^{v_i} F(x) dx$).

By revenue equivalence, i's unconditional expected payment is the same in an "all-pay" auction (i.e., under current US rules).

We assumed that $F(\cdot)$ is strictly increasing and atomless, that bidders are risk-neutral, and that the "all-pay" equilibrium is symmetric and increasing with type $\underline{v}$ bidding zero.

(ii) Revenue equivalence implies that the expected legal expenses of a bidder with value v are the same under both rules, assuming Quayle's rules also result in a symmetric and increasing equilibrium with type $\underline{v}$ bidding zero (this is justified in part iv).

(iii) Now the expected payments of the lowest type are positive, since that type will lose and pay some of the opponent's cost. So every type's expected legal expenses are higher (by the expectation of the lowest type's payment, since the incentive compatibility condition is unchanged for every type; see Appendix 1.A) (assuming a symmetric, increasing, equilibrium, etc.; see part v).

(iv) Under Quayle's rules, spending $l(v_i)$ yields total expected payment

$$E(i\text{'s payment}) = \underbrace{l(v_i)}_{\text{Direct Cost}} + \underbrace{(1 - F(v_i))l(v_i)}_{\text{Pr(Lose)} * \text{Transfer}} - \underbrace{F(v_i) \int_{\underline{v}}^{v_i} l(x) \frac{f(x)}{F(v_i)} dx}_{\text{Pr(Win)} * E(\text{Transfer}|\text{Win})} .$$

Using parts (i) and (ii) we also have $E(i\text{'s payment}) = \int_{\underline{v}}^{v_i} xf(x)dx$. Equating these two expressions yields a differential equation which is satisfied by the (increasing) function

$$l(v_i) = \frac{v_i^2}{3} \frac{3 - v_i}{(2 - v_i)^2}$$

if $F(v_i) = v_i$ (noting that $\int_0^{v_i} l(x)dx = [v_i^3/6(2 - v_i)]$).

(v) A party's deservingness may influence the judgment, as may other asymmetries, risk aversion, etc.

Furthermore, *which* lawsuits are brought is a crucial issue not captured in the model. In particular, under the European systems low types will prefer not to participate (see part iii). This suggests the number of trials will be lower. (But note that if in our model low types are permitted to withdraw, there can be no increasing equilibrium, so we no longer have revenue equivalence with an ascending auction.)

However, the model does capture the intuition that the larger stakes in the European and the Quayle systems increase the incentives to spend. In the European system this means higher expenses. In Quayle's it counteracts the fact that paying your lawyer another $1 may cost you $2. [See section 2.2.1 and Appendix 2.A, and Baye, Kovenock, and de Vries (1997) for further discussion.]

5. (i) Bidder i's expected utility from behaving as type $\tilde{v}$, given her opponents behave according to the (to be determined) equilibrium bidding function $b(v)$ is

$$EU_i = \tilde{v}^{n-1}\left(v_i - b(\tilde{v}) - k\left[b(\tilde{v}) - E\left[\max_{j \neq i} b(v_j) \mid v_j < \tilde{v}, \; \forall j \neq i\right]\right]\right).$$

Bidder i's optimal bidding choice of $\tilde{v}$ satisfies $\partial EU_i/\partial \tilde{v} = 0$, so:

$$(n - 1)\tilde{v}^{n-2}\left(v_i - b(\tilde{v}) - k\left[b(\tilde{v}) - E\left[\max_{j \neq i} b(v_j) \mid v_j < \tilde{v}, \; \forall j \neq i\right]\right]\right)$$

$$+ \tilde{v}^{n-1}\left(-b'(\tilde{v}) - k\left[b'(\tilde{v}) - \frac{\partial}{\partial \tilde{v}} E\left[\max_{j \neq i} b(v_j) \mid v_j < \tilde{v}, \; \forall j \neq i\right]\right]\right)$$

$$= 0$$

and in equilibrium $\tilde{v} = v_i$. Assuming there is a linear equilibrium $b(v) = \beta v$, and noting $E[\max_{j\neq i} b(v_j) \mid v_j < v_i, \forall j \neq i] = \beta[(n-1)/n]v_i$ (see note 2), we have

$$(n-1)v_i^{n-2}\left(v_i - \beta v_i - k\left[\beta v_i - \frac{n-1}{n}\beta v_i\right]\right)$$

$$+ v_i^{n-1}\left(-\beta - k\left[\beta - \frac{n-1}{n}\beta\right]\right) = 0$$

$$\Rightarrow \quad \beta = \left(\frac{n-1}{n+k}\right).$$

(ii) Bidder i's unconditional expected utility is

$$EU_i = v_i^{n-1}\left(v_i - \beta v_i - k\left(\beta v_i - \frac{n-1}{n}\beta v_i\right)\right) = \frac{v_i^n}{n}.$$

The seller's expected revenue is

$$E\left[\max_i \; (\beta v_i)\right] = \frac{n-1}{n+k}\frac{n}{n+1}.$$

(iii) EU_i is independent of k: since the highest type wins, the lowest type makes zero surplus, and the other conditions for revenue equivalence are satisfied for all k, the bidders are equally well off for all k. $E[\max_i \; (\beta v_i)]$ decreases in k: since there is social waste (embarrassment), and the allocation and bidders' expected utilities are unchanged, the seller is worse off than if $k = 0$.

[The revenue equivalence theorem might more helpfully have been named the bidders'-surpluses equivalence theorem, since in a case like this (or in many wars of attrition, lobbying games, etc.) bidders' utilities are equivalent, but revenue is only equivalent if we think of the social waste as a part of revenue. That is, we have revenue equivalence in our problem if we think of revenue as $b_i + k(b_i - \max_{j\neq i} b_j)$.]

The intuition is that the risk of winning by a large amount depresses bids so that the seller is worse off. But for the buyers, the positive effect of lower bids and the negative cost of embarrassment exactly cancel.

(iv) If losers suffer embarrassment also, then the lowest type makes strictly negative surplus. This raises the issue of whether the lowest possible type would actually bid at all. If not, then under reasonable assumptions the seller is worse off.

If we assume that all bidders participate, then by the usual revenue equivalence argument (the incentive compatibility condition is unchanged for every type) every type's expected utility is reduced by the same amount. Bids are increased by losers' embarrassment costs (the lowest type bids a strictly positive amount, and so pushes up others' bids), so the seller might be better off than with no embarrassment. [For example, if a loser's (dis)utility is $u_i = -l(\max_{j \neq i} b_j - b_i)$ and $n = 2$, then equilibrium bidding strategies are $b(v_i) = [(v_i + l)/(k + l + 2)]$, so if $2l > k$ the seller is better off than with no embarrassment, while if $0 < 2l < k$ both buyers and seller are worse off.]

(v) In an ascending auction the winner pays just a little more than the runner-up bid so suffers no embarrassment. But part (iii) shows the view expressed in the first sentence of the question is wrong in the model of part (i). The view is correct in the model of part (iv) (and, I conjecture, also for some bidders in asymmetric versions of model i). However, more important reasons for bidders to lobby against sealed-bid auctions are discussed in parts C and D of this volume.

6. (i) Conditional on a bidder with value x winning, her opponent's value, v_{opp}, is uniform on $[0, x]$, so bidder x expects to pay $\frac{1}{2}x$.

(ii) Conditional on winning, a bidder pays v_{opp} if $v_{\text{opp}} < p(x)$, and b otherwise. Thus, her conditional expected payment is

$$\Pr\left(v_{\text{opp}} < p(x) \mid v_{\text{opp}} < x\right) E\left(v_{\text{opp}} \mid v_{\text{opp}} < p(x)\right) + \Pr\left(v_{\text{opp}} > p(x) \mid v_{\text{opp}} < x\right) b$$

$$= \frac{p(x)}{x} \frac{1}{2} p(x) + \frac{x - p(x)}{x} b = \frac{1}{x}\left(\frac{1}{2}(p(x))^2 + b(x - p(x))\right).$$

(iii) By revenue equivalence between (i) and (ii) (note $p'(x) > 0$ ensures that the highest value bidder wins),

$$\frac{1}{2}x = \frac{1}{x}\left(\frac{1}{2}(p(x))^2 + b(x - p(x))\right) \quad \Rightarrow \quad (p(x) - x)(p(x) + x - 2b) = 0.$$

The relevant root is $p(x) = 2b - x$.
[Note that $b \geq 0.5$ ensures $p(x) > 0$. If $b < 0.5$ a set of types would bid b immediately, resulting in possible inefficiency, and meaning that revenue equivalence with the ascending auction no longer holds.]

(iv) (a) Conditional on type x winning the auction, if the runner-up's value is below $p(x)$ both the buy-price and the ascending auction yield the same actual revenue, but if the runner-up's value exceeds $p(x)$ the buy-price auction yields b while the ascending auction revenue is variable with the same average (since conditional on type x winning expected revenue is $\frac{1}{2}x$ in both auctions). Therefore, conditional on type x winning the auction, the distribution of revenues from the ascending auction can be derived by a sequence of mean-preserving spreads from the distribution of revenues from the buy-price auction. So any risk-averse seller will have a higher expected utility from the buy-price than from the ascending auction, for each x, by Rothschild and Stiglitz's (1970) standard result. Since this expected utility ranking of the auctions holds for all x, it also holds for the ex ante expected utilities, that is, when the expectation is taken before knowing x.

(b) The argument parallels that for (a): conditional on *any* given x winning, the buy price auction has the same expected revenue, $\frac{1}{2}x$, as the first-price auction, but is riskier (the first-price auction always yields exactly $\frac{1}{2}x$), so a risk-averse seller prefers the (unconditional) distribution of revenues from the first-price auction to that from the buy-price auction.

(v) Bidders' risk-aversion does not affect bids in the ascending auction, but will result in more aggressive bidding and higher profits in buy-price and first-price auctions (see question 11 and section 1.5). A natural conjecture is that the first-price auction will be even more profitable than the buy-price auction (since the bidding of low-value bidders is unaffected in the latter auction; also with sufficient risk-aversion a set of types might immediately offer the buy-price, resulting in inefficiency). [Budish and Takeyama (2001) provide the first analysis of "buy-prices" of which I am aware, and compare the revenues from the buy-price and the first-price auctions when the type space is discrete.]

7. (i) Marginal revenues in markets 1 and 2 are $MR_1 = 1 - 2q_1, MR_2 = 2 - 2q_2$ (this can be written $MR_1 = 2p_1 - 1$, $MR_2 = 2p_2 - 2$, see (ii)). To maximize total revenue, set $MR_1 = MR_2$, with $q_1 + q_2 = 1$. So $q_1 = \frac{1}{4}, q_2 = \frac{3}{4}$ and $p_1 = \frac{3}{4}, p_2 = \frac{5}{4}$ (since this yields $MR_i > 0$, the monopolist wants to sell the whole unit).

(ii) In an auction context "price" $p = v$ and $MR_i = v_i - [(1 - F(v_i))/f(v_i)]$ (see Appendix 1.B). Since $F(v_1) = v_1$, $F(v_2) = v_2 - 1$, we again have $MR_1 = 2v_1 - 1$, $MR_2 = 2v_2 - 2$. The optimal auction allocates the unit to the bidder who has the highest marginal revenue (bidder 1 if $2v_1 - 1 \geq 2v_2 - 2$, that is $v_1 \geq v_2 - \frac{1}{2}$, and bidder 2 otherwise), at a price equal to the lowest valuation he could have had and still won (since $MR_2 \geq 0$ the auctioneer always wants to sell the unit). (With this pricing rule, bidders will report their MRs truthfully; see Bulow and Roberts, 1989.)

(iii) A monopolist sells to its highest marginal revenue customers, and an optimal auctioneer sells to the highest marginal revenue bidder, in both cases at the highest prices that satisfy incentive compatibility. The difference is that in (i) expected sales to market 1 are $\frac{1}{4}$, and total revenue is $\frac{9}{8}$; in (ii) expected sales to buyer 1 are $\frac{1}{8}$ (bidder 2 always wins if $v_2 > \frac{3}{2}$ or $v_1 < \frac{1}{2}$, and wins in half the cases where both $v_2 < \frac{3}{2}$ and $v_1 > \frac{1}{2}$), and total revenue is $\frac{25}{24}$. Price discrimination is like an auction with a flexible capacity constraint; an auctioneer who was permitted to give out units to both bidders or to neither bidder, such that the same number of units was given out on average, would face the same problem (and so earn the same revenue) as the price-discriminating monopolist (our auctioneer would give units to both bidders if $v_1 \geq \frac{3}{4}$ and $v_2 \geq \frac{5}{4}$, to neither bidder if $v_1 < \frac{3}{4}$ and $v_2 < \frac{5}{4}$, and sell one unit otherwise).

8. (i) See Appendix 1.B. The result extends to other auction forms whenever the revenue equivalence theorem applies.

(ii) The optimal auction allocates the item to the bidder who reports the highest marginal revenue, $v_i - [(1 - F(v_i))/f(v_i)]$, at the lowest valuation she could have had and still won (since $MR_A \geq 0$ the auctioneer always wants to sell the unit). (With this pricing rule, bidders will report their MRs truthfully; see Bulow and Roberts, 1989.) The bidders' marginal revenues are $MR_A = 10$, $MR_B = 2v_B - 30$, and $MR_C = 2v_C - 50$. So if $v_B < 20$ and $v_C < 30$, A gets the item at price $p = 10$. If $v_B > 20$ and $v_C < 30$, B wins at $p = 20$. If $v_B < 20$ and $v_C > 30$, C wins at $p = 30$. Finally, if $v_B > 20$ and $v_C > 30$, then if $v_B - 20 > v_C - 30$, B wins at $p = v_C - 10$, otherwise C wins at $p = v_B + 10$.

(iii) This is the "Maximum Game" of Bulow and Klemperer (2002). Bidder i's marginal revenue is

$$MR_i = v - \frac{1 - F_i(t)}{f_i(t)} \frac{\partial v}{\partial t_i}.$$

Writing t_{max} for the highest signal,

$$MR_i = \begin{cases} t_i - (1 - t_i) & \text{if } i \text{ has the highest signal} \\ t_{max} & \text{if } i \text{ has one of the two lower signals (since then } \dfrac{\partial v}{\partial t_i} = 0). \end{cases}$$

So, since $E(t_{max}) = \frac{3}{4}$ (see note 2), the expected marginal revenue of the winning bidder equals $\frac{1}{2}$ conditional on the highest-signal bidder winning, and equals $\frac{3}{4}$ conditional on the highest-signal bidder not winning. By part (i), therefore:

(a) The bidder with the highest signal wins: $E[\pi(\text{seller})] = \frac{1}{2}$.

(b) The bidder with the highest signal wins $\frac{2}{3}$ of times while a bidder with a lower signal wins $\frac{1}{3}$ of times (when the highest is excluded):

$$E[\pi(\text{seller})] = \frac{2}{3}\frac{1}{2} + \frac{1}{3}\frac{3}{4} = \frac{7}{12}.$$

(c) The bidder with the highest signal wins $\frac{1}{3}$ of times while a bidder with a lower signal wins $\frac{2}{3}$ of times:

$$E[\pi(\text{seller})] = \frac{1}{3}\frac{1}{2} + \frac{2}{3}\frac{3}{4} = \frac{2}{3}.$$

(d) The price is *decreasing* in the number of bidders because higher-signal bidders have lower marginal revenues (and higher information rents). Reducing the number of bidders increases the probability of selling to a lower-signal bidder. (See also chapter 1, note 63.)

[A direct, but more cumbersome, approach to part (iii) is: (a) the symmetric equilibrium bidding strategy is $b(t) = t$ (no bidder will drop out before her signal and, since the bidder with the highest signal wins, a bidder who stays in past her signal, and wins, will have negative profits), so $E\pi = E(\text{second-highest signal}) = \frac{1}{2}$. (b) If bidders i and j participate, then bidder i with signal t_i bids up to $E(v \mid t_i = t_j)$ (see Appendix 1.D). This equals $t_i t_i + (1 - t_i)\frac{1}{2}(1 + t_i) = \frac{1}{2}(1 + t_i^2)$ (because, conditional on $t_i = t_j$, with probability $1 - t_i$ the excluded signal is the highest with expected value $\frac{1}{2}(1 + t_i)$). Since the density of the lower of two uniform signals is $2(1 - t)$, the expected price at which the lower signal of the two participants quits is $E\pi = \int_0^1 2(1 - t)\frac{1}{2}(1 + t^2)dt = \frac{7}{12}$. (c) The lowest type estimates the value as the expectation of the highest of the other two signals, which is $\frac{2}{3}$. So, this is the take-it-or-leave-it price.]

9. (i) Bidder i remains in the bidding until the price where, if $z_i = z_j$, she is exactly indifferent between winning and quitting, that is, she bids up to $3z_i + z_i = 4z_i$. (See Appendix 1.D, for discussion.)

(ii) (a) Conditional on i winning, j's signal is uniformly distributed on $[0, z_i]$. Thus, i's conditional expected payment in the ascending auction is $4z_i/2$. By revenue equivalence, the expected payment conditional on winning is the same in the Dutch auction, hence i bids $b(z_i) = 2z_i$.

(b) If type z_i bids $b(\tilde{z})$, she wins with probability $\tilde{z}$, and her prize is worth $3z_i + (\tilde{z}/2)$ on average (since she beats types below $\tilde{z}$), so her surplus is $S = \tilde{z}(3z_i + \frac{1}{2}\tilde{z} - b(\tilde{z}))$. Her optimal choice of $\tilde{z}$ satisfies

$$\frac{\partial S}{\partial \tilde{z}} = 0 \quad \Rightarrow \quad \left(3z_i + \frac{1}{2}\tilde{z} - b(\tilde{z})\right) + \left(\frac{1}{2} - b'(\tilde{z})\right)\tilde{z} = 0.$$

In equilibrium, $\tilde{z} = z_i$, so $b'(\tilde{z}_i) = 4 - (b(z_i)/z_i)$ and $b(0) = 0$ (in symmetric equilibrium type $z_i = 0$ wins only when $z_j = 0$, so type 0 cannot bid more). So, $b(z_i) = 2z_i$.

(iii) (a) Buyers' strategies in ascending auctions are not affected by their risk preferences. However, in a Dutch auction, risk-neutral bidders bid $b(z_i) = 2z_i \le 3z_i + z_j$, so are guaranteed profits, conditional on winning. So risk-averse bidders bid a little higher, trading lower payoffs for a higher probability of winning. [For example, if bidders' utilities are $\sqrt{v_i - b(v_i)}$, then in a Dutch auction they bid up to $b(z_i) = (\frac{3}{2} + \sqrt{\frac{11}{12}})z_i$.] So the seller prefers a Dutch auction.

(b) Conditional on type z_i winning, in the Dutch auction *actual* revenue is $2z_i$, whereas in the ascending auction *expected* revenue is also $2z_i$ but *actual* revenue is variable (since it depends on the loser's signal), so the distribution of ascending auction revenues is a mean-preserving spread of the Dutch revenues. Therefore any risk-averse seller will have a higher expected utility from the Dutch auction than from the ascending auction, for each z_i, by Rothschild and Stiglitz's (1970) standard result. Since this expected utility ranking of the auctions holds conditional on *any* z_i, it also holds for the ex ante expected utilities, that is, when the expectation is taken with respect to z_i. So a risk-averse seller prefers the Dutch auction.

10. (i) See Appendix 1.A.

(ii) This is a version of the "Wallet Game" analyzed in Klemperer (1998) and Bulow and Klemperer (2002). Write $t_{(j)}$ for the jth highest actual signal. In a symmetric equilibrium, type t expects to win if her signal is not lowest, so remains in the bidding until the price at which, if she is tied with another bidder for lowest signal, she is exactly indifferent between winning and losing. (See Appendix 1.D for a similar argument.) Since $E[t_{(1)} \mid t_{(2)} = t_{(3)} = t] = \frac{1}{2}(1 + t)$, this price is $b(t) = \frac{1}{3}(t + t + \frac{1}{2}(1 + t)) = \frac{1}{6} + \frac{5}{6}t$.

(iii) Type t's expected surplus is

$$S(t) = \Pr(t \text{ is highest}) \cdot E[v - b(t_{(3)}) \mid t_{(1)} = t]$$

$$+ \Pr(t \text{ is second highest}) \cdot E[v - b(t_{(3)}) \mid t_{(2)} = t].$$

Type t is highest with probability t^2, and in this case $E[t_{(2)}] = \frac{2}{3}t$, $E[t_{(3)}] = \frac{1}{3}t$ (see note 2), and hence $E[v] = \frac{2}{3}t$ and $E[b(t_{(3)})] = (\frac{1}{6} + \frac{5}{6}(\frac{1}{3}t))$. Type t is second-highest with probability $2t(1 - t)$, and in this case $E[t_{(1)}] = \frac{1}{2}(1 + t)$, $E[t_{(3)}] = \frac{1}{2}t$, and hence $E[v] = \frac{1}{6}(4t + 1)$ and $E[b(t_{(3)})] = (\frac{1}{6} + \frac{5}{6}(\frac{1}{2}t))$. Therefore

$$S(t) = t^2 \left(\frac{2}{3}t - \left(\frac{1}{6} + \frac{5}{6}\left(\frac{1}{3}t \right) \right) \right) + 2t(1 - t)\left(\frac{1}{6}(4t - 1) - \left(\frac{1}{6} + \frac{5}{6}\left(\frac{1}{2}t \right) \right) \right)$$

$$= \frac{1}{9}t^2(3 - t).$$

(iv) Similarly, the surplus of type t in a first-price auction is

$$t^2 \left(\frac{2}{3}t - b(t) \right) + 2t(1 - t)\left(\frac{1}{6}(4t + 1) - b(t) \right)$$

(in which $b(t)$ is now the first-price bid).

By revenue equivalence, and part (iii), this equals $\frac{1}{9}t^2(3 - t)$, so

$$b(t) = \frac{-5t^2 + 6t + 3}{9(2 - t)}.$$

11. (i) (a) It is a dominant strategy for each bidder to remain in the bidding until the price reaches her value. So the bidder with the highest value wins and pays the second highest value, and expected revenue is $E(\text{2nd highest } v_i) = \frac{1}{3}$ (see note 2).

(b) Assuming the other bidder bids according to the (to be determined) equilibrium bidding strategy $b(v)$, i's surplus from bidding as type $\tilde{v}$ is $S = (v_i - b(\tilde{v}))\tilde{v}$ (since i then wins with probability $\tilde{v}$). Bidder i's optimal choice of $\tilde{v}$ satisfies $\partial S/\partial \tilde{v} = 0 \Rightarrow (v_i - b(\tilde{v})) + \tilde{v}(-b'(\tilde{v})) = 0$. In equilibrium, $\tilde{v} = v_i$, so $b'(v_i) = [(v_i - b(v_i))/v_i]$ which, since $b(0) = 0$, has solution $b(v_i) = \frac{1}{2}v_i$. So expected revenue is $\frac{1}{2}E(\text{highest } v_i) = \frac{1}{3}$.

(c) Expected revenue is the same across auction types, illustrating the revenue equivalence theorem.

(ii) (a) Bidding up to v_i remains the dominant strategy, so expected revenue is unaffected by the risk-aversion.

(b) Following the same method as in (i)(b):

$$S = \left(\sqrt{v_i - b(\tilde{v})}\right)\tilde{v}.$$

$$\frac{\partial S}{\partial \tilde{v}} = 0 \quad \Rightarrow \quad \sqrt{v_i - b(\tilde{v})} + \frac{\tilde{v}(-b'(v_i))}{2\sqrt{v_i - b(\tilde{v})}} = 0.$$

For $\tilde{v} = v_i$, $b'(v_i) = 2(v_i - b(v_i))/v_i$ which, using the condition $b(0) = 0$, has solution $b(v_i) = \frac{2}{3}v_i$. So expected revenue is $\frac{2}{3}E(\text{highest } v_i) = \frac{4}{9}$.

(c) Risk-averse players bid uniformly higher in first-price auctions than their risk-neutral counterparts. Taking one's opponent's bid as fixed, a higher bid is less risky—it gives a higher probability of a lower prize—so is preferred by a risk-averse bidder. Since (i) satisfied revenue equivalence, first-price auctions are more profitable than ascending ones in (ii).

12–20. Outlines for some of the essays can be found at www.paulklemperer.org.

References

Abbink, K., Irlenbusch, B., Pezanis-Christou, P., Rockenbach, B., Sadrieh, A., and Selten, R. (2001a) An Experimental Test of Design Alternatives for the British 3G/UMTS Auction. Working paper, University of Bonn.

Abbink, K., Irlenbusch, B., Rockenbach, B., Sadrieh, A., and Selten, R. (2001b) The Behavioural Approach to the Strategic Analysis of Spectrum Auctions: The Case of the German DCS-1800 Auction. Working paper, Universities of Nottingham, Erfurt, Tilburg, and Bonn.

_____ (2002) The Behavioural Approach to the Strategic Analysis of Spectrum Auctions: The Case of the German DCS-1800 Auction. *ifo Studien*, 48, 457–480.

Abreu, D. and Gul, F. (2000) Bargaining and Reputation. *Econometrica*, 68, 85–117.

Anton, J. J. and Yao, D. A. (1989) Split Awards, Procurement, and Innovation. *The RAND Journal of Economics*, 20, 538–552.

_____ (1992) Coordination in Split Award Auctions. *Quarterly Journal of Economics*, 107, 681–701.

Armstrong, M. (2000) Optimal Multi-Object Auctions. *Review of Economic Studies*, 67, 455–481.

Ashenfelter, O. (1989) How Auctions Work for Wine and Art. *Journal of Economic Perspectives*, 3, 23–36.

Athey, S. (2001) Single-Crossing Properties and the Existence of Pure Strategy Equilibrium in Games of Incomplete Information. *Econometrica*, 69, 861–890.

Athey, S., Bagwell, K., and Sanchirico, C. (forthcoming) Collusion and Price Rigidity. *Review of Economic Studies*.

Ausubel, L. M. (forthcoming) An Efficient Ascending-Bid Auction for Multiple Objects. *American Economic Review*.

Ausubel, L. M. and Cramton, P. (1998a) Demand Reduction and Inefficiency in Multi-Unit Auctions. Mimeo, University of Maryland.

_____ (1998b) The Optimality of Being Efficient. Mimeo, University of Maryland.

Ausubel, L. M., Cramton, P., McAfee, R. P., and McMillan, J. (1997) Synergies in Wireless Telephony: Evidence from the Broadband PCS Auctions. *Journal of Economics and Management Strategy*, 6, 497–527.

Ausubel, L. M. and Milgrom, P. R. (2002) Ascending Auctions with Package Bidding. *Frontiers of Theoretical Economics*, 1, 1–42.

Ausubel, L. M. and Schwartz, J. A. (1999) The Ascending Auction Paradox. Working paper, University of Maryland.

Avery, C. (1998) Strategic Jump Bidding in English Auctions. *Review of Economic Studies*, 65, 185–210.

Avery, C. and Hendershott, T. (2000) Bundling and Optimal Auctions of Multiple Goods. *Review of Economic Studies*, 67, 483–497.

Back, K. and Zender, J. F. (1993) Auctions of Divisible Goods. *Review of Financial Studies*, 6, 733–764.

———— (2001) Auctions of Divisible Goods with Endogenous Supply. *Economics Letters*, 73, 29–34.

Ballard, C. L., Shoven, J. B., and Whalley, J. (1985) General Equilibrium Computations of the Marginal Welfare Costs of Taxes in the United States. *American Economic Review*, 75, 128–138.

Banks, J. S., Ledyard, J. O., and Porter, D. (1989) Allocating Uncertain and Unresponsive Resources: An Experimental Approach. *The RAND Journal of Economics*, 20, 1–25.

Bartolini, L. and Cottarelli, C. (1997) Designing Effective Auctions for Treasury Securities. *Current Issues in Economics and Finance*, Federal Reserve Bank of New York, 3(9), 1–6.

Baye, M. R., Kovenock, D., and de Vries, C. (1997) Fee Allocation of Lawyer Services in Litigation. Mimeo, Indiana University, Purdue University, and Tinbergen Institute, Erasmus University.

———— (1998) A General Linear Model of Contests. Working paper, Indiana University, Purdue University, and Tinbergen Institute, Erasmus University.

Baye, M. R. and Morgan, J. (1999a) A folk theorem for one-shot Bertrand games. *Economics Letters,* 65, 59–65.

———— (1999b) Bounded Rationality in Homogeneous Product Pricing Games. Working paper, Indiana University and Princeton University.

———— (2001) Information Gatekeepers on the Internet and the Competitiveness of Homogeneous Product Markets. *American Economic Review*, 91, 454–474.

Beggs, A. W. and Graddy, K. (1997) Declining Values and the Afternoon Effect: Evidence from Art Auctions. *The RAND Journal of Economics*, 28, 544–565.

Beggs, A. W. and Klemperer, P. D. (1992) Multi-Period Competition with Switching Costs. *Econometrica*, 60, 651–666.

Benoit, B. (2000) Bidders Warned in German 3G Phone Auction. *The Financial Times,* 2 August, 28.

Benoît, J.-P. and Krishna, V. (2001) Multi-Object Auctions with Budget Constrained Bidders. *Review of Economic Studies*, 68, 155–179.

Bernhardt, D. and Scoones, D. (1994) A Note on Sequential Auctions. *American Economic Review*, 84, 653–657.

Bernheim, B. D. and Whinston, M. D. (1986) Menu Auctions, Resource Allocation, and Economic Influence. *Quarterly Journal of Economics,* 101, 1–31.

Betton, S. and Eckbo, E. B. (1995) Toeholds, Competition and State-contingent Payoffs: An Experimental Investigation. *Journal of Economics and Management Strategy*, 6, 573–603.

Bikhchandani, S. (1988) Reputation in Repeated Second-Price Auctions. *Journal of Economic Theory*, 46, 97–119.

———— (1999) Auctions of Heterogeneous Objects. *Games and Economic Behavior*, 26, 193–220.

Bikhchandani, S. and Huang, C-F. (1993) The Economics of Treasury Securities Markets. *Journal of Economic Perspectives*, 7, 117–134.

Bikhchandani, S. and Riley, J. G. (1991) Equilibria in Open Common Value Auctions. *Journal of Economic Theory*, 53, 101–130.

Black, J. and de Meza, D. (1992) Systematic Price Divergences Between Successive

Auctions Are No Anomaly. *Journal of Economics and Management Strategy*, 1, 607–628.

Bliss, C. and Nalebuff, B. (1984) Dragon-Slaying and Ballroom Dancing: The Private Supply of a Public Good. *Journal of Public Economics*, 25, 1–12.

Board, S. A. (1999) Commitment in Auctions. M.Phil Thesis, Nuffield College, Oxford University.

Bolle, F. (1992) Supply Function Equilibria and the Danger of Tacit Collusion: The Case of Spot Markets for Electricity. *Energy Economics*, 14, 94–102.

Börgers, T. and Dustmann, C. (2002a) Rationalizing the UMTS Spectrum Bids: The Case of the UK Auction. *ifo Studien* 48, 77–109.

———— (2002b) Strange Bids: Bidding Behavior in the United Kingdom's Third Generation Spectrum Auction. Working paper, University College London.

Branco, F. (1997) The Design of Multidimensional Auctions. *The RAND Journal of Economics, 28,* 63–81.

Brusco, S. and Lopomo, G. (2002a) Collusion via Signaling in Simultaneous Ascending Bid Auctions with Heterogeneous Objects, With and Without Complementarities. *Review of Economic Studies*, 69, 407–436.

———— (2002b) Simultaneous Ascending Auctions with Budget Constraints. Working Paper, Stern School of Business, New York University.

Budish, E. B. and Takeyama, L. (2001) English Auctions with Buy Prices: Irrationality on the Internet? *Economics Letters*, 72, 325–333.

Bulow, J. I., Geanakoplos, J. D., and Klemperer, P. D. (1985a) Multimarket Oligopoly: Strategic Substitutes and Complements. *Journal of Political Economy*, 93, 488–511.

———— (1985b) Holding Idle Capacity to Deter Entry. *Economic Journal*, 95, 178–182.

Bulow, J. I., Huang, M., and Klemperer, P. D. (1995) Toeholds and Takeovers: General Characterization, Existence, and Uniqueness of Equilibrium. Mimeo, Stanford University and Nuffield College, Oxford University.

———— (1999) Toeholds and Takeovers. *Journal of Political Economy*, 107, 427–454 (also reprinted in Biais, B. and Pagano, M. (eds.) (2002) *New Research in Corporate Finance and Banking*, Oxford University Press, pp. 91–116).

Bulow, J. I. and Klemperer, P. D. (1994) Rational Frenzies and Crashes. *Journal of Political Economy*, 102, 1–23 (also reprinted in Biais, B. and Pagano, M. (eds.) (2002) *New Research in Corporate Finance and Banking*, Oxford University Press, pp. 91–116).

———— (1996) Auctions vs. Negotiations. *American Economic Review*, 86, 180–194.

———— (1998) The Tobacco Deal. *Brookings Papers on Economic Activity (Microeconomics)*, 323–394.

———— (1999) The Generalized War of Attrition. *American Economic Review*, 89, 175–189.

———— (2002) Prices and the Winner's Curse. *The RAND Journal of Economics*, 33, 1–21.

———— (forthcoming) Privacy and Prices. Discussion paper, Nuffield College, Oxford University.

Bulow, J. I. and Roberts, D. J. (1989) The Simple Economics of Optimal Auctions. *Journal of Political Economy*, 97, 1060–1090.

Burguet, R. and Sákovics, J. (1996) Reserve Prices without Commitment. *Games and Economic Behavior*, 15, 149–164.

———— (1999) Imperfect Competition in Auction Designs. *International Economic Review*, 40, 231–247.

Burrough, B. and Helyar, J. (1990) *Barbarians at the Gate: The Fall of RJR Nabisco*. London: Arrow.

Cable, J., Henley, A., and Holland, K. (2002) Pot of Gold or Winner's Curse? An Event Study of the Auctions of 3G Mobile Telephone Licences in the UK. *Fiscal Studies*, 23, 447–462.

Cai, H.-B. (2000) Delay in Multilateral Bargaining under Complete Information. *Journal of Economic Theory*, 93, 260–276.

Caillaud, B. and Jehiel, P. (1998) Collusion in Auctions with Externalities. *The RAND Journal of Economics*, 29, 680–702.

Cane, A. and Owen, D. (2000) The UK Cellular Phone Auction. *Financial Times*, London, 28 April, 23.

Capen, E. C., Clapp, R. V., and Campbell, W. M. (1971) Competitive Bidding in High-Risk Situations. *Journal of Petroleum Technology*, 23, 641–653.

Cassady, R. Jr. (1967) *Auctions and Auctioneering*. Berkeley and Los Angeles, CA: University of California Press.

Cauley, L. and Carnevale, M. L. (1994) Wireless Giants, Some Surprise Players to Seek New Generation of Licenses. *The Wall Street Journal*, October 31, A4.

Chatterjee, K. and Samuelson, W. (1983) Bargaining under Incomplete Information. *Operations Research*, 31, 835–851.

Che, Y.-K. (1993) Design Competition through Multidimensional Auctions. *The RAND Journal of Economics*, 24, 668–680.

Che, Y.-K. and Gale, I. L. (1996) Expected Revenue of All-Pay Auctions and First-Price Sealed-Bid Auctions with Budget Constraints. *Economics Letters*, 50, 367–371.

———— (1998) Standard Auctions with Financially Constrained Bidders. *Review of Economic Studies*, 65, 1–21.

Clark, C. (1939) *The Conditions of Economic Progress*. London: Macmillan.

Coase, R. H. (1959) The Federal Communications Commission. *Journal of Law and Economics*, 2, 1–40.

Cramton, P. (1997) The FCC Spectrum Auctions: An Early Assessment. *Journal of Economics and Management Strategy*, 6, 431–495.

Cramton, P., Gibbons R., and Klemperer, P. D. (1987) Dissolving a Partnership Efficiently. *Econometrica*, 55, 615–632.

Cramton, P. and Schwartz, J. A. (2000) Collusive Bidding: Lessons from the FCC Spectrum Auctions. *Journal of Regulatory Economics*, 17, 229–252.

———— (2002) Collusive Bidding in the FCC Spectrum Auctions. *Contributions to Economic Analysis & Policy*, 1, article 11 (http://www.bepress.com/bejeap/contributions/vol1/iss1/art11).

Crossland, D. (2000) Austrian UMTS Auction Unlikely to Scale Peaks. Reuters, October 31. Available at http://www.totaltele.com.

Crémer, J. and McLean, R. P. (1985) Optimal Selling Strategies under Uncertainty for a Discriminatory Monopolist when Demands Are Interdependent. *Econometrica*, 53, 345–361.

_____ (1988) Full Extraction of the Surplus in Bayesian and Dominant Strategy Auctions. *Econometrica*, 56, 1247–1257.

Daniel, K. and Hirshleifer, D. (1995) A Theory of Costly Sequential Bidding. Mimeo, Universities of Chicago and Michigan.

Daripa, A. (1996a) Quantities Rather Than Prices: Market Allocation, Informational Free-Rides and the Value of Inside Information. Mimeo, Birkbeck College, London.

_____ (1996b) A Theory of Treasury Auctions. Mimeo, Birkbeck College, London.

Dasgupta, P. S., Hammond, P. J., and Maskin, E. S. (1979) The Implementation of Social Choice Rules: Some General Results on Incentive Compatibility. *Review of Economic Studies*, 46, 185–216.

Dasgupta, P. S. and Maskin, E. (2000) Efficient Auctions. *Quarterly Journal of Economics*, 115, 341–388.

Engelbrecht-Wiggans, R. (1987) Optimal Reservation Prices in Auctions. *Management Science*, 33, 763–770.

_____ (1993) Optimal Auctions Revisited. *Games and Economic Behavior*, 5, 227–239.

_____ (1994) Sequential Auctions of Stochastically Equivalent Objects. *Economics Letters*, 44, 87–90.

Engelbrecht-Wiggans, R. and Kahn, C. M. (1998a) Multi-unit Auctions with Uniform Prices. *Economic Theory*, 12, 227–258.

_____ (1998b) Multi-Unit Pay-Your-Bid Auctions with Variable Awards. *Games and Economic Behavior*, 23, 25–42.

_____ (1998c) Low Revenue Equilibria in Simultaneous Auctions. Working paper, University of Illinois.

Engelbrecht-Wiggans, R., Milgrom, P. R., and Weber, R. J. (1983) Competitive Bidding and Proprietary Information. *Journal of Mathematical Economics*, 11, 161–169.

Esteves, R. (forthcoming) Targeted Advertising and Price Discrimination in the New Media. DPhil thesis, Oxford University.

Esö, P. (1999) Optimal Auctions with Correlated Information and Risk Aversion. Mimeo, Harvard University.

Ewerhart, C. and Moldovanu, B. (2001) A Stylized Model of the German UMTS Auction. Working paper, University of Mannheim, Germany.

_____ (2002) The German UMTS Design: Insights from Multi-Object Auction Theory. *ifo Studien*, 48, 158–174.

Feddersen, T. J. and Pesendorfer, W. (1996) The Swing Voter's Curse. *American Economic Review*, 86, 408–424.

_____ (1998) Convicting the Innocent: The Inferiority of Unanimous Jury Verdicts under Strategic Voting. *American Political Science Review*, 92, 23–35.

Federico, G. and Rahman, D. (2000) Bidding in an Electricity Pay-As-Bid Auction. Working paper, Nuffield College.

von der Fehr, N.-H. (1994) Predatory Bidding in Sequential Auctions. *Oxford Economic Papers*, 46, 345–356.

von der Fehr, N.-H. and Harbord, D. (1993) Spot Market Competition in the UK Electricity Industry. *Economic Journal*, 103, 531–546.

_____ (1998) Competition in Electricity Spot Markets: Economic Theory and International Experience. Memorandum No. 5/1998, Department of Economics, University of Oslo.

von der Fehr, N.-H. and Riis, C. (1999) Option Values in Sequential Markets. Mimeo, University of Oslo and Norwegian School of Management.

Feldstein, M. (1999) Tax Avoidance and the Deadweight Loss of the Income Tax. *Review of Economics and Statistics*, 81, 674–680.

Fishman, M. J. (1988) A Theory of Pre-emptive Takeover Bidding. *The RAND Journal of Economics*, 19, 88–101.

Fortis Bank (2000) The UMTS Report, Brussels.

Friedman, L. (1956) A Competitive Bidding Strategy. *Operations Research*, 4, 104–112.

Friedman, M. (1953) *Essays in Positive Economics*, Chicago: University of Chicago Press.

Fudenberg, D. and Kreps, D. M. (1987) Reputation in the Simultaneous Play of Multiple Opponents. *Review of Economic Studies*, 54, 541–568.

Fudenberg, D. and Tirole, J. (1986) A Theory of Exit in Duopoly. *Econometrica*, 54, 943–960.

———— (1991) *Game Theory*. Cambridge, MA: MIT Press.

Fudenberg, D., Gilbert, R., Stiglitz, J., and Tirole, J. (1983) Preemption, Leapfrogging and Competition in Patent Races. *European Economic Review*, 22, 3–31.

Fullerton, R. and McAfee, R. P. (1999) Auctioning Entry into Tournaments. *Journal of Political Economy*, 107, 573–605.

Gale, I. L. and Hausch, D. B. (1994) Bottom-Fishing and Declining Prices in Sequential Auctions. *Games and Economic Behavior*, 7, 318–331.

Gale, I. L., Hausch, D. B., and Stegeman, M. (2000) Sequential Procurement with Subcontracting. *International Economic Review*, 41, 989–1020.

Gale, I. L. and Stegeman, M. (2001) Sequential Auctions of Endogenously Valued Objects. *Games and Economic Behavior*, 36, 74–103.

Gibbon, E. (1776) *History of the Decline and Fall of the Roman Empire*. London: Strahan and Cadell.

Gibbons, R. (1992) *Game Theory for Applied Economists*. Princeton, NJ: Princeton University Press.

Gilbert, R. and Klemperer, P. D. (2000) An Equilibrium Theory of Rationing. *The RAND Journal of Economics,* 31, 1–21.

Ginsburgh, V. (1998) Absentee Bidders and the Declining Price Anomaly in Wine Auctions. *Journal of Political Economy*, 106, 1302–1319.

Graham, D. A. and Marshall, R. C. (1987) Collusive Bidder Behavior at Single-Object Second-Price and English Auctions. *Journal of Political Economy*, 95, 1217–1239.

Graham, D. A., Marshall, R. C., and Richard, J.-F. (1990) Differential Payments within a Bidder Coalition and the Shapley Value. *American Economic Review*, 80, 493–510.

Green, R. J. (1996) Increasing Competition in the British Electricity Spot Market. *Journal of Industrial Economics*, 44, 205–216.

Green, R. J. and Newbery, D. M. (1992) Competition in the British Electricity Spot Market. *Journal of Political Economy*, 100, 929–953.

Griesmer, J. H., Levitan, R. E., and Shubik, M. (1967) Toward a Study of Bidding Processes Part IV: Games with Unknown Costs. *Naval Research Logistics Quarterly*, 14, 415–433.

Grimm, V., Riedel F., and Wolfstetter, E. (2002) The Third Generation (UMTS) Spectrum Auction in Germany. *ifo Studien*, 48, 123–143.

———— (2003) Low Price Equilibrium in Multi-Unit Auctions: The GSM Spectrum Auction in Germany. *International Journal of Industrial Organization*, 21, 1557–1569.

Haigh, J. and Cannings, C. (1989) The n-Person War of Attrition. *Acta Applicandae Mathematicae,* 14, 59–74.

Haile, P. (1996) Auctions with Resale Markets. PhD dissertation, Northwestern University.

Hall, R. E. (2001) *Digital Dealing*. New York: W. W. Norton.

Hansard (1998), written answer to Parliamentary Question, 18 May.

Hansen, R. G. (1986) Sealed Bids versus Open Auctions: The Evidence. *Economic Inquiry*, 24, 125–142.

———— (1988) Auctions with Endogenous Quantity. *The RAND Journal of Economics*, 19, 44–58.

Hansen, R. G. and Lott, J. R., Jr. (1991) The Winner's Curse and Public Information in Common Value Auctions: Comment. *American Economic Review*, 81, 347–361.

Harford, T. (1998) Sequential Auctions with Financially Constrained Bidders. MPhil thesis, Oxford University, available at www.timharford.com.

Harris, M. and Raviv, A. (1981) Allocation Mechanisms and the Design of Auctions. *Econometrica*, 49, 1477–1499.

Harris, M. and Townsend, R. M. (1981) Resource Allocation Under Asymmetric Information. *Econometrica*, 49, 33–64.

Harstad, R. M. (1990) Alternative Common Values Auction Procedures: Revenue Comparisons with Free Entry. *Journal of Political Economy*, 98, 421–429.

Harstad, R. M., Kagel, J., and Levin, D. (1990) Equilibrium Bid Functions for Auctions with an Uncertain Number of Bidders. *Economics Letters*, 33, 35–40.

Harstad, R. M. and Rothkopf, M. H. (1994) Modeling Competitive Bidding: A Critical Essay. *Management Science*, 40, 364–384.

Hausch, D. B. (1986) Multi-Object Auctions: Sequential vs. Simultaneous Sales. *Management Science*, 32, 1599–1610.

Hendricks, K. and Paarsch, H. J. (1995) A Survey of Recent Empirical Work Concerning Auctions. *Canadian Journal of Economics*, 28, 403–426.

Hendricks, K. and Porter, R. H. (1988) An Empirical Study of an Auction with Asymmetric Information. *American Economic Review*, 78, 865–883.

———— (1989) Collusion in Auctions. *Annales D'Économie et de Statistique*, 15/16, 217–230.

Hendricks, K., Porter, R. H., and Tan, G. (1999) Joint Bidding in Federal Offshore Oil and Gas Lease Auctions. Working paper, University of British Columbia.

Holt, C. A. Jr. (1980) Competitive Bidding for Contracts under Alternative Auction Procedures. *Journal of Political Economy*, 88, 433–445.

Holt, C. A. Jr. and Sherman, R. (1982) Waiting-Line Auctions. *Journal of Political Economy*, 90, 280–294.

Hughes, J. W. and Snyder, E. A. (1995) Litigation and Settlement Under the English and American Rules: Theory and Evidence. *Journal of Law and Economics,* 38, 225–250.

Jehiel, P. and Moldovanu, B. (1996) Strategic Nonparticipation. *The RAND Journal of Economics*, 27, 84-98.

⸻ (2000) A Critique of the Planned Rules for the German UMTS/IMT-2000 License Auction. Working paper, University College London and University of Mannheim.

⸻ (2001a) Efficient Design with Interdependent Valuations. *Econometrica*, 69, 1237–1259.

⸻ (2001b) The European UMTS/IMT-2000 License Auctions. Working paper, University College London and University of Mannheim.

⸻ (2002) An Economic Perspective on Auctions. Working Paper, University College London and University of Mannheim.

Jehiel, P., Moldovanu, B., and Stacchetti, E. (1996) How (Not) to Sell Nuclear Weapons. *American Economic Review*, 86, 814–829.

Kagel, J. H. (1995) Auctions: A Survey of Experimental Research. In Kagel, J. H. and Roth, A. E. (eds.), *The Handbook of Experimental Economics*. Princeton, NJ: Princeton University Press, pp. 501–586.

Kagel, J. H. and Roth, A. E. (eds.) (1995) *The Handbook of Experimental Economics*. Princeton, NJ: Princeton University Press.

Kambe, S. (1999) Bargaining with Imperfect Commitment. *Games and Economic Behavior*, 28, 217–237.

Kaplan, T. and Wettstein, D. (2000) The Possibility of Mixed-Strategy Equilibria with Constant-Returns-to-Scale Technology under Bertrand Competition. *Spanish Economic Review*, 2, 65–71.

Keynes, J. M. (1933) *Essays in Biography*. London: Macmillan.

Klemperer, P. D. (1987a) Markets with Consumer Switching Costs. *Quarterly Journal of Economics*, 102, 375–394.

⸻ (1987b) The Competitiveness of Markets with Switching Costs. *The RAND Journal of Economics*, 18, 138–150.

⸻ (1995) Competition when Consumers have Switching Costs: An Overview with Applications to Industrial Organization, Macroeconomics, and International Trade. *Review of Economic Studies*, 62, 515–539.

⸻ (1998) Auctions with Almost Common Values. *European Economic Review*, 42, 757–769.

⸻ (1999a) Auction Theory: A Guide to the Literature. *Journal of Economic Surveys*, 13, 227–286 (also reprinted in Dahiya, S. (ed.) (1999) *The Current State of Economic Science*, vol. 2. India: Spellbound Publications, pp. 711–766; also reprinted as chapter 1 of this volume).

⸻ (1999b) Applying Auction Theory to Economics. 1999 draft of Invited Lecture to Eighth World Congress of the Econometric Society, at www.paulklemperer.org.

⸻ (ed.) (2000a) *The Economic Theory of Auctions*. Cheltenham, UK: Edward Elgar.

⸻ (2000b) What Really Matters in Auction Design. May 2000 Working paper, Nuffield College, Oxford University (revised version reprinted as chapter 3 of this volume).

⸻ (2000c) Spectrum on the Block. *Wall Street Journal*, 5 October, p. 8 and available at www.paulklemperer.org.

———— (2002) Using and Abusing Economic Theory. Working paper, Nuffield College, Oxford (revised version reprinted as chapter 4 of this volume).

Klemperer, P. D. and Meyer, M. A. (1986) Price Competition vs. Quantity Competition: The Role of Uncertainty. *The RAND Journal of Economics*, 17, 618–638.

———— (1989) Supply Function Equilibria in Oligopoly Under Uncertainty. *Econometrica*, 57, 1243–1277.

Klemperer, P. D. and Pagnozzi, M. (forthcoming) Advantaged Bidders and Spectrum Prices: An Empirical Analysis. Working paper, Nuffield College, Oxford University.

Klemperer, P. D. et al. (forthcoming) Auctions for Environmental Improvements: the UK ETS Auction. Working paper, Nuffield College, Oxford.

Koselka, R. (1995) Playing Poker with Craig McCaw. *Forbes*, July 3, 62–63.

Kremer, I. (2002) Information Aggregation in Common Value Auctions. *Econometrica*, 70, 1675–1682.

Krishna, K. (1993) Auctions with Endogenous Valuations: The Persistence of Monopoly Revisited. *American Economic Review*, 83, 147–160.

Krishna, V. (2002) *Auction Theory*, San Diego, CA: Academic Press.

Krishna, V. and Morgan, J. (1997) An Analysis of the War of Attrition and the All-Pay Auction. *Journal of Economic Theory*, 72, 343-3-62.

Kühn, K.-U. and Vives, X. (1995) *Information Exchanges Among Firms and their Impact on Competition*. European Commission Document. Luxembourg: Office for Official Publications of the European Communities, pp. 146.

Laffont, J.-J. (1997) Game Theory and Empirical Economics: The Case of Auction Data. *European Economic Review*, 41, 1–35.

Laffont, J.-J., Ossard, H., and Vuong, Q. (1995) Econometrics of First-Price Auctions. *Econometrica*, 63, 953–980.

Laffont, J.-J. and Tirole, J. (1987) Auctioning Incentive Contracts. *Journal of Political Economy*, 95, 921–937.

Laffont, J.-J. and Vuong, Q. (1996) Structural Analysis of Auction Data. *American Economic Review*, 86, 414–420.

Lebrun, B. (1996) Existence of an Equilibrium in First Price Auctions. *Economic Theory*, 7, 421–443.

Lee, H. G. (1998) Do Electronic Marketplaces Lower the Price of Goods? *Communications of the ACM*, 41, 73–80.

Lee, H. G., Westland, J. C., and Hong, S. (1999) The Impact of Electronic Marketplaces on Product Prices: An Empirical Study of AUCNET. *International Journal of Electronic Commerce* 4(2), 45–60.

Leininger, W., Linhart, P. B., and Radner, R. (1989) Equilibria of the Sealed Bid Mechanism for Bargaining with Incomplete Information. *Journal of Economic Theory*, 48, 63–106.

Levin, D., Kagel, J. H., and Richard, J.-F. (1996) Revenue Effects and Information Processing in English Common Value Actions. *American Economic Review*, 86, 442–460.

Levin, D. and Smith, J. L. (1994) Equilibrium in Auctions with Entry. *American Economic Review*, 84, 585–599.

———— (1996a) Optimal Reservation Prices in Auctions. *Economic Journal*, 106, 1271–1283.

_____ (1996b) Ranking Auctions with Risk Averse Bidders. *Journal of Economic Theory*, 68, 549–561.

Levin, J. (1996) Auctions for Complements and Substitutes. MPhil thesis, Oxford University.

Lizzeri, A. and Persico, N. (2000) Uniqueness and Existence of Equilibrium in Auctions with a Reserve Price. *Games and Economic Behavior*, 30, 83–114.

Lopomo, G. (1998) The English Auction is Optimal among Simple Sequential Auctions. *Journal of Economic Theory*, 82, 144–166.

Lucking-Reiley, D. (2000) Vickrey Auctions in Practice: From Nineteenth-Century Philately to Twenty-First-Century E-Commerce. *Journal of Economic Perspectives*, 14, 183–192.

Maasland, E. (2000) Veilingmiljarden Zijn een Fictie (Billions from Auctions: Wishful Thinking). *Economisch Statistische Berichten*, June 9, 479; translation available at www.paulklemperer.org.

Machlup, F. (1946) Marginal Analysis and Empirical Research. *American Economic Review*, 36, 519–554.

Mailath, G. J. and Zemsky, P. (1991) Collusion in Second Price Auctions with Heterogeneous Bidders. *Games and Economic Behavior*, 3, 467–486.

Malvey, P. F., Archibald, C. M., and Flynn, S. T. (1996) Uniform-Price Auctions: Evaluation of the Treasury Experience. Working Paper, US Treasury.

Manelli, A. M. and Vincent, D. R. (1995) Optimal Procurement Mechanisms. *Econometrica*, 63, 591–620.

Marshall, A. (1890) *Principles of Economics*. London: Macmillan.

_____ (1906) Letter to A. L. Bowley, February 27, 1906. In Pigou, A. C. (ed.), *Memorials of Alfred Marshall*. London: Macmillan, pp. 427–428.

Marshall, R. C. and Meurer, M. J. (2002) The Economics of Bidder Collusion. In Chatterjee, Kalyan (ed.), *Game Theory and Business Applications*. Norwell, MA: Kluwer.

Marshall, R. C., Meurer, M. J., Richard, J.-F., and Stromquist, W. (1994) Numerical Analysis of Asymmetric First Price Auctions. *Games and Economic Behavior*, 7, 193–220.

Maskin, E. S. (1992) Auctions and Privatization. In Siebert, H. (ed.), *Privatization: Symposium in Honor of Herbert Giersch*. Tübingen: Mohr (Siebeck), pp. 115–136.

Maskin, E. S. and Riley, J. G. (1984) Optimal Auctions with Risk Averse Buyers. *Econometrica*, 52, 1473–1518.

_____ (1985) Auction Theory with Private Values. *American Economic Review*, 75, 150–155.

_____ (1989) Optimal Multi-Unit Auctions. In Hahn, F. (ed.), *The Economics of Missing Markets, Information, and Games*. Oxford: Oxford University Press, Clarendon Press, pp. 312–335.

_____ (2000a) Equilibrium in Sealed High Bid Auctions. *Review of Economic Studies*, 67, 439–454

_____ (2000b) Asymmetric Auctions. *Review of Economic Studies*, 67, 413–438.

_____ (forthcoming) Uniqueness of Equilibrium in Sealed High-Bid Auctions. *Games and Economic Behavior*.

Matthews, S. A. (1983) Selling to Risk Averse Buyers with Unobservable Tastes. *Journal of Economic Theory*, 3, 370–400.

_____ (1984) Information Acquisition in Discriminatory Auctions. In Boyer, M. and Kihlstrom, R. E. (eds), *Bayesian Models in Economic Theory*. New York: North-Holland, pp. 181–207.

_____ (1987) Comparing Auctions for Risk-Averse Buyers: A Buyer's Point of View. *Econometrica*, 55, 633–646.

Maxwell, C. (1983) *Auctioning Divisible Commodities: A Study of Price Determination*. PhD dissertation, Harvard University.

Maynard Smith, J. (1974) The Theory of Games and the Evolution of Animal Conflicts. *Journal of Theoretical Biology*, 47, 209–219.

McAdams, D. (1998), Adjustable Supply and 'Collusive-seeming Equilibria' in the Uniform-price Share Auction. Working paper, Stanford University.

McAfee, R. P. (1992) A Dominant Strategy Double Auction. *Journal of Economic Theory*, 56, 434–450.

_____ (1993) Mechanism Design by Competing Sellers. *Econometrica*, 61, 1281–1312.

McAfee, R. P. and McMillan, J. (1986) Bidding for Contracts: A Principal-Agent Analysis. *The RAND Journal of Economics*, 17, 326–338.

_____ (1987a) Auctions and Bidding. *Journal of Economic Literature*, 25, 699–738.

_____ (1987b) Auctions with a Stochastic Number of Bidders. *Journal of Economic Theory*, 43, 1–19.

_____ (1987c) Auctions with Entry. *Economics Letters*, 23, 343–347.

_____ (1987d) Competition for Agency Contracts. *The RAND Journal of Economics*, 18, 296–307.

_____ (1988) Search Mechanisms. *Journal of Economic Theory*, 44, 99–123.

_____ (1989) Government Procurement and International Trade. *Journal of International Economics*, 26, 291–308.

_____ (1992) Bidding Rings. *American Economic Review*, 82, 579–599.

_____ (1994) Selling Spectrum Rights. *Journal of Economic Perspectives*, 8, 145–162.

_____ (1996) Analyzing the Airwaves Auction. *Journal of Economic Perspectives*, 10, 159–175.

McAfee, R. P., McMillan, J., and Reny, P. J. (1989) Extracting the Surplus in the Common Value Auction. *Econometrica*, 57, 1451–1460.

McAfee, R. P. and Reny, P. J. (1992) Correlated Information and Mechanism Design. *Econometrica*, 60, 395–421.

McAfee, R. P. and Vincent, D. (1993) The Declining Price Anomaly. *Journal of Economic Theory*, 60, 191–212.

_____ (1997) Sequentially Optimal Auctions. *Games and Economic Behavior*, 18, 246–276.

McMillan, J. (1994) Selling Spectrum Rights. *Journal of Economic Perspectives*, 8, 145–162.

Mead, W. J. and Schneipp, M. (1989) Competitive Bidding for Federal Timber in Region 6, An Update: 1983–1988. Santa Barbara, CA: Community and Organization Research Institute, University of California.

Meeks, R. (2001) An Event Study of the Swiss UMTS Auction. Research Note, Nuffield College, Oxford University.

Menezes, F. (1996) Multiple-unit English Auctions. *European Journal of Political Economy*, 12, 671–684.

Menezes, F. M. and Monteiro, P. K. (2000) Auctions with Endogenous Participation. *Review of Economic Design*, 5, 71–89.

_____ (in preparation) *An Introduction to Auction Theory.*

Menezes, F., Monteiro P. K. and Temimi, A. (2000) Discrete Public Goods with Incomplete Information. Working paper, EPGE/FGV.

Michelson, M. (2000) Swiss 3G auction set to become battle of giants. *Reuters*, November 9; available at http://www.totaltele.com/.

Milgrom, P. R. (1979) A Convergence Theorem for Competitive Bidding with Differential Information. *Econometrica*, 47, 679–688.

_____ (1981) Rational Expectations, Information Acquisition, and Competitive Bidding. *Econometrica,* 49, 921–943.

_____ (1985) The Economics of Competitive Bidding: A Selective Survey. In Hurwicz, L., Schmeidler, D. and Sonnenschein, H. (eds.), *Social Goals and Social Organization: Essays in Memory of Elisha Pazner.* Cambridge: Cambridge University Press.

_____ (1987) Auction Theory. In Bewley, T. F. (ed.), *Advances in Economic Theory: Fifth World Congress.* Cambridge: Cambridge University Press.

_____ (1989) Auctions and Bidding: A Primer. *Journal of Economic Perspectives*, 3, 3–22.

_____ (2000) Putting Auction Theory to Work: The Simultaneous Ascending Auction. *Journal of Political Economy*, 108, 245–272.

_____ (2004) *Putting Auction Theory to Work.* Cambridge, UK: Cambridge University Press.

Milgrom, P. R. and Roberts, D. J. (1982) Limit Pricing and Entry under Incomplete Information: An Equilibrium Analysis. *Econometrica*, 50, 443–459.

Milgrom, P. R. and Weber, R. J. (1982a) A Theory of Auctions and Competitive Bidding. *Econometrica*, 50, 1089–1122.

_____ (1982b) The Value of Information in a Sealed-Bid Auction. *Journal of Mathematical Economics*, 10, 105–114.

_____ (2000) A Theory of Auctions and Competitive Bidding II. In Klemperer, P. (ed.), *The Economic Theory of Auctions*, Cheltenham, UK: Edward Elgar, vol. II, pp. 179–194.

Mirrlees, J. A. (1971) An Exploration in the Theory of Optimum Income Taxation. *Review of Economic Studies*, 38, 175–208.

Mussa, M. and Rosen, S. (1978) Monopoly and Product Quality. *Journal of Economic Theory*, 18, 301–317.

Myerson, R. B. (1979) Incentive Compatibility and the Bargaining Problem. *Econometrica*, 47, 61–73.

_____ (1981) Optimal Auction Design. *Mathematics of Operations Research*, 6, 58–73.

Myerson, R. B. and Satterthwaite, M. A. (1983) Efficient Mechanisms for Bilateral Trade. *Journal of Economic Theory*, 29, 265–281.

National Audit Office (2001) *The Auction of Radio Spectrum for the Third Generation of Mobile Telephones.* London: The Stationery Office, and available at www.nao.gov.uk.

Newbery, D. M. (1998) Competition, Contracts, and Entry in the Electricity Spot Market. *The RAND Journal of Economics,* 29, 726–749.

Nyborg, K. G. (1997) On Complicity in Share Auctions. Mimeo, London Business School.

Nyborg, K. and Sundaresan, S. (1996) Discriminatory Versus Uniform Treasury Auctions: Evidence from When-issued Transactions. *Journal of Financial Economics*, 42, 63–104.

Office of Gas and Electricity Markets (1999) *The New Electricity Trading Arrangements,* July, available at www.open.gov.uk/offer/reta.htm.

Ortega Reichert, A. (1968a) Models for Competitive Bidding Under Uncertainty. PhD thesis, Stanford University (and Technical Report No. 8, Department of Operations Research, Stanford University).

_____ (1968b) A Sequential Game with Information Flow. Chapter 8 in *Models for Competitive Bidding Under Uncertainty*, PhD thesis, Stanford University, pp. 232–254. Also in Klemperer, P. D. (ed.) (2000) *The Economic Theory of Auctions* (with foreword by S. A. Board and P. D. Klemperer). Cheltenham, UK: Edward Elgar.

Paarsch, H. J. (1991) Empirical Models of Auctions and an Application to British Columbian Timber Sales. Discussion paper, University of British Columbia.

Pagnozzi, M. (2002) Sorry Winners. Working paper, Oxford University.

_____ (forthcoming) Post-auction Takeovers. Working paper, Oxford University.

Palfrey, T. R. (1983) Bundling Decisions by a Multiproduct Monopolist with Incomplete Information. *Econometrica*, 51, 463–484.

Perry, M. and Reny, P. J. (1998) Ex-Post Efficient Auctions for Agents with Interdependent Values. Working paper, Hebrew University of Jerusalem and University of Pittsburgh.

_____ (1999) On the Failure of the Linkage Principle in Multi-Unit Auctions. *Econometrica*, 67, 895–900.

Persico, N. (2000a) Games of Redistribution Politics are Equivalent to All-Pay Auctions with Consolation Prizes. Working paper, University of Pennsylvania.

_____ (2000b) Information Acquisition in Auctions. *Econometrica*, 68, 135–148.

Pesendorfer, W. and Swinkels, J. M. (1997) The Loser's Curse and Information Aggregation in Common Value Auctions. *Econometrica*, 65, 1247–1281.

_____ (2000) Efficiency and Information Aggregation in Auctions. *American Economic Review*, 90, 499–525.

Peters, M. and Severinov, S. (1997) Competition Among Sellers Who Offer Auctions Instead of Prices. *Journal of Economic Theory*, 75, 141–179.

Piccione, M. and Tan, G. (1996) A Simple Model of Expert and Non Expert Bidding in First Price Auctions. *Journal of Economic Theory*, 70, 501–515.

Pitchik, C. (1995) Budget-Constrained Sequential Auctions with Incomplete Information. Mimeo, University of Toronto.

Pitchik, C. and Schotter, A. (1988) Perfect Equilibria in Budget Constrained Sequential Auctions: An Experimental Study. *The RAND Journal of Economics*, 19, 363–388.

Plott, C. (1997) Laboratory Experimental Testbeds: Application to the PCS Auction. *Journal of Economics and Management Strategy*, 6, 605–638.

Plott, C. and Salmon, T. (forthcoming) The Simultaneous, Ascending Auction: Dynamics of Price Adjustment in Experiments and in the UK 3G Spectrum Auction. *Journal of Economic Behavior and Organization*.

Porter, R. H. (1995) The Role of Information in U.S. Offshore Oil and Gas Lease Auctions, *Econometrica*, 63, 1–27.

Power U.K. (1999) The Problems with the Pool. Issue 66, August 31, 14.

Radiocommunications Agency (1998a) UMTS Auction Design. UMTS Auction Consultative Group Paper 14 of 1998, available as UACG(98)14 at www.spectrumauctions.gov.uk.

_____ (1998b) UMTS Auction Design 2. UMTS Auction Consultative Group Report, 98, 16, available at www.spectrumauctions.gov.uk.

Reece, D. K. (1979) An Analysis of Alternative Bidding Systems for Leasing Offshore Oil. *Bell Journal of Economics*, 10, 659–669.

Reinhert, V. and Belzer, G. (1996) Some Evidence on Bid Sharing and the Use of Information in the U.S. Treasury's Auction Experiment. Working Paper, Board of Governors of the Federal Reserve System.

Riley, J. G. (1980) Strong Evolutionary Equilibrium and The War of Attrition. *Journal of Theoretical Biology*, 82, 383–400.

_____ (1988) Ex Post Information in Auctions. *Review of Economic Studies*, 55, 409–430.

_____ (1989a) Expected Revenue from Open and Sealed Bid Auctions. *Journal of Economic Perspectives*, 3, 41–50.

_____ (1989b) An Introduction to the Theory of Contests. In Kuhn, H. W. and Szego, G. (eds.), *Incomplete Information and Bounded Rationality Decision Models*. Berlin: Springer-Verlag.

Riley, J. G. and Li, H. (1997) Auction Choice: A Numerical Analysis. Mimeo, University of California at Los Angeles.

Riley, J. G. and Samuelson, W. F. (1981) Optimal Auctions. *American Economic Review*, 71, 381–392.

Riordan, M. H. and Sappington, D. E. M. (1987) Awarding Monopoly Franchises. *American Economic Review*, 77, 375–387.

Robert, J. (undated, ≈1995) Sequential Descending-Price Auctions with Multi-Unit Demand. Mimeo, Université de Montreal.

Robert, J., Laffont, J.-J., and Loisel, P. (1994) Repeated Descending-Price Auctions I: Theory. Mimeo, Université de Montreal, Université de Toulouse, and INRA.

Roberts, D. (2000) Phone Numbers that Could Well Result in Panic. *The Financial Times,* October 19, 38.

Roberts, D. and Ward, A. (2000) Little Gold at the End of the Spectrum. *The Financial Times,* November 3, 21.

Robinson, M. S. (1985) Collusion and the Choice of Auction. *The RAND Journal of Economics*, 16, 141–145.

Rosenthal, R. W. (1980) A Model in which an Increase in the Number of Sellers Leads to a Higher Price. *Econometrica*, 48, 1575–1579.

Roth, A. E. (2002) The Economist as Engineer: Game Theory, Experimentations, and Computation as Tools for Design Economics. *Econometrica*, 70, 1341–1378.

Rothkopf, M. H. (1969) A Model of Rational Competitive Bidding. *Management Science*, 15, 362–373.

_____ (1980) On Multiplicative Bidding Strategies. *Operations Research*, 25, 570–575.

_____ (1994) Models of Auctions and Competitive Bidding. In Pollock, S. M., Rothkopf, M.H., and Barnett, A. (eds.), *Handbooks in Operations Research and Management Science*. New York: North-Holland, volume 6, chapter 19.

Rothkopf, M. H. and Engelbrecht-Wiggans, R. (1993) Misapplications Reviews: Getting the Model Right—The Case of Competitive Bidding. *Interfaces*, 23, 99–106.

Rothkopf, M. H., Harstad, R. M., and Fu, Y. (2003) Is Subsidizing Inefficient Bidders Actually Costly? *Management Science*, 49, 71–84.

Rothkopf, M. H., Pekeč, A., and Harstad, R. M. (1998) Computationally Manageable Combinational Auctions. *Management Science*, 44, 1131–1147.

Rothkopf, M. H., Teisberg, T. J., and Kahn, E. P. (1990) Why are Vickrey Auctions Rare, *Journal of Political Economy*, 98, 94–109.

Rothschild, M. and Stiglitz, J. E. (1970) Increasing Risk I: A Definition. *Journal of Economic Theory*, 2, 225–243.

Rustichini, A., Satterthwaite, M. A., and Williams, S. R. (1994) Convergence to Efficiency in a Simple Market with Incomplete Information. *Econometrica*, 62, 1041–1063.

Salant, D. (1997) Up in the Air: GTE's Experience in the MTA Auction for Personal Communication Services Licenses. *Journal of Economics and Management Strategy*, 6, 549–572.

———— (2000) Auctions and Regulation: Reengineering of Regulatory Mechanisms. *Journal of Regulatory Economics*, 17, 195–204.

Satterthwaite, M. A. and Williams, S. R. (1989a) The Rate of Convergence to Efficiency in the Buyer's Bid Double Auction as the Market Becomes Large. *Review of Economic Studies*, 56, 477–498.

———— (1989b) Bilateral Trade with the Sealed Bid k-Double Auction: Existence and Efficiency. *Journal of Economic Theory*, 48, 107–133.

Schmidt, K. (2002) Efficiency of the British UMTS Auction: A Comment on Börgers and Dustmann. *ifo Studien*, 48, 111–114.

Scott Morton, F., Zettelmeyer, F., and Silva Risso, J. (2001) Internet Car Retailing. *Journal of Industrial Economics*, 49, 501–519.

Shubik, M. (1983) Auctions, Bidding, and Markets: An Historical Sketch. In R. Engelbrecht-Wiggans, M. Shubik, and J. Stark (eds), *Auctions, Bidding, and Contracting*. New York: New York University Press, pp. 33–52.

Sills, D. L. (ed.) (1968) *International Encyclopedia of the Social Sciences*. New York: Macmillan and The Free Press, vol. 10.

Simon, D. (1994) The Treasury's Experiment with Single-Price Auctions in the Mid-1970's: Winner's or Taxpayer's Curse? *Review of Economics and Statistics*, 76, 754–760.

Spence, M. A. (1972) Market Signalling: The Informational Structure of Job Markets and Related Phenomena. PhD thesis, Harvard University.

Spulber, D. F. (1990) Auctions and Contract Enforcement. *Journal of Law, Economics and Organization*, 6, 325–344.

———— (1995) Bertrand Competition when Rivals' Costs are Unknown. *Journal of Industrial Economics*, 43, 1–12.

Stevens, M. (1994) Labour Contracts and Efficiency in On-the-Job Training. *Economic Journal*, 104, 408–419.

———— (2000) Reconciling Theoretical and Empirical Human Capital Earnings Functions. Working paper, Nuffield College, Oxford University.

Stigler, G. J. (1964) A Theory of Oligopoly. *Journal of Political Economy*, 72, 44–61.

Stuewe, H. (1999) Auktion von Telefonfrequenzen: Spannung bis zur letzten Minute. *Frankfurter Allgemeine Zeitung,* October 29.

Swinkels, J. M. (2001) Efficiency of Large Private Value Auctions. *Econometrica,* 69, 37–68.

Thisse, J. and Vives, X. (1988) On the Strategic Choice of Spatial Price Policy. *American Economic Review,* 78, 122–137.

Total Telecom (2000) Italy's UMTS auction to start October 19. Reuters staff, October 12; available at http://www.totaltele.com/.

U.K. Monopolies and Mergers Commission (1999) British Sky Broadcasting Group plc and Manchester United plc: A Report on the Proposed Merger. Cm 4305. London: The Stationery Office.

Ulph, D. and Vulkan, N. (2001) E-Commerce, Mass Customisation and Price Discrimination. Mimeo, UCL and University of Bristol.

van Damme, E. (1999) The Dutch DCS-1800 Auction. In Patrone, Fioravante, Garcia-Jurado, Ignacio, and Tijs, Stef (eds.), *Game Practice: Contributions from Applied Game Theory.* New York: Kluwer, pp. 53–73.

——— (2002) The European UMTS Auctions. *European Economic Review,* 45, 846–858.

Vickrey, W. (1961) Counterspeculation, Auctions and Competitive Sealed Tenders. *Journal of Finance,* 16, 8–37.

——— (1962) Auction and Bidding Games. In *Recent Advances in Game Theory.* Princeton, NJ: The Princeton University Conference, pp. 15–27.

——— (1976) Auctions Markets and Optimum Allocations. In Amihud, Y. (ed.), *Bidding and Auctioning for Procurement and Allocation: Studies in Game Theory and Mathematical Economics.* New York: New York University Press, pp. 13–20.

Vives, X. (2002) Private Information, Strategic Behavior, and Efficiency in Cournot Markets. *The RAND Journal of Economics,* 33, 361–376.

Waehrer, K. (1995) A Model of Auction Contracts with Liquidated Damages. *Journal of Economic Theory,* 67, 531–555.

Waehrer, K., Harstad, R. M. and Rothkopf, M. H. (1998) Auction Form Preferences of Risk-Averse Bidtakers. *The RAND Journal of Economics,* 29, 179–192.

Wang, J. J. D. and Zender, J. F. (2002) Auctioning Divisible Goods. *Economic Theory,* 19, 673–705.

Waterson, M. (1984) *Economic Theory of the Industry.* Cambridge, UK: Cambridge University Press.

Weber, R. J. (1983) Multi-Object Auctions. In Engelbrecht-Wiggans, R., Shubik, M., and Stark, R. M. (eds.), *Auctions, Bidding, and Contracting.* New York: New York University Press, pp. 165–191.

——— (1985) Auctions and Competitive Bidding. In Young, H. P. (ed.), *Fair Allocation, American Mathematical Society Proceedings of Symposia in Applied Mathematics.* Providence, RI: American Mathematical Society, pp. 143–170.

——— (1997) Making More from Less: Strategic Demand Reduction in the FCC Spectrum Auctions. *Journal of Economics and Management Strategy,* 6, 529–548.

Wighton, D. (1995a) Wellcome Accepts Glaxo Bid and Criticises Trust. *The Financial Times,* March 8, 27.

——— (1995b) Wellcome Still Smarting Over Handling of Trust's Stake. *The Financial Times,* March 8, 32.

Williams, S. R. (1991) Existence and Convergence of Equilibria in the Buyer's Bid Double Auction. *Review of Economic Studies*, 58, 351–374.

Wilson, R. (1967) Competitive Bidding with Asymmetric Information. *Management Science*, 13, A816–A820.

_____ (1969) Competitive Bidding with Disparate Information. *Management Science*, 15, 446–448.

_____ (1977) A Bidding Model of Perfect Competition. *Review of Economic Studies*, 44, 511–518.

_____ (1979) Auctions of Shares. *Quarterly Journal of Economics*, 93, 675–689.

_____ (1985) Incentive Efficiency of Double Auctions. *Econometrica*, 53, 1101–1115.

_____ (1992) Strategic Analysis of Auctions. In Aumann, R. J. and Hart, S. (eds.), *Handbook of Game Theory, Volume 1*. Amsterdam: Elsevier, pp. 228–279.

_____ (1998) Sequential Equilibria of Asymmetric Ascending Auctions: The Case of Log-Normal Distributions. *Economic Theory*, 12, 433–440.

_____ (2002) Architecture of Power Markets. *Econometrica*, 70, 1299–1340.

Wolfram, C. D. (1998) Strategic Bidding in a Multiunit Auction: An Empirical Analysis of Bids to Supply Electricity in England and Wales. *The RAND Journal of Economics*, 29, 703–725.

_____ (1999) Measuring Duopoly Power in the British Electricity Spot Market. *American Economic Review*, 89, 805–826.

Wolfstetter, E. (1996) Auctions: An Introduction. *Journal of Economic Surveys*, 10, 367–420.

_____ (2003) The Swiss UMTS Spectrum Auction Flop: Bad Luck or Bad Design? In Nutzinger, H.-G. (ed.), *Regulation, Competition, and the Market Economy*. Festschrift for C. C. v. Weizsäcker. Göttingen: Vandenhoek & Ruprecht, pp. 281–294.

Wruck, K. H. (1994) Financial Policy, Internal Control, and Performance: Sealed Air Corporation's Leveraged Special Dividend. *Journal of Financial Economics*, 36, 157–192.

Zheng, C. Z. (2001) High Bids and Broke Winners. *Journal of Economic Theory*, 100, 129–171.

Index

n after a page number denotes a footnote.